A
Bastard's
TALE

To Brian —
With very best wishes

A
Bastard's
TALE

THE POLITICAL
MEMOIRS OF

GEORGE
GARDINER

AURUM PRESS

First published in Great Britain 1999
by Aurum Press Ltd
25 Bedford Avenue, London WC1B 3AT

The author and publisher wish to thank Lady Empson and The Hogarth Press
for permission to reproduce the verses from 'Just a Smack at Auden' from
Collected Poems by William Empson.

A catalogue record for this book is available from the British Library.

ISBN 1 85410 637 6

1 3 5 7 9 10 8 6 4 2
1999 2001 2003 2002 2000

Book design by Roger Lightfoot
Typeset by York House Typographic, London
Printed and bound in Great Britain by MPG Books Ltd, Bodmin

Contents

*To Douglas and Tarzi Simpson
and Bill and Ena Westnedge,
as true Conservatives
as any I have known*

'The first duty of a Member of Parliament is to do what in his faithful and disinterested judgement he believes is right and necessary for the honour and safety of our beloved country. The second duty is to his constituents, of whom he is the representative but not the delegate. It is only in the third place that a man's duty to party organisation or programme takes rank. All three loyalties should be observed, but there is no doubt of the order in which they stand in any healthy manifestation of democracy.'

Winston S. Churchill, Woodford (1955)

FOREWORD

―――――――――・✢・――――――――

When Parliament Mattered

'Sir George is like a sinister figure with a taste for conspiracy. Were all the world a stage, he would be played by Vincent Price.'
Julian Critchley, former MP for Aldershot

'Gaunt and emaciated, the Angel of Death so far as Conservative Wets, liberals and lefties are concerned, [Sir George] clanks and gibbers his way round the committee rooms ...'
Ian Aitken, former political editor, the *Guardian*

ONE OF THE myths most destructive to a healthy democracy, peddled frequently by the media, is that the sole purpose of being a Member of Parliament is to gain promotion to office. Never mind what political principles you hold dear, never mind whether you achieve some success in projecting them – all that matters is how far you manage to shin up the greasy pole before sliding down again.

Soon after my election in 1974 I became a confirmed Thatcherite, though the seed was sown in childhood; mine was a single-parent family, my mother coping with post-war austerity in decidedly straitened circumstances. As a conviction politician, I warmed to Margaret Thatcher, yet despite my contribution to her successful leadership campaign in 1975 and active support thereafter she never offered me promotion. For that I am profoundly grateful. Perhaps I could have served a few years as some parliamentary undersecretary, with little influence at all, then with good fortune as a Minister of State which brings some real power, but before long the ladder would have been pulled away and I would have found myself sliding down the snake. I am sure I did not have the temperament for cabinet office. My vocation was as a back-bench mover and polemicist – and for me that is cause for pride.

The one conclusion I hope will emerge from reading this book is how fulfilling life as a back-bench activist can be. But to achieve that fulfilment a backbencher must be prepared to organise with like-minded colleagues to achieve specific political ends. I set out on this road soon after being elected in February 1974, long before I became chairman of the 92, the right-of-centre group that became the largest on the Tory benches. Throughout Margaret Thatcher's time as Tory leader, from February 1975 till she was ousted in November 1990, I was dedicated to ensuring that the principles and policies for which she stood were not obstructed by the old Heathites on our benches. This also meant organising pressure on certain ministers. I supported John Major through the bulk of his time as leader too, urging on him policies which if heeded might just have saved the party from defeat – but alas, they fell on deaf ears.

However, being a back-bench organiser carries its price tag, and for me it was to be cast as the arch-plotter. The quotes from my old Wet sparring partner Julian Critchley and my former press gallery colleague Ian Aitken, printed above, were fairly typical, though others too portrayed me as the right-wing fixer, just as Tristan Garel-Jones was cast as the Prince of Darkness organising the Tory Wets and Europhiles from his position on the government benches. In Tristan's case his reputation was perhaps merited, but mine was a character portrayal I strongly disputed; so far as I was concerned I was a conviction politician who simply knew how to organise. But no, my political reputation was that of a back-bench plotter, and that I had to accept. No doubt this was enhanced by my physical appearance – slightly stooping, hooded eyes, full lips, lugubrious manner – and I can understand why left-of-centre colleagues I managed to displace from party committees were eager to promote this sinister-figure image. But from the moment I joined the campaign team to get Margaret Thatcher elected leader in place of the calamitous Edward Heath, I knew what I wanted from political life, and most of the time I got it.

There is also the question how such a back-bench role can fit in with the demands of a party machine. All party machines are tempted to draw on totalitarian instincts. The Tory machine from 1992 to 1997 certainly did, and the 'New Labour' Government has made a virtue of doing the same. But for the public good, and indeed for the long-term good of the parties themselves, such instincts must be resisted. If backbenchers are not permitted to exercise their own judgement on important issues regardless of instructions from party whips, then democracy will be the poorer and their parties will simply fossilise over time.

Parliament *is* important - or at least it was. I am not the first to object to the way the House of Commons has been bypassed by Tony Blair's administration. This is not a necessary consequence of a 179 steam-roller majority; over two successive Parliaments Margaret Thatcher had majorities of 145 and 103, yet she was always held to account not just by an Opposition, albeit enfeebled, but also by her own backbenchers. I sometimes wonder whether during my twenty-three years as a back-bencher I saw the end of a democratic Golden Age in which Parliament mattered. Now it seems the Prime Minister keeps his appearances in the voting lobbies to the barest minimum; do new Labour back-benchers ever ponder why they bothered to get elected to Parliament, when they have no chance of meeting their leader except at a reception or briefing session at which he is their host? Policy changes are often announced without a statement first to MPs, with no opportunity for questions; Labour backbenchers are actively encouraged to take a week at a time away from Westminster during sessions when their public duty is to be there to hold the administration to account, while total compliance is expected from them when they are actually present. Has the back-bench plotter become an endangered species? It is not simply what happens on the floor of the Commons – the importance of this has been exaggerated for many years. What *is* important is what happens on the government back benches, and on its committees, to shape and influence government policy. On all the evidence to date, I fear this will go down in history as the poodle Parliament.

To be fair, this is not solely the doing of the Blair administration. The contempt for Parliament began under John Major after 1992 over the handling of European policy: first the lies over what the Maastricht Treaty really signified, before the translation into English revealed what had actually been negotiated; then the draconian abuse of the whipping system to compel MPs to vote against their party's basic instincts; the persistent denials of free votes, even on the referendum amendment, through to the adamant refusal at the end of 1996 to allow a Commons debate on the EMU 'stability pact' before the Chancellor of the Exchequer agreed to it in Paris. The results of the Maastricht Treaty have also had an increasingly debilitating effect on Parliament, as more and more of our laws are dictated by European directives regardless of the judgement of elected MPs.

The focus of this book is intended to explain the important role played by Tory backbenchers during my years in Parliament, from February 1974 to the election of 1997, though it will also explain how I became the politician that I am. It will show how training in journalism shaped my free-thinking approach, and how I used writing to back up my political campaigning. I hope this will help readers to see what were momentous political events through a back-bench activist's eyes; it might even help explain how the Conservative Party came to reverse the long decline of post-war Britain before it was dragged to the very brink of oblivion under the well-intentioned but disastrous leadership of John Major. Yet most of all I hope to show how, provided that Britain's government *is* saved for Westminster by keeping out of a European single currency, and powers already ceded to European Union institutions are returned to our own Parliament, backbenchers will continue to have a rewarding and above all necessary role to play.

CHAPTER ONE

Our Blind Bargain

'Sir! You have disappointed us!*
We had intended you to be
The next Prime Minister but three:
The stocks were sold; the Press was squared;
The Middle Class was quite prepared.
But as it is! ... My language fails!
Go out and govern New South Wales!'
    Hilaire Belloc, *Cautionary Tales* (1907)

'Like Caesar's wife, all things to all men.'
    G.W.E. Russell, *Collections and Recollections* (1898)

NOVEMBER 26, 1990. As we entered 10 Downing Street the heavy scent of flowers was all around us. Every few minutes yet another bouquet or exotic plant arrived at the front door from people devastated that Margaret Thatcher was resigning as Prime Minister, deserted not by the majority of her party but by cabinet ministers whose careers she had supported. The sides of the hallway and the walls all the way up the stairs to the dining and reception rooms were lined with flowers in every imaginable kind of container; not even the Chelsea Flower Show could produce blooms in such profusion. We went into the drawing room where Margaret was giving her final lunch to a couple of dozen close supporters and friends.

Those present were by no means all hard Thatcherites. The most honoured guest was Lord Joseph, certainly the first of that breed, but Lord Thorneycroft, who had to be relieved of his job as Party Chairman when he questioned publicly the direction of her policies, was there too, since he had served her loyally. She was always loyal to those who had been loyal to her. There was Nick Ridley, who could claim to have been a Thatcherite before she was. That was not the case with John Gummer, who had also served her as party chairman, and who was sitting next to me. His eyes were streaming and his tears ran throughout the meal; he claimed that the pollen that lay heavy in the air was activating his hay fever. But most of us were fighting hard to control our emotions.

My mind went back to 1975, when as a new MP I fought under Airey Neave on the campaign committee to make her leader and, as an experienced journalist, had drafted the final part of her leadership manifesto; to the back-bench battles to support her successful crusade to restore the nation's achievement and pride; but most of all to the night less than a week before when, after her spirit had been broken by a succession of interviews with her cabinet ministers, I led a delegation urging her to stay on to fight the second round of the leadership election. The previous day she had just failed to get sufficient votes to defeat outright the challenge mounted by Michael Heseltine, and I remain convinced to this day she would have seen him off had she stayed to fight a second ballot. But she had chosen to walk away from all that treachery.

As coffee was served Lord Joseph proposed a toast to the retiring Prime Minister, in which he struck an upbeat note. In her reply she reminded us briefly of all we had managed to achieve together before getting to her real message: 'Whatever we do now, we must protect our *philosophy* – and that means throwing all our support behind John Major.' Some of us were a bit taken aback by this. Major had never been known for being guided by philosophy at all, though he had been a late recruit to the Blue Chips, a tight Tory group made up of avowed left-wingers. In truth Margaret was in a difficulty of her own creation; her most notable failure had been to promote and foster a successor in her own mould. Once upon a time it was thought this would be Norman Tebbit or John Moore, but both fell by the wayside. Cecil Parkinson, too, was once favoured, but a year before she had passed over him in favour of Major when she had to find a new Chancellor. Now she obviously wanted to ensure the defeat of Heseltine, whose ruthless challenge had brought her to this pass. She had promoted Major ahead of his experience; he was a stronger candidate than the somewhat stuffy Douglas Hurd, but many of us doubted whether he had the conviction to protect or indeed build upon her legacy. But she made the point several times over, always in terms of 'protecting our philosophy'. As we left she directed her pleas personally to two of her guests, Edward Leigh and Michael Brown, who were inclined to support Heseltine as the most charismatic candidate. 'No,' she repeated, 'no. You just *can't* do that.' Most of us accepted her advice, but for us Major was a blind bargain.

As a Thatcherite, I have to admit: he was her creation. In this and the next chapter I will offer one Tory backbencher's perspective of how John Major, despite all efforts from well-wishers to save him, brought about his own decline and fall, dragging the Tory Party to its worst election defeat for more than ninety years. It is not a story of heroes and villains, goodies and baddies; rather it is a sad tale of courage sustained by self-delusion, of poor judgement and of good intentions in a vacuum of ideals.

The right-of-centre 92 Group, of which I was chairman and which had around a hundred MPs as members, was split in all directions. I decided we should hold a meeting at the Commons at which all three candidates would outline their platforms for fifteen minutes, then answer questions for a further fifteen. If this was to succeed I would have to be scrupulously neutral myself. Heseltine came on first; his speech went way beyond fifteen minutes, leaving little time for questions – just as well for him, perhaps, since his answers concerning Europe hardly endeared him to many present. He left to make way for Hurd, who stuck to his time and was competent but dull; at one stage I feared the questions would dry up. Then Major, whose speech was very well-tailored for that audience, very Thatcherite. When questioned over how he would handle the coming Inter-Governmental Conference to negotiate a new European Treaty he gave replies that would satisfy the most ingrained Euro-sceptic. I estimated that he secured more than 70 per cent of 92 Group votes in the ballot; I certainly voted for him. In the division lobby that night, as hundreds swarmed around congratulating him, I slipped him a note which he put in his side pocket to read later, congratulating him and warning him that, as Chief Whip, Tim Renton had lost the confidence of the right.

So we had a new Government. Renton was shunted aside to become minister for the arts, though whether this had anything to do with my note or with Major's own observation of the 'support' Renton gave Margaret as her chief whip we will never know. More ominously, Tristan Garel-Jones, who shouldered such heavy responsibility in bringing about her downfall, was made Minister of State at the Foreign Office in charge of European negotiations, and Chris Patten, who on the fateful night had done so much to undermine her, became party chairman.

From then to the general election of April 1992 was one long battle for Major's ear. Was he living up to the high hopes that Thatcher held for him, or was he leaning towards his old Wet friends in the party?

No-one could properly tell. There was no doubt that those of us on the right wanted him to succeed. Many of his public speeches were reassuringly Thatcherite, yet the word coming from Patten in off-the-record briefings to the press was that Thatcher's philosophy was a spent force, that Major was distancing himself from her legacy as fast as he could, and that 'Majorism' – whatever that meant – was the inspiration for the future. When later Patten made a botch of CCO's election campaign launch and Thatcher had to be called in as star speaker at the election rally in the QEII Centre, his grovelling introduction gave many of her old supporters wry satisfaction, though coupled with the uneasy feeling that we would soon need to use a sick bag.

It was on a chill January night in 1992 that Mark Allatt asked to see me in my Commons office. I had known Mark since his days as a activist in the Federation of Conservative Students (FCS), the wing of the party dissolved by Norman Tebbit when party chairman in one of the worst mistakes he ever made. Allatt brought with him two other veterans of the FCS, John Swannick and Adrian Lee. Their message was simple: they wanted me to take the lead in setting up a movement in the party to promote the principles that made our governments so successful in the 1980s, and to act as a counter to the Tory Reform Group (TRG), focus for the left and old Tory Wets, which had signed up many of Thatcher's ministers as patrons. It was all very well having a group like the 92 battling for these principles within Parliament, they argued, but an equivalent body was needed to bring together all those supporting Thatcherite philosophy in the party at large. Many of these were under thirty – what came to be called 'Thatcher's Children'.

Thus was Conservative Way Forward (CWF) born. Margaret Thatcher, still in the Commons, agreed to be its president, Lord Joseph her deputy and Cecil Parkinson its chairman. But before going ahead I wanted to get Major's approval, and this proved surprisingly difficult. Of course we had to contend with the Tory Establishment, eager as always to laud the new leader while turning their backs on his predecessor. Patten campaigned hard to stop us ever getting off the ground, but of course we expected that from one of TRG's heroes. Old fogeys from the National Union were wheeled out to plead with 1922 chairman Cranley Onslow to intervene to stop the creation of a group which they claimed would split the party 'at this time', but that was beyond Onslow's control. I discussed it with Major in his room a couple of times; he was clearly fearful of Thatcher's shadow, and asked me how I would feel if I were in his shoes and someone proposed setting up a group to honour his predecessor. I replied he should feel no differently to Margaret Thatcher, who happily accepted the creation of TRG even though it took a line critical of her. As for CWF, I saw no reason why he should regard it as anything other than supportive. But still he demurred, spoke to Margaret, and persuaded her to postpone its launch until the Gulf War was over – though what the Gulf had to do with it was beyond anyone's understanding. In the end CWF was set up, with a regular magazine, *Forward*, which I edited; it proved to be the most successful group, working within the party until the 1997 election, attracting young people into its ranks and providing many new candidates.

Meanwhile the Inter-Governmental Conference was under way, culminating in the Maastricht Treaty. Years before I had been a founder member of the Conservative Group for Europe, and an enthusiastic Marketeer, but I now understood that Ted Heath's pledge that no loss of political sovereignty was involved in signing up to the Rome Treaty had been a downright deception. I subscribed to the ideal of a Europe of nation states expounded by Margaret Thatcher in her famous 1988 Bruges speech. Several times during this period I discussed the matter with Major, either at meetings with the 1922 executive, on which I sat, or leading the steering committee which ran the 92. He agreed with all our fears, but invariably ended up with the words: 'I just ask that you trust me.' And that, alas, was what we did.

———— ∽◇∾ ————

Penny Junor got it about right when, in her sympathetic biography of Major published in 1993, she described him as an enigma. 'He is as much an enigma today as he was when he stepped into Mrs Thatcher's shoes,' she wrote. Many of us who watched his movements closely came to the same conclusion before the 1992 election. He had good reason to feel proud of his ascent from such humble origins, yet there was something of a chip on his shoulder. Because he had never been to university, as most of those around him had, he often saw himself as the victim of intellectual snobbery. Though there was no doubting his intelligence, he nevertheless felt intellectually insecure. Besides this, he seemed to have no political credo of his own, and thus absorbed the current orthodoxy of cabinet friends or civil servants with whom he worked regularly, or even worse the opinions of those with whom he had last spoken. It was quite usual to come away from a meeting with him believing he had accepted your analysis, but within a week hear him say something quite different. He was usually courteous, good at handling people, and in the election was presented as 'a decent chap'. It was not till later that some of his supporters discovered his vicious streak.

Major had been lucky to be the only leading minister acceptable to the right at the time of Thatcher's downfall, and in the 1992 election he was lucky in his opponents. He entered the election well behind in the opinion polls, but the ominous triumphalism of Neil Kinnock at Labour's televised Sheffield rally reminded too many of newsreels of a much earlier rally at Nuremberg, and contrasted badly with Major's more basic campaigning by loudhailer from his soapbox. Conservative propaganda pointed to a Britain about to emerge from economic recession, against which the tax and national insurance increases promised by shadow chancellor John Smith presented a dismal prospect. With the uncertainty of the election behind us, economic recovery would soon be evident. Major emerged with an overall majority of twenty-one.

Though there was a short passage in the Conservative manifesto commending the Maastricht Treaty, which had yet to be formally ratified, it played no part whatsoever in the campaign. It never featured in election broadcasts, nor was it ever raised with me on doorsteps in Reigate. All parties appeared to accept it, though it was very relevant that the text had yet to be published in English. All we had to go on was foreign office propaganda that it pulled us *away* from a federal Europe; Major stressed the new concept of 'subsidiarity', which apparently meant that nothing would be decided at European level that could be decided nationally. This was still the position when the bill making the consequent changes to our laws came to the Commons for its second reading. I spoke in its favour, though against a federal Europe and against Britain ever joining a single currency; I accepted the foreign office line and congratulated Major for 'halting the progress of federalism, and in some respects reversing it'. Foreign Secretary Douglas Hurd sat just two benches down from me, nodding furiously. The treaty was only published in English shortly before the debate; several newspapers carried it in small-print supplements, but it was largely unintelligible. Not until a few weeks later were expert commentaries published which set the text alongside the Treaty of Rome and other concordats agreed since, revealing what a huge step *was* being taken towards a federal Europe, and how many of Parliament's powers were being transferred under our noses to European Union institutions. It was then I realised I had been duped, and with bitter feelings decided to do all I could to oppose ratification of this disastrous treaty. The fact that the

Government had not been honest over what it had negotiated undoubt-edly intensified opposition on the Tory benches.

Such peace as existed on the Maastricht front in the Tory Party was shattered when, in June, the Danes voted narrowly in their referendum to reject the treaty. A feeling of relief swept across our benches; many had suppressed their doubts about Maastricht but now it no longer mattered, since unless all the parties ratified to it, it would fall. Pressed by Neil Kinnock from the opposition benches, Major agreed to post-pone any further proceedings on the Maastricht Bill until the situation became clearer. Straight away Michael Spicer, MP for Worcestershire South and former junior minister, was at work collecting signatures to an early day motion; EDMs are rarely debated, but appear on the Commons Order Paper as strong expressions of back-bench opinion. Spicer's motion called on the Government to use this opportunity to 'make a fresh start with the future development of the EEC', and was quickly dubbed the 'Fresh Start motion'. Some 86 Tories signed it, including half the 1922 executive, and future whips like David Willetts, Liam Fox and Peter Ainsworth. Major was furious; I recall him throw-ing on the table a copy of the *Evening Standard* headlined 'Revolt' and shouting 'How can I be expected to lead when my achievements are questioned like this?' He was always far too sensitive to newspaper headlines, taking them as personal attacks on himself. The whips per-suaded five MPs to withdraw their names from the motion, under threat that unless they did, future promotion would be denied them. That did them little good, since they were never promoted anyway.

The result of the first Danish referendum and the success of the Fresh Start motion proved to be a catalyst for those opposing Maastrict within the Tory ranks. Michael Spicer drew the strongest opponents together to form the Fresh Start Group, with Bill Cash at his side, which from then on met regularly to work out how best to press our case. The battle lines were becoming firmly drawn.

John Major often claimed to be a pragmatic politician, yet once an idea or a doctrine became firmly embedded in his mind he would stick to it stubbornly regardless of the cost, whereas a truly pragmatic politician at least allows for the possibility of change. So it was over the Exchange Rate Mechanism. When as Chancellor in October 1990 he finally per-suaded Margaret Thatcher to drop her opposition to British member-ship, he was accepting the current Establishment orthodoxy; the Treasury, the Foreign Office, the City, the CBI, even the press and the leaders of all political parties were urging that we should join. The familiar mantra we have heard so often since was chanted: being in the ERM would bring stability, lower interest rates, and control inflation while strengthening our voice in Europe. But by early 1992 the system was in serious trouble, largely because the high costs of German reunification dictated high interest rates, and with the Deutschmark as the ERM's benchmark currency that meant keeping UK interest rates way above what was appropriate at our stage in the economic cycle. The effect was to prolong the UK recession. Towards the end of that summer Chancellor Norman Lamont warned the Prime Minister that it might become necessary for Britain to leave the ERM until the different economies of the member countries were more attuned, but Major would hear none of it. In speech after speech all through the summer he insisted there was no question of Britain *ever* leaving the ERM and that, were we to do so, the consequence would be higher inflation and still higher interest rates; on one occasion he happily described his economic critics as 'quack doctors'. He even kidded the *Sunday Times* to run a story that it was a realistic ambition to make sterling Europe's benchmark currency in place of the Deutschmark – and he really meant it. Walter Mitty was there, alive and well, in Downing Street.

It was this stubborn refusal even to contemplate any alternative that made the total collapse of Wednesday 16 September so ruinous politically. Those away from Downing Street listened to the news with incredulity as interest rates rose first to 12 then to 15 per cent in a desperate bid to stem the flood from sterling. But neither this nor throwing more than £10 billion of our currency reserves into supporting the pound had any effect; the dam was well and truly burst. Major's economic policy lay in ruins. Yet so total had been his commitment to that policy that he could not bring himself to admit he had got it wrong. Instead the blame was first put on the Germans for 'letting us down', though given their own national needs their actions made perfect economic sense. Next in line of fire were the 'speculators' – and this coming from a Government that was supposed to believe in free markets! Harold Wilson's handy 'Gnomes of Zurich' were riding high again.

Most commentators chart the long decline of Major and his Government from 'Black Wednesday', as ministers came to call it, though it turned out to be more like 'Golden Wednesday' so far as the UK economy was concerned. It shattered any public confidence in the Government's ability to manage the economy – the traditional advantage the Tories had over Labour – and made Major look like a small man who would never admit he had been wrong. Even then his Government could have recovered from the debacle had they but understood the opportunities that lay before them, and had they handled differently the supreme issue of relations with the rest of Europe. Yet such a reassessment of strategy was never made.

The Brighton conference showed clearly how much the Government had lost touch with Tory activists over Europe. When Norman Tebbit was called to speak from the rostrum he had some hard words for Major: 'I hope, Prime Minister, you will stand by your Chancellor. After all, it was not Norman Lamont's decision to enter the ERM. [The decision, of course, was Major's.] He did his best to make the unworkable work.' The delegates went wild with cheering. 'This conference wants policies for Britain first, Britain second and Britain third. Politics, like charity, begins at home.' Deafening cheers, before Tebbit went on: 'Do we want to be citizens of the European Union?' 'No!' came the thundering response. 'Do we want a single currency?' 'No!' again. 'Do we want other countries interfering in our immigration controls?' 'No, no, no.' The standing ovation went on and on; delegates would not let Tebbit resume his seat. Major and Douglas Hurd, both ashen-faced on the platform, gritted their teeth – yet still they refused to hear the message.

Two weeks later those of us on the executive of the 1922 Committee gathered at the Carlton Club to mark the seventieth anniversary of the meeting there in 1922 when Tory MPs, led by one Stanley Baldwin, turned on their leaders to bring down the Lloyd George coalition. The 1922 Committee was formed the following year, with the purpose of ensuring that in future the party's leaders kept more in tune with their backbenchers. Now its chairman, two vice-chairmen, one treasurer, two secretaries and twelve members of its executive are elected when the party is in Government by Tory backbenchers at the start of each session. We were effectively the 'shop stewards' for Tory MPs outside Government. Invited to the lunch were Major, chief whip Richard Ryder and Lord Wakeham, together with the chairmen of the Carlton Club and of its political committee. So auspicious was the occasion deemed to be that the Carlton brought out its Disraeli table, circular in form with added circular extensions, used only on very rare occasions. The lunch certainly proved memorable, though for very different reasons.

It was on the Monday that the Commons returned from the summer recess – and the Tories were in turmoil. The previous week had seen the leak, then confirmation, that President of the Board of Trade Heseltine had decided to shut down thirty-one coal pits and scrap 30,000 miners' jobs. There had been minimal consultation with other cabinet ministers, none at all within the party, and no preparation of public opin-

ion; that was it, and Heseltine was adamant. The Opposition were
pressing a motion of censure the following Wednesday, and countless
Tories were threatening to abstain or vote against. Even 1922 chairman
Sir Marcus Fox, normally totally supportive of the Government, said
the plan was unacceptable. Meanwhile the unemployment figures were
rising. The Government was in deep crisis only six months after winning the election. It promised to be an interesting lunch.

Major arrived late, looking harassed. After setting him up with a
restorative drink we took our places, feeling rather like the Knights of
the Round Table. The first course was a salmon terrine, and when the
plates were cleared away Sir Marcus said a few words about the historic
event we were commemorating. Major then rose to reply, and most of
us were expecting a few flattering words about the 1922. But no, he
launched into a full explanation of how the pits crisis had come about,
and spelt out in detail the Cabinet's U-turn that morning to grant a
temporary reprieve to twenty-one of the thirty-one pits, pending a full
review. After fifteen minutes he turned to the economy. If he were to
take as long explaining that, we would never reach the roast lamb, so
Sir Marcus suggested tactfully that perhaps he could conclude his
remarks and take questions after the sweet.

The account of the discussion circulated to the press by Major's
aides had it that the premier's critics on the executive were given a
severe reprimand, told not to offend again and left shamefaced. There
is nothing new about spin-doctoring. The reality was very different. By
his honest account of the Cabinet's U-turn Major defused much of the
criticism on that score, though some, like Sir Rhodes Boyson and
Elizabeth Peacock, were clearly still not satisfied. But when it came to
questions there was a feeling that the discussion should be broadened,
which as always meant the executive divided into two schools. The first,
consisting of those who I am sure nursed the ambition of being given a
peerage after the next election, spent their slot telling Major how well
he was doing and that all that was necessary was to improve his publicity machine. The second, consisting of Boyson, Sir Ivan Lawrence,
Bob Dunn, John Townend, Jim Pawsey and myself, tried to make him
understand what was happening out there in the real world. One of
them asked whether the Maastricht Treaty really was worth splitting the
party over, given the anxiety felt by the bulk of grassroots workers. That
was the cue for Major to go onto autopilot, pointing to the danger of
Britain being marginalised in Europe and the rest.

My turn came to contribute. The pits crisis, I said, was but the latest example of the poor government we had suffered since the ERM
debacle; in the weeks since we had been given no new strategy for

recovery; the Cabinet had not even agreed whether they wanted to get back into the ERM in the foreseeable future or to exploit the advantages of being outside it. I appealed to him to give some clear leadership to the country; indecision meant we would go on being buffeted by events. My remarks were meant constructively, but were not well received. Major regarded me coldly, and gave a brush-off reply; more particularly, he gave no clue to his position over rejoining the ERM. Looking back, I doubt whether he even had one. The following day the 1922 executive met Heseltine and dictated further concessions, enabling him to climb out of the hole he had dug himself, so saving the Government from defeat in Labour's censure motion.

----------·◁◯▷·----------

Mine was not the only voice calling on Major to give a clear lead, by which I meant on economic policy, but the Tory press and others were lamenting the absence of any 'smack of firm government'. Major decided the time had come to deliver this smack, but the issue on which he chose to do it proved near disastrous. He *could* have spelt out a clear policy to revive the economy, then invited the Commons to endorse it; this would have united the Tory Party behind him. Instead he chose to make approval of the Maastricht Treaty the test, thus throwing the gauntlet down to all those in his own party who had deep misgivings, and splitting the party from top to bottom. Whose advice pushed him to take this almost suicidal course cannot be said for certain, but it was strongly believed that Kenneth Clarke, renowned for his 'gung-ho' approach, urged this as a means of bringing the Maastricht rebels to heel. Another possible motive was to demonstrate that *he*, Major, controlled the Tory Party and not Tebbit, as the recent party conference might have suggested.

The promise to hold a full Commons debate before moving to the committee stage of the Maastricht Bill had been given to Kinnock while he was still opposition leader, and of course had to be honoured. But it did not have to be honoured yet; indeed, only a month before, Major had said it would not make sense to bring the Maastricht Bill back to the House till the Danes had conducted their second referendum, which they did not do till the following May. Similarly, there was no commitment to a debate on a substantive resolution; it could have been simply on a 'take note' motion, which would have presented no challenges to anybody. But no; it was decreed that the paving motion had to be a test of the Government's virility – with a three-line whip to prove it.

From this, things went from bad to worse. On Saturday 23 October

I was speaker at a Tory supper club in the Vale of Glamorgan, which revealed the habitual majority against the provisions of Maastricht. That night we stayed with old family friends in Penarth, and next morning while everyone else was still in bed I walked to the local newsagent to buy my usual range of Sunday papers. When I read the *Sunday Times* front-page headline I fell about laughing: 'Major threatens general election if he fails to win Maastricht vote,' it said. Why my mirth? The very idea that the Queen would grant a dissolution only six months after an election, and without the Government losing a vote of confidence in the House, was patently ludicrous. I also imagined how that headline would ruin party chairman Norman Fowler's breakfast, since Central Office was still £18 million in the red following that election. Furthermore, given the Government's low standing in the opinion polls, the Cabinet would never allow Major to draw them into collective suicide. Major had been to Egypt to celebrate the fiftieth anniversary of victory at El Alamein, and apparently there had been much aggressive talk to British correspondents on the plane there and back. Major later claimed he had been misunderstood, but I had verification from two separate witnesses that his threat to the party was delivered with total conviction, besides which the Downing Street press machine was ordered not to deny the story. Major was playing Walter Mitty yet again.

The 92 Group, which I chaired, was the largest grouping in the party with nearly a hundred backbenchers, though with support outside its ranks, which explains why we held almost all the chairmanships of the back-bench subject committees. It was run by a steering committee of seven, who held morning meetings once a fortnight in my office over a glass of chilled sherry or wine, to chew over what was happening in the party. The 92's machinery provided me with an intelligence-gathering machine second only to the whips' office, and I soon learned that the possibility of defeat for the Government on the paving motion loomed large. Major's threat, which few took seriously, was proving counter-productive. I thought a policy meeting of the 92 to discuss the state of the party might restore some stability to the situation; some of the hardline Euro-sceptics were among our members, but so too were many habitual Major loyalists. Our whip members were excluded from these policy meetings, though by common consent I reported the drift of the discussion to the chief whip afterwards. The meeting revealed how opinion was swinging against Maastricht; those who sought to defend it got a pretty rough ride. Many said the election threat was pathetic. But the biggest cheer went to Alan Duncan, a new Member who had lent his Westminster home to Major for his leadership campaign. The reason why we were getting poor government and so many foolish decisions, said Duncan, was the imbalance between a substantially right-of-centre parliamentary party and a left-of-centre Cabinet. This was, indeed, the nub of the matter. Only four in the Cabinet – Norman Lamont, Michael Howard, Peter Lilley and Michael Portillo – were properly of the right; the priorities of the rest reflected a fairly narrow band of backbenchers. Until we got the balance right in Cabinet, Duncan argued, the Cabinet would go on getting things wrong. I reported the point to Chief Whip Richard Ryder later, but there was no chance of rectifying this before the paving resolution the following week, which Ryder too feared would be lost. The same point was frequently put direct to Major subsequently, but he never listened; his was largely a Cabinet of chums.

The situation was very worrying. The next day I went on the radio to plead for a conciliatory approach in the paving motion: 'Please, John, don't split the party on this issue.' The day after that I had an article in *The Times* warning that Major's survival was at stake: 'I hope desperately that he does survive ... but for him to do so requires an instinct for survival that for the moment seems to have deserted him.' I pleaded for a genuine free vote. 'The Opposition would have to allow a free vote too, and it is possible this might give him the majority he seeks.' The alternative was to order the whips to twist so many arms that a majority could be secured – just. 'Yet the price of that will be a bitterly divided party at Westminster, and a party smitten to its knees outside. Is this what John Major wants? I just cannot believe it. There has to be a better way of party management than this.' How prophetic those words turned out to be.

That Thursday Major put his case to a full meeting of the 1922 Committee. He was well received, and won over a few doubters. 'I am the Cabinet's greatest Euro-sceptic,' he told us. The trouble was that few people on either side of the argument believed him. Meanwhile the Whips' arm twisting was well under way. I was left alone by this; Ryder had the wisdom not to try these tactics on me, but I learned of many colleagues who had felt the hot breath of burly whip David Lightbown down their necks, coupled with threats over their political future. A few were blackmailed over the odd sexual indiscretion: 'You wouldn't want your wife to hear about that, would you?' I kept my ear to the ground, and knew that Michael Spicer had enough pledges to secure the Government's defeat – provided all held true. I agonised; I wanted to kill that abominable treaty stone dead, but I did not particularly want to lose Major, since Clarke – the most likely replacement after Heseltine's pits fiasco – would be even more disastrous.

The twelve members of the 1922 executive included six Euro-sceptics

– Ivan Lawrence, Rhodes Boyson, John Townend, Bob Dunn, Jim
Pawsey and myself. All apart from Lawrence felt ourselves torn apart
over the paving motion; Lawrence was in no doubt that he would vote
against the Government, but the remaining five agonised over what we
should do. Every one of us was in close touch with Tory grassroots
opinion, as a result of frequent Friday and Saturday evenings as guest
speakers at Tory supper clubs the length and breadth of the land.
Boyson, after a famous stint as headmaster of a comprehensive school,
knew all there was to know about education; a former minister of state,
he had strong views on most things, was inclined to take 'populist'
stances, and went door-knocking in his constituency every weekend to
find out what was worrying his voters. Dunn, too, was a former minister, acerbic in manner with a shrewd sense of what the party could take
and what it could not. Townend was the blunt Yorkshireman, wine merchant and chartered accountant, chairman of our back-bench treasury
committee, and hardline on all matters penal and economic. Pawsey,
too, was a businessman who, short of being a minister, had served the
party in every conceivable way; he was chairman of the back-bench
education committee, had been at the right hand of every Tory
Education Secretary on the standing committees of every bill they had
presented, and was as 'loyal' as you could ever wish. He, if any backbencher, richly deserved a knighthood, yet as Birthday Honours succeeded New Year Honours he was passed over in favour of yes men
whose service to the party was not a fraction of his. It was very indica-
tive of Major's character that he never chose to elevate this man whose
service to the party was unquestioned; instead, Pawsey's freely given
advice was held against him. All, apart from Boyson, were on my 92
group steering committee.

We met in Dunn's office to try to work out a common position. The
Government was staring defeat in the face. Dunn wanted to abstain,
and so did Pawsey; Boyson, Townend and I were inclined to vote
against. We decided the least we could do was see Major, and a meeting was fixed for 5 p.m. in his room behind the Speaker's Chair. That
afternoon I told Spicer what we were doing, and he gave me his figures,
which pointed to a Government defeat. So when Boyson, Dunn,
Townend, Pawsey and I went in to see Major we knew we held his fate
in our hands.

I have never seen Major in such a forlorn state he was then – bat-
tered, utterly washed out. He pleaded that he had had a busy day,
which was doubtless true. His manner was limp, his eyes vacant as if he
were finding it hard to concentrate on anything. We told him why we
were so opposed to the Maastricht Treaty, Pawsey speaking most elo-

quently from the heart. Major, in turn, did not give us the usual hog-wash about being marginalised in Europe. Contemplating the possibility of defeat, he said he had been misreported in threatening to call an election, nor did he threaten resignation, as the whips were doing on his behalf, though he came near to saying it would be hard to continue as Prime Minister in such circumstances. He appealed to us for our help, if only to keep the party together. For our part we sought no bargains, but simply promised to consider what he had said.

We returned to Dunn's room, astounded by what we had seen. We agreed Major was very near the end of his tether. Perhaps he might not resign if he lost the vote next day, but he was more than likely to throw in the towel the moment the next crisis hit him. We came to the conclusion he had to be shored up. I was deputed to write him a letter, which I handed to his PPS, Graham Bright, in the division lobby at 10 p.m. This said we would back the paving motion next day for no other reason than personal loyalty to him, and that he should not see our decision as in any way supporting the Maastricht Treaty. So five 1922 executive votes went to Major, and I know that several others in the 92 Group took their cue from us. In the event Major survived by just three votes. We had saved his bacon.

There were bitter recriminations from my friends in the Fresh Start Group of hardline Maastricht rebels, chaired by Spicer, though these were overcome once the committee-stage battle over the Maastricht Bill had begun. In time, too, Major turned on those who had saved him, forgetting the wise maxim that loyalty is a two-way street. So looking back, am I proud of the role I played then? With the wisdom of hindsight, I have to say I am not. We had the chance to abort that bill, and had we done so we would have wrecked the treaty, forcing its participants back to the negotiating table. The Tory Party would have been pitched into turmoil, of course, but then there was at least time for recovery; instead, far worse turmoil, procrastination and fudge afflicted the party until the 1997 election put us out of our misery.

Over the next two years and more the Tory leadership nailed their party to the cross of Maastricht, and as each nail was hammered in, blood flowed from the party at every level. All the high command's resources were thrown into crushing dissent. Many from the 1992 intake faced the choice of sticking to their principles and so forfeiting all hope of promotion, or shutting up and doing as they were told; unsurprisingly most chose the latter, but their morale was sapped and they lost pride in themselves. Few in the parliamentary party except a small band of Euro-enthusiasts ever sought to justify Maastricht to their local party workers. As for opinion among those workers, those of us who fulfilled regular weekend speaking dates knew the score. A debate in my own constituency, with me as a neutral chairman, on a motion that 'This meeting would ratify the Maastricht Treaty' produced a 2–1 majority *against* ratification, and wherever I went I found Tory audiences breaking down in much the same proportion. At the same time they wanted to be loyal to Major, so they were being torn apart within themselves. Public opinion polls told the same story. Meanwhile grassroots support was haemorrhaging; by 1997, most local associations had little more than a third of the members they had in 1990.

Tory back-bench opposition to the Maastricht Bill was co-ordinated by the Fresh Start Group, which included many of the old anti-Marketeers like Teddy Taylor, but also many like myself, as well as some very brave new Members who could see all the dangers of ceding yet more powers to European Union institutions. Though we came to the group from different directions we were cohesive; Spicer was careful to let everyone have their say at the regular weekly meetings. But equally influential was Bill Cash, who had recently established the European Foundation, with help from Sir James Goldsmith, Lord McAlpine and others. The foundation provided us with expert and very useful briefs at every stage of the bill's progress. Those in the group became used to a degree of 'creative tension' between Spicer and Cash. James Cran and Chris Gill, both from the 1992 intake, performed splendidly as unofficial whips and 'floor managers'. Other valued members of the Group included Sir John Biffen, Nick Budgen, Iain Duncan-Smith, Teresa Gorman, Bernard Jenkin, Roger Knapman, Sir Ivan Lawrence, Barry Legg, Tony Marlow, Richard Shepherd, Sir Trevor Skeet, Sir Peter Tapsell, Bill Walker and Nick and Ann Winterton.

Cash was the real driving force within Fresh Start, and was often portrayed by the Government's lackeys as a xenophobic Little Englander. They could not have been more wrong. His interests were international; a strong Francophile who spoke French fluently, he travelled in all the countries of the European Union frequently and was on friendly terms with many of their national politicians. In consequence his knowledge of what was really happening below government level in European politics vastly exceeded that of any Foreign Office minister of the period. It is a grave pity that this knowledge was never tapped by the Foreign Office, for all his warnings have proved to be right. Today's Tory Party should recognise just how much it owes to Cash's diligence.

The Maastricht Bill took twenty-two days and nights in committee, before even getting to report stage and third reading. For night after night up to fifty rebels voted against the Government on every amendment, as well as on closure motions to conclude debate on one amendment in order to pass on to the next. We often felt we were the only ones left speaking for the Tory Party across the country, though we knew from our weekend speaking visits that we were not alone. Occasionally there were lengthy filibuster speeches to delay business further, though for the most part telling points were made. However, very rarely were they answered. More often than not it fell to Tristan Garel-Jones, Minister of State for Europe at the Foreign Office, to reply for the Government, and his attitude was one of bored indifference; he knew that points of substance made in the late hours of the night would never get reported, so why should he bother? All but one vote went in the Government's favour, thanks to Lib-Dem support (that is assuming they were there) and Labour front-bench abstention. The strong-arm tactics of the Tory whips did the rest.

Only on occasion during this time of agony did I get the chance to talk to Major, the first as chairman of the 92 Group. After his narrow paving-motion survival we invited him to speak at one of our dinners, if only to help him rehabilitate himself. Naturally he asked us to put recent troubles behind us, and wisely spent much time on the prospects for economic recovery. When it came to questions the Euro-sceptics chose not to come on strong, but there were many endorsements of the plea I made direct to him to make the Cabinet more representative of the parliamentary party by securing a better balance between right and left. That would help him to govern with the grain of the party and not against it, as so often happened. Major did not respond directly, but he knew the strength of our feeling. Neither was he very keen on further discussion with the 1922 executive, after his bruising Carlton Club lunch with us. During this crucial period the executive were invited to his room only once, when the old stagers made the usual cop-out calls for better public relations. I pleaded for a free vote on the amendment to hold a referendum before Maastricht was ratified, but was told there was no way he would take such a risk. By having so little contact with the 1922 executive he made himself even more out of touch with feeling in the party.

The Fresh Start Group met weekly to discuss tactics. Spicer, its chairman, maintained friendly relations with Chief Whip Ryder, as indeed I did myself. At one stage we conveyed through him to Major that if only he would concede a referendum, such as the Danes and French had enjoyed, then we would do what we could to facilitate the bill's passage, but Major set his face against such a course. Then the

Government offered us its own deal – a pledge not to rejoin ERM in the course of that Parliament in return for us calling off our hounds. But rejoining ERM in that time scale was never on the cards anyway, and we turned the offer down flat.

Every year in March, the party's National Union holds a meeting of its central council – a kind of mini-party conference, but attended by far fewer people, and usually held in one of the spa towns. 1993's was in Harrogate, and the Euro-enthusiasts in the Cabinet used it to try to divide the Euro-sceptics at Westminster from the party in the country. Few MPs attend the central council, but word reached us quickly that we were being made the scapegoats for the Government's continued unpopularity. Heseltine, Hurd and Party Chairman Norman Fowler made speeches claiming that we were siding with Labour to force Britain into the Social Chapter – a ludicrous suggestion. Worse still, Fowler was reported to be dropping hints that Euro-rebels might be deselected by their local parties in revenge. Fowler then tried to back-track, but the bitter seed had been sown. I contacted Ryder, only to discover he was in hospital with an injured back. Had he been at Harrogate I am sure he would never have allowed this to happen.

It was not till May 1993 that Major eventually shuffled his Cabinet in response to the party's rout in the county council elections and the humiliating loss of Newbury, hitherto a safe Tory seat, with a spectacular by-election swing against the Government of 28.4 per cent. I and my political friends saw this as proof of the gap opening up between the Government and its habitual supporters, who if they were not registering a protest vote by supporting Lib-Dem candidates, were choosing instead to stay at home. But the leadership saw it differently. The Euro-sceptics were to blame for parading Tory splits; if it were not for us, all would be well. Meanwhile Party Chairman Norman Fowler had his own scapegoat to offer to Major for public sacrifice – Chancellor Norman Lamont, whom he persuaded Major either to demote or drop. Lamont's value as a shield to prevent Major taking the blame over the ERM debacle was over, so dropped he was. To those who remembered how Lamont had served as Major's campaign manager in his battle for the leadership, this was proof of the scant loyalty Major felt for his political friends.

Two were qualified to take Lamont's place – Michael Howard, underemployed as Environment Secretary, and Kenneth Clarke, who was not making a great success of the Home Office. Michael Portillo, Chief Secretary at the Treasury, was not senior enough for such rapid promotion. The choice of successor was bound to give an important signal to the Tory benches. Howard was Euro-sceptic, and Major probably felt this would cramp his style with other European leaders, but appointing him would have avoided all the ambiguity over the European single currency that was to dog Major till the election. Instead he settled for the Europhile Clarke, arguably making his worst mistake in cabinet reconstruction, for Clarke was to use his position and threat of resignation to box Major in for the rest of the Parliament. So the signal was given – despite the obvious mood of the party, Major had aligned himself with the Europhile camp. So much for his claim to be the 'greatest Euro-sceptic in the Cabinet'.

Despite all this, Major still had the support of the right. The following month I chaired a 92 policy group meeting to discuss the state of the party, and apart from one dissident it was decided to convey to him our full support as leader. I reported this afterwards to the press. As it happened, Baroness Thatcher issued a statement the same evening urging the party to unite behind Major, though we did not know of this at our meeting. There was no collusion, but both moves probably owed much to the fact that there was no alternative in sight acceptable to the right.

The final vote on the Maastricht Bill, and hence on the treaty, loomed at the end of July. With thirty or more Tory Euro-sceptics threatening to vote against the Government, Ryder predicted defeat. Even the promise of support from the Ulster Unionists was not enough, so there was renewed arm twisting. A few of us were conversing on the bench outside the whips' office in the Members' Lobby when we heard a cracking sound, and someone joked: 'Ah well, that's another arm broken.' I have to say I was never the subject of whips' bullying, possibly because I led by far the strongest grouping on the Tory benches, but more likely because the whips, being for the most part intelligent men, knew that such tactics would only increase my intransigence.

The first vote on 'Maastricht Night' was on a Labour amendment to make Britain part of the Social Chapter, the second on a government motion to approve all the amendments necessary to our existing laws so that the remaining provisions of the treaty could be applied. My intention was to abstain in the first – I could never see how embracing the Social Chapter could kill off the treaty – and to vote against the Government in the second. That evening I was with Barry Legg, a consistent critic of the treaty, in his room discussing the situation when there was a knock on the door; it was Portillo, dispatched on a ritual round to try to win over rebels. We told him no straight away; he grinned and joined in our conversation, confirming that the Government expected defeat and would table a motion of confidence the following day. After I left Legg I was approached by Irvine Patrick, a friendly whip, who said that Major would like to see me alone in his room. I knew this would prove a pointless exercise, but no Member of Parliament ever refuses such a request from a Prime Minister.

Major waved me to sit on the sofa opposite him. His approach was not bullying, simply businesslike. He began with flattery. 'George, you know you're the best tactician on our backbenches.' Presumably this was a reference to my achievement in building up the 92 as the most influential grouping, controlling the chairmanships of all the significant back-bench committees; in addition, more than half the 1922 executive were 92 members. 'We need your help to get the party out of this mess. If the rebels win tonight we'll only be back for a vote of confidence tomorrow – so what will have been achieved?' I replied that he already knew my detestation of the treaty, and that having opposed the Bill through all its Commons stages I was hardly likely to shy at the final fence. But still he tried to hammer out a deal. 'I accept you'll abstain on the Labour amendment,' he said, 'but that's not what worries me. Abstain on that by all means, but I need you to help save us from humiliation by supporting the main resolution.' I repeated my answer, but still Major would not give up. 'All right, so why not abstain on both?' I decided it was time to draw the discussion politely to a close. 'John,' I said, 'I have to tell you that if I were to do anything that helped to ratify a treaty so damaging to our national interest I would never be able to live with myself again. Your time really would be better spent trying to persuade others.' He got up to see me out, then I turned and said to him finally: 'John, you do understand it's the *treaty* I object to? I have nothing personal against *you*.' 'Yes, George, I understand.' But he did not understand, nor did he ever.

Voting on Labour's Social Chapter amendment produced a tie, 317–317, though when the count was scrutinised more carefully the Government had a majority of one. But the main government motion was defeated by 324–316. Several rebels had their arms twisted or found limp excuses for supporting the Government after all, but still twenty-six of us fought the treaty to the bitter end. The following day the Government won its confidence motion easily; we had made our point to good effect, and I am sure a Tory Government will never again seek to bludgeon through a treaty surrendering constitutional powers against such a significant proportion of its own party, both in Westminster and beyond. For us to have abstained on the crucial confidence motion, thus securing our Government's defeat, would have meant an autumn general election and totally predictable Labour victory. A chastened Tory Government was certainly better than that. On the evening of the confidence vote Major's pent-up frustration broke through in an inadvertently recorded conversation with ITN's Michael Brunson after an interview, when he famously referred to three of his Euro-sceptic cabinet ministers – Portillo, Lilley and Redwood – as 'bastards'. Predictably the comment was leaked to the *Observer*, but the three who were thus maligned received it with amusement rather than anger. At the same time all the Maastricht rebels happily accepted the tag – hence the title of this book. The passage of the Maastricht Bill had been throughout a searing experience for Major.

Major set about recreating unity in the party with a signed article in *The Economist* at the end of September in which he swung back to a Euro-sceptic line, warning other European heads of government that reciting 'the mantra of full economic and monetary union' would 'have all the quaintness of a rain dance and about the same potency'. This pleased the Euro-sceptics, who wanted to use the forthcoming party conference to show that if this did represent a new approach by the Government after the humiliations of Maastricht then we were happy to support it. In fact, it was Major returning to his old game of saying one thing to reassure one wing of his party before saying something totally different to reassure the other.

In fact, the new theme that Major used to inspire the Blackpool Conference was 'Back to Basics' – the promise to return to and strengthen traditional values in education, family responsibility, and better enforcement of law and order. This was well received, and was in part featured in other cabinet speeches. But not enough thought had been put into defining where its margins lay, and through succeeding months it became a laughing stock as the press revealed a succession of public scandals involving ministers and MPs. Perhaps this reflected Major's lack of confidence in handling intellectual concepts. At the time of the Blackpool conference many commentators asserted that he was responding to a right-wing agenda, but that was a gross over-simplification. Quite apart from European policy, pressure from the right was for cuts in public spending to enable lower personal taxes, more self-reliance within the welfare state, more effective deterrents to crime and carrying further the education reforms already under way, and we were certainly making headway with Portillo, Howard, Lilley and John Patten. As policy goals each of these was free-standing. In truth, 'Back to Basics' as a concept owed far more to Sarah Hogg, head of Number Ten's policy unit, than to any pressure from the Tory right.

I had to pay a price that autumn for my Maastricht rebellion. There
was one other leading Euro-sceptic on the executive of the 1922, Ivan
Lawrence, with a record of rebellion identical to mine, but the Euro-
enthusiast Positive European Group together with the leaders of the
Lollards, the Tory Wet grouping that had so often been trounced by the
92 in back-bench committee elections (in practice the two groups overlapped), decided that I was the demon who had to be exorcised.
Anonymous press briefings were given throughout the summer, stepping up during the Blackpool Conference, that I was to be targeted in
the new session's elections to the executive. A new umbrella group was
formed by Peter Temple-Morris called Mainstream, made up of these
two groups together with some old whips' 'trusties', sharing two immediate objectives – to remove me from the executive and John Townend,
renowned for his hardline thrust on public spending, from being chairman of the back-bench finance committee. A special dinner was organised in St Stephen's Club, also used by the 92 for its regular dinners, to
co-ordinate strategy. As well as having BBC cameras at the door, two
activist friends took their own camcorder to record those arriving, after
which one stood on the other's shoulders to film through an uncur-
tained window the gathering assembled inside. By the end of the
evening I was given a tape which Dunn, Pawsey and I watched in the
video room in the vaults of the Commons. I was amused to see Sir
Cranley Onslow, who a few years back had won the 1922 chairmanship
largely thanks to the 92 slate I had organised, apparently giving his support to this dubious exercise.

But dubious or not, the exercise succeeded. After the ballot in committee room 14 to decide who should sit on the executive I waited in a
room below the Speaker's Chair for Alan Duncan, a good radical friend
from the new intake, to bring me the result when it was posted in the
whips' office. The moment he was inside the door he turned his thumb
down. I had lost my battle, giving way ironically to David Evans, the
outspoken millionaire with a Cockney accent who was further to the
right than I was. It was Evans who once said of his contract-cleaning
business: 'I trousered £20 million.' The voting figures in 1922 elections
are never published, but a friendly whip told me that I lost by only a
handful of votes; however, whether you lose by one or by fifty, the outcome is the same. The important question was how far Major encouraged this move against me. Anthony Seldon, in his biography of Major,
records that 'Number Ten were glad to see [me] voted off the 1922
executive', but I still have no positive evidence that Major gave verbal
encouragement to my opponents. What is undoubtedly true is that
Tristan Garel-Jones, who boasted of having the Prime Minister's ear,

was making it clear to all who cared to listen that Major wanted me off the executive. Over this period there were also some very spiteful personal attacks in the still Majorite *Daily Express* which could only have been inspired from Downing Street, but whether with Major's blessing I will never know. However, we did manage to save Townend as chairman of finance.

The 92 had just two officers, a chairman and a secretary who also managed the group's finances. In addition a steering committee of five elected members met fortnightly in my room over dry sherry or white wine to direct the group's affairs and test one another's views on the latest political developments. At this time Townend was secretary, and on the steering committee were Dame Jill Knight, a doughty Tory of the old school; Marion Roe, who had been eased out as a junior minister following a sniping campaign which appeared to have been orchestrated by Tristan Garel-Jones; Bob Dunn, also a former junior minister; Jim Pawsey, chairman of the back-bench education committee; and Vivian Bendall, who filled my office with cigarette smoke and whose ear was as close to Tory activists in North London as anyone I knew. The group did not hold annual elections; instead they were held whenever there was a consensus that new blood might be brought on. In January 1994, we decided the time had come to put ourselves to the test of what was now a membership of more than a hundred. First, however, there was business to be done; as a steering committee we had often had consultations with the party leader, first with Margaret Thatcher and then John Major, and it was time for us to renew this contact. I wrote to Major, and a meeting was fixed in his room at the Commons for 1 February.

We knew we wanted to put to him again the point made at our last 92 dinner with him – that one reason the Government was suffering was that the Cabinet was not properly representative of back-bench opinion, which all evidence showed was certainly inclined to the right. We also had some ideas how to reunite the party following the Maastricht schism, but our meeting was overshadowed by some unwelcome press publicity. Though we never announced when we were due to meet the Prime Minister, the resourceful Nick Wood and Arthur Leathley of *The Times* learned of our meeting and two days beforehand wrote a speculative story on the demands we were supposed to be making as a condition of our continued support. If we *had* intended to put such demands they could easily be worked out from the public comments of myself and Townend over recent weeks. In fact, we did not see it this way, and had no intention of sitting before him to reconstruct his Cabinet; rather we wanted to offer some constructive advice, as we had on occasions before. I had no idea where the source of the leak lay, though subsequently I suspected a set-up by Downing Street. We met in my room the morning before the meeting to agree the line we wanted to put; Jill Knight and Marion Roe had already given notice they could not attend the meeting that afternoon. The rest of us wondered whether it would be better to postpone it, in view of the press build-up, but decided that to cancel at such short notice would be discourteous to the Prime Minister.

However, courtesy was not the name of the game that evening. As we entered we could see that Major was clearly agitated; he motioned us to be seated, but remained standing himself. Graham Bright, his PPS and known to most backbenchers as 'Graham Dim', was also present. Major then referred to the press reports and said he had no intention of taking our advice on how to construct his Cabinet. He then made the remark – the full import of which I did not appreciate straight away – that he understood we were all facing re-election within the 92, and that in view of this would defer the meeting until new officers had been elected. Since we had already considered seeking a postponement we readily agreed. Even as we left Bright's hand was itching on the handle of the door, betraying his eagerness to spread the word among lobby correspondents that the Prime Minister had sent us away 'with fleas in our ears'. Despite my protestations, the national press had a field day: 'Two-minute hearing for Gardiner', shouted the headlines, and, 'Rightwingers rebuffed by angry Major'. Obviously Major's action had been carefully planned, and it was probably a whip's tip-off that kept Jill Knight away. We had been set up to show the country that 'Major was boss'. But why did he choose to insult so gratuitously a group of Members who had met him previously for such discussions, who had always supported him personally, and four of whom had compromised their own beliefs to save his bacon when he faced defeat over the paving motion only a year or so before? One theory was that Christopher Meyer, who had moved into position as his press chief just two days earlier, had put him up to 'playing it macho'. Another was that his judgement had deserted him, inducing him to declare war on the right in his party. A third, put forward later and which gave point to his remark about the coming 92 elections, was that he wanted to target me specifically. Whatever his motive, there were that night four senior and angry Tory Members who would never trust Major again.

Almost straight away stories were planted with the press that many in the 92 felt that I had overstepped the mark, and that I would face a challenge as 92 chairman. And sure enough a challenger came forward – Sir Anthony Durant, a pure product of the whips' office, older than me and due to stand down in the next election anyway. I quite liked Durant; I had known him before we entered the Commons together in February 1994. He was a dependable fellow, but totally lacking in imagination. Having been a whip, he was destined forever to think like one. He put himself forward as 'Major's man', with obvious support from the remaining Europhiles in the 92. I made it known I intended to stand down as chairman before the next election, since I had already served for ten years – but not now. We fought a vigorous campaign, 101 of the 107 in the 92 voted in the postal ballot, and I was re-elected chairman by 60–41. 'Rebuff for Major', said the headlines. I made clear that I would continue to support him, but George Jones, political editor of the *Daily Telegraph*, got it right when he described the result as 'a clear signal from the right that Mr Major should not ride roughshod over its views in trying to reassert his authority'. It was indeed a triumph for back-bench independence, and delivered a blow to Major's esteem which he richly deserved.

CHAPTER TWO

The Lost Leader

'Life's night begins, let him never come back to us!
There would be doubt, hesitation and pain,
Forced praise on our part – the glimmer of twilight,
Never glad confident morning again!'
Robert Browning, 'The Lost Leader' (1895)

'I'm going to fucking crucify the right for what they've done.'
John Major to Michael Brunson (1994)

T HROUGHOUT THIS PERIOD it was frequently alleged by those close to John Major that I and my friends were plotting to replace him as leader with Michael Portillo. Portillo entered the House in 1984, and his clear thinking and radical ideas marked him clearly from the start as a right-winger. He was quickly welcomed into the 92 Group, and later gave immense encouragement to the Thatcherite group Conservative Way Forward outside Parliament. I found his company and ideas stimulating, and became a great admirer. After he entered the Cabinet in 1992 I had regular meetings with him.

On 27 September, 1993, during the summer recess, I arranged a dinner for those on the 92's steering committee still in London; this was barely two months after the bloody climax of the Maastricht Bill and just a week before the Tory conference, and we felt an urgent need to take stock of what was happening in the party. We gathered in a private room upstairs at the Gran Paradiso, a restaurant in Wilton Road and a favourite haunt of Tory MPs. Present were Vivian Bendall, Bob Dunn, Jim Pawsey, Marion Roe and myself – quite enough for a stimulating discussion.

We were deeply aware that the leadership was unstable. No-one knew whether Major could pull the party together, or whether in some future crisis he would decide to throw in the towel. Three of us could recall the abject state in which we found him before we bailed him out over the paving motion. We also felt the frequent jibe from press commentators that the right had no-one of leadership potential; the 'big beasts' in the Cabinet – Clarke, Heseltine, Hurd – were all from the left. I think it was Marion Roe who said: 'We've been caught in this situation before, when Margaret suddenly went, with no-one of our own to push in her place,' and we all concurred. So it was agreed we should soon identify a potential leader acceptable to the right, which after all constituted the majority in the parliamentary party, and do all we could to promote respect for him or her. The next question was – who? The answer really boiled down to Lilley or Portillo; Redwood was mentioned, but at that time he had been in the Cabinet only three months. We had great respect for Lilley's intellect, but could not see him developing the necessary charisma to fight off the likes of Clarke or, despite his recent heart attack, Heseltine. Portillo was the natural choice, having the necessary strength, guts and potential to appeal to younger members of the party. However, I must stress that we never saw him as a leadership candidate *against* Major, but as the man we would support *in case* Major were to quit.

However, this brought us face to face with a big problem, for Portillo – and, to a lesser extent, Lilley too – was the subject of vicious rumours concerning alleged previous and current homosexual practices. You could not take a taxi from the House of Commons without the driver shouting back through his window: 'What's all this about Portillo, then?' before launching into a highly colourful account of alleged incidents involving male prostitutes and sometimes Lilley as well. I did not believe the rumours for one minute, but it was exceedingly irksome to hear conversations in restaurants where some loud-mouth at the next table was imparting 'inside knowledge' of such a scandal, supposedly just about to break. Even six months after our Gran Paradiso supper I was amazed when my party agent in Reigate came back from a Central Office agent's seminar believing every lurid detail of the gossip which had sustained him and his colleagues over drinks well into the night. I remembered witnessing much the same rumour factory at work when I was a political correspondent during and after the famous Profumo scandal: accounts of how a masked man wearing only a masonic apron serving canapes at a degenerate party attended by Stephen Ward was in fact a cabinet minister, or how Christine Keeler gave oral sex to another respected minister on the back seat of his official limousine. It took a painstaking inquiry by Lord Denning to sweep away all that nonsense. Now, two perfectly respectable ministers, both good friends, were being put through the same agony with almost no possibility of redress. But what worried my 92 friends over that dinner was the danger that some press 'revelation' would be sprung in the course of a leadership election, thereby nobbling our candidate. I insisted there was no truth in the rumours, but I had to acknowledge their anxiety. I therefore promised to conduct what investigations I could, and to report back.

Where did the rumours start? None of the leads I followed took me to the Labour HQ in Walworth Road, nor even to some mischievous Labour MP. When I consulted Michael Forsyth, then a Minister of State, he blamed elements in the Tory Reform Group for seeking to destroy the reputations of those right-wing ministers they feared. Apparently similar rumours had been circulated against him when the Scottish TRG were seeking to undermine his position in the party in Scotland, but thankfully the Scots were too canny to believe such far-fetched nonsense. I next spoke to old friends in the national press, and learned that some newspapers had invested thousands of pounds in investigations to obtain an exclusive story that would support the rumours, but had got nowhere and so had aborted these exercises. This was most instructive. If even a fraction of the tales being circulated in London were true, then surely there would be *at least one* rent boy willing to earn a few thousand pounds for himself by spilling the beans – rent boys are hardly known for their loyalty – yet none had been found who were willing to make a statement on oath. Finally, I spoke to a number of women who knew Portillo reasonably well (women, I have found, are often far more perceptive in detecting homosexuality than men), and they all found the rumours frankly ludicrous. I therefore reported back to my friends that not only I but also the combined efforts of the national press had found nothing to sustain the rumours, and that the moment they heard someone repeating them they should themselves use the same arguments in refutation.

One underground publication did publish the rumours, and indeed sought to embellish them – a gutter sheet called *Scallywag*. I asked Portillo whether he should consider a libel action, but he thought not. A totally different rumour had been used by *Scallywag* in a bid to discredit Major, and stupidly this was alluded to in a much more respected magazine, the *New Statesman & Society*. Major had sued, and rightly so, but the outcome was unsatisfactory with no admission of libel, though the *New Statesman* had to bear all its own costs. Besides, in Portillo's case the libel had got no further than *Scallywag*; a libel action would simply have shut the gutter sheet down, whereupon its writers would go on peddling the same filth in another under a different title.

If a national newspaper had repeated the libel then Portillo would have sued, but for reasons I have just described no newspaper ever did. With stoical self-discipline, Portillo simply waited for the unfounded rumours to run themselves into the ground. Their final death was helped by the publication of an unauthorised biography, Michael Gove's *Michael Portillo: The Future of the Right*, in 1995, which charted his years at Cambridge and since, showing clearly how heterosexual he was and is. Neither Portillo nor Lilley has suffered from such rumours since.

Portillo had been a strong supporter of Conservative Way Forward from the beginning, so was invited to be guest speaker at CWF's second president's dinner in January 1994. Lord Parkinson, our chairman, presided, and I was asked to propose the vote of thanks. Portillo had delivered a well-thought-out speech, in which he castigated 'the new British disease ... the self-destructive sickness of national cynicism' which was undermining so many of our national institutions. This received much national publicity, as did my remark at the end. In thanking him for all his past encouragement, I said that, in return, he could count on CWF's support 'when the time comes'. This was greeted by deafening applause, and was seen by some in the press as a bugle call to unseat Major. In fact, my intention was to demonstrate to Portillo that he enjoyed more personal support in the party outside the Commons than he realised.

Throughout his time as Chief Secretary to the Treasury, Portillo produced a number of speeches, articles and interviews in which he developed his thoughts on future Conservative philosophy for the remainder of the 1990s, and which had a remarkable impact on the development of Tory thinking. Taken together they provided the intelligently argued, inspirational spark which was so obviously lacking from Major's pronouncements, so I decided to bring them together and edit them in a booklet to be published by CWF. *Clear Blue Water*, with a foreword by Lord Parkinson, came to fruition in the summer of 1994 and was in demand by party activists way beyond the ranks of CWF. By this time there was little doubt that Portillo was the Tory rank and file's favourite to succeed Major *if* the Prime Minister resigned or unforeseen circumstances led him to quit. Heseltine still had his fans, but his illness had damaged his prospects. Clarke would probably have been the left's choice, though there were others in the Cabinet who thought that mantle would be better draped around their own shoulders. For this reason we kept pressing Portillo's attributes, but *only* in case the still unstable situation led to a vacancy opening up.

The 1994 party conference at Bournemouth was a triumph for

Portillo, without any prior planning at grassroots level, which we have learned subsequently caused 'deep irritation' at Number Ten. His platform speech as Secretary of State for Employment, declaring it was time to 'stop the rot from Brussels', got a rapturous reception. Wherever he went at fringe meetings he was mobbed; when I chaired a CWF lunchtime fringe meeting for him we had to throw open the French windows of the Connaught Hotel meeting room so that the ten-deep crowd on the patio outside could hear his words. For his conference address Major delivered a 'consolidating' speech which, though well received, hardly inspired. My reading was that, though few of the party faithful wanted to see Major go, they were in little doubt that Portillo would be a better bet than Heseltine to succeed if he did.

Meanwhile, since our steering committee supper a year before I had been at work. I knew from my close involvement in Margaret Thatcher's leadership campaign, and from my observation of how slowly Major's had got under way, that if something unexpected were to happen Portillo would need an organisation in being to start work straight away, so without any word with him I set about creating one. By the spring of 1995 I had an embryo campaign team, drawn from inside the House and out. Of course if the time were to come Portillo would want to make all kinds of changes to such plans, including a campaign manager drawn from the Cabinet, but at least he would not be starting from scratch. I secured the promise of an ideal campaign headquarters within walking distance of the Commons, which already had multiple phone outlets installed. I also made tentative arrangements for a substitute HQ, less well appointed, in case unforeseen circumstances should make use of the first venue impossible. I was extremely worried that some hint of these preparations would leak to the press, and I deliberately never told Portillo; if a journalist were to ask him, he could reply with total honesty that he knew nothing whatsoever about any such plans. Ironically, when in the summer of 1995 Major did stake all by resigning as leader and offering himself for re-election, Portillo's private adviser David Hart quite independently came to the same conclusion: that if the contest did get as far as a second round then his master would need an HQ. Alas, he was caught by the press installing phone cables outside a house in nearby North Street at the same time as Portillo was expressing his support for Major, thereby embarrassing Portillo considerably. In fact none of this was necessary at all; a mothball campaign team and wired-up campaign HQ were already there, waiting to be mobilised.

Throughout 1994 Major was being hammered by the media, and few Sundays passed without reference to the possibility that he would be challenged for the leadership that autumn. Lamont was mentioned; John Carlisle (jokingly called the Member for Pretoria South due to his staunch support for South Africa) said that if no-one else came forward, he might; while Tony Marlow was huffing and puffing in the wings. Though there were several Tory MPs who thought Major was a walking disaster, much of the speculation was press led; it was not until the summer of that year that I heard serious talk of an attempt to depose him. Roger Knapman was a friend dating from the 1987 intake, a consistent opponent of Maastricht and a man of sober judgement. During the recess he asked if I could meet him and Chris Gill, another conviction politician of immense courage, over lunch to discuss something that was worrying them. Both were members of the 92 and were looking to me for guidance. In the end Gill was not able to make the date I suggested, so Knapman and I lunched together that September in Soho. He and Gill had discussed the situation at length, and concluded there was no way the Tories could win the next election under Major's leadership. They were sure that many from their political generation thought the same. The question was, how to get rid of him. They knew of my reputation as a back-bench tactician, even plotter, and Knapman suggested I should take the task in hand.

I pointed out that it would be most unwise to embark on such a project without having a replacement in mind, so who did he suggest? His answer was Portillo or Redwood; I responded by saying I knew Portillo was certainly not minded to mount a challenge, nor was it in his interest to do so. A 'stalking horse' from the back benches was the only way the leadership question could be opened up; we both remembered Anthony Meyer's challenge to Margaret Thatcher in 1989. But I reminded Knapman how the rules governing leadership elections had since been changed: for a contest to take place at all, the rules now required 10 per cent of the parliamentary party to write to the 1922 chairman asking him to institute an election and invite nominations. That meant assembling thirty-four Tory MPs, and all my experience as chairman of the 92 told me there were not that number whose courage was sufficiently strong. 'You and Chris are simply counting up the grumblers,' I told him, 'but if it came to the crunch, I guess very few would actually put their names on paper.'

The following month Major found himself embroiled in the Neil Hamilton saga. Though Hamilton protested he had never been paid by

Harrods owner Mohammed Fayed to table parliamentary questions, and Major had initially supported the minister's efforts to clear his name, he unfortunately accepted Heseltine's advice that this was politically inconvenient for the Government and so sacked Hamilton without any idea whether the accusations against him were true. This affronted the right in the party, who saw this as weak leadership, allowing Heseltine – from the opposite wing of the party to Hamilton and to us – to call the shots.

By the time the Commons returned from the summer recess and the fortnightly meetings of the 92 steering committee resumed over sherry in my room, it was clear that – contrary to my advice to Knapman only weeks before – pressure was building up in the parliamentary party for a challenge to Major's leadership to be mounted once the Queen's Speech was behind us. However, I still advised caution, saying that the 92 should never be seen as being part of such manoeuvres. There were rumours that Lamont would be a stalking horse, and if not him, then Carlisle – all with a view to denying Major a sufficient majority to avoid a second ballot, when the race would be opened up to all comers. Edward Leigh began sounding out opinion on whether the thirty-four names required to trigger a contest could be found.

I steered clear of this, though some close to Major were bent on identifying *me* as the 'guilty plotter'. Terry Dicks, a voluble MP who was putty in the hands of Major's aides, claimed in a *Newsnight* interview that I was the one canvassing for names. He later told a journalist that my approach to Tory backbenchers was: 'Look, we need 34 names; we've already got 32, so if you sign now, I'll add mine and we've got him!' Fortunately the journalist checked this story out with me and, when I denied it vehemently, made no further use of it. Clearly I had to do something to shut up the loud-mouth Dicks, so I engaged a solicitor to warn him that if he repeated his alleged libel he would face court action. This was expensive, but thankfully it worked. The very fact that a Tory MP had to threaten a libel action against a colleague speaks volumes about how bitter the internal warfare was becoming.

I find no national anniversary more moving than Remembrance Sunday, as wreaths of poppies are laid and the Last Post sounded at precisely the same moment at Whitehall's Cenotaph and at war memorials across the land, in memory of those who gave their lives to safeguard our freedom in two World Wars and since. But for six carefully chosen members of John Major's Cabinet, Remembrance Sunday in 1995 was to acquire a different significance: with the poppies discarded from their buttonholes they arrived for a supper at 10 Downing Street with a far more brutal purpose – to work out how to crush those back-bench Tories who had put their political lives at risk in defence of that self-same national freedom. This was a significant landmark in Major's decline and fall and, like the rest, was totally unnecessary and self-inflicted.

The danger was seen to come from the European Communities (Finance) Bill, which would implement the decisions over further funding to the European Union reached at the Edinburgh Summit the previous December. The Government had a Commons majority of fourteen, which should have become thirty-two with the promised support of the Ulster Unionists – but was that enough to survive a rebellion by Tory Euro-sceptics? Chief whip Ryder was convinced it was not.

Those invited to the discussion over supper were Hurd, Clarke, Heseltine, Howard, Rifkind and Ryder. Howard was the sole Euro-sceptic; the gathering was kept secret from Portillo, Lilley and Redwood. The inclusion of Howard was seen as a deft move to separate him from these three, though how he came to agree to the final decision is a matter of mystery. This decision was to turn the Bill's second reading into a vote of confidence in the Government. The tactic had worked before at the end of the Maastricht saga, and was clearly to be wheeled out again whenever the Government sensed trouble. The fateful decision had all the hallmarks of Clarke's gung-ho approach – he was said to have urged that the Euro-sceptics be 'crushed like beetles' – but according to Anthony Seldon's biography of Major, this aggressive line was also taken by Hurd and by Major himself. Perhaps he was acting out his dream when he confided to ITN's political editor Michael Brunson at a private dinner back in June: 'I'm going to fucking crucify the right.' But I doubt whether he and his close colleagues ever understood that back-bench objection to European policy now ran so deep that some would abstain on a confidence vote. It was a fatal error of judgement.

On the Thursday before Monday's vote I passed Chris Gill in the Central Lobby; I knew his name was early in the list of parliamentary questions to the Prime Minister that afternoon, and I asked what line he was going to take. I could tell at once he had reached a decision after days of agonising. 'I can't tell anyone, even you,' he said, 'but I don't imagine I'll be popular.' When his supplementary question came it was devastating: did the Prime Minister understand he would rather resign the whip than vote for a Bill with which he and so many of his colleagues disagreed with such intensity? Whatever accusations might be made against Gill, lack of courage will never be one of them. My own courage was not of the same order. I too objected to tipping still more taxpayers' money into the bottomless pit of Europe, but I argued this was a straight consequence of the Maastricht Treaty, which we had failed to defeat. With a heavy heart I voted with the Government. But eight honoured their consciences to the end – Gill, Nick Budgen, Michael Cartiss, Teresa Gorman, Tony Marlow, Richard Shepherd, Teddy Taylor and John Wilkinson.

With a Commons majority of just fourteen I never imagined that Major and Ryder would be so insane as to wipe out that majority by withdrawing the whip from these eight, yet withdrawn it was. 'Those whom the gods wish to destroy they first make mad', and this was suicidal madness. Another Euro-sceptic who had given the Government the benefit of his doubts, Richard Body, promptly resigned the whip by way of protest. By implementing the threat agreed at that Downing Street 'suicide supper' the Tory Party was rent asunder as it had never been even during the entire passage of the Maastricht Bill. Amidst all the wreckage there was just one consolation for Major: if any of the banished nine had been minded to sign a letter to Marcus Fox calling for a leadership election, they were no longer in a position to do so. There was now no question that the required thirty-four names could ever be obtained.

The business of the Tory Party could never be conducted but for a whole range of private lunch, dining, even breakfast clubs at which like-minded backbenchers, often with help from ministers, put their heads together regularly to work out where their party was going and what they should do about it. The biggest were the 92 on the right, and the Lollards (superseded by Mainstream) on the left; smaller groups like One Nation, Nick's Diner, No Turning Back and, over a briefer period, the Blue Chips which overlapped the first two, but even smaller groupings came into being as needs dictated. It was in the summer of 1994 that I invited a few radical colleagues, mostly from the 92, to lunch in the upstairs room at the Gran Paradiso restaurant to discuss how we could best press the Government into pursuing policies more to the liking of natural Conservatives – for instance, on taxation – that would help bring back those voters who were so conspicuously deserting us. Fewer than ten were at the first lunch, yet the discussion was so stimulating that we decided to make it a regular gathering to which more sympathisers would be invited. The Upstairs Club, as we came to call ourselves, met at intervals of two months or more until late 1996. Altogether twenty-two colleagues attended at one time or another, but as usual there was a hard core of around ten, made up of David Amess,

Vivian Bendall, Alan Duncan, Iain Duncan-Smith, Bernard Jenkin, Barry Legg, David Martin, Graham Riddick, David Shaw and John Townend.

We were worried over security. To reach the upstairs room at Gran Paradiso you had to walk through the restaurant, much frequented by Tory colleagues and even ministers. Over the past three years there had been an increasingly totalitarian tendency in the Tory Party: every suggestion or idea had to survive the test of whether it was 'loyal to Major' or not, and in this gulag atmosphere any rumour that backbenchers were meeting in secret would soon reach the whips' office and offered to Downing Street as evidence of 'plotting'. For this reason we met occasionally at L'Amico's restaurant in Horseferry Road, but we preferred Gran Paradiso, where we avoided attention by staggering our times of arrival and departure.

The purpose of the lunches was to discuss *policy*, not personality, but we were drawn up sharply at our second gathering. I had invited David Evans, whose apparent lack of sophistication was well compensated by his instinctive understanding of how the man-in-the-street thinks. We were barely out of our first course before Evans let rip: 'Yer all kiddin' yerselves. Come on, be honest – we all know what the *real* trouble is. It's 'im, Major. Fat lot of use sittin' on yer arses and talkin' abaht gettin' 'im to adopt sensible policies – 'e'll never do it. 'E's a dead loss. What we ought to be talkin' abaht is 'ow to get rid of 'im.' Rarely are politicians lost for words, but his outburst was followed by stunned silence. Evans had brought us face the face with the unmentionable. Each one of us felt in our hearts that he was probably right, yet we could not face the implications. We settled instead for the vain hope that we could still win the next election, even under Major – if only he could be persuaded to get his policies right, especially over taxation and Europe. The next lunch invitation I sent stressed that our purpose was '*not* to plot the downfall of John Major or even to discuss the possibility of stalking horses, etc. Rather it is how we might best act to strengthen the Government in pursuing the kind of policies that will win back our natural supporters in time for the next election.' I can record with total honesty that the Upstairs Club was never a vehicle for leadership plotting. Perhaps it should have been.

Our hopes were raised again at the start of 1995, when Major appeared to be moving towards a credible European policy. In a TV interview with David Frost he took a hard line over any additional powers for the European Parliament and against any extension of qualified majority voting. By this time he had the veteran John Ward as his PPS in place of the ineffectual Graham Bright, and Ward could give him far

shrewder briefing on the state of feeling on the back benches. In his
Frost interview Major hinted at a national referendum on whether to
join a European single currency, and looked forward to the whipless
nine being back within the fold fairly soon. By then there was overwhelming evidence of the support they were getting from their own
constituents for taking their principled stand. Most were members of
the 92, and I made it clear that withdrawal of the whip made no difference to their membership; indeed, I urged them personally to continue
to attend our regular meetings. Towards the end of January they held a
press conference, and said that when they resumed the whip they
would do so together – a perfectly reasonable position. On important
matters they still voted with the Government, and furthermore voted to
ensure it was not endangered as a result of their expulsion when it came
to appointing members of standing committees.

When, well into February, there had still been no movement to bring
the whipless nine back, the 92's steering committee decided I should
offer to serve as a go-between. After checking again that they were all
willing to accept the whip if asked, I wrote to Major assuring him that
an invitation would not be rejected. He replied that there was no
impediment to them returning, provided they accepted the obligations
of membership of the parliamentary party. Yet still nothing happened,
and further inquiries established that the blockage came from Ryder,
who wanted a pledge from them first that they would never defy the
whip on European business again. This amounted to a far more stringent condition than even those of us in receipt of the whip could ever
accept, so not surprisingly deadlock continued. Not until mid-April,
when the Tories faced near wipeout in the local elections, did Major
bypass Ryder and call in Michael Spicer as a go-between. The whole
sorry saga, which was unnecessary in the first place and could have
been ended in January, was not concluded until 24 April. In the next
reshuffle, Ryder went.

It was a frequent cry from the blind loyalists in the party that the reason for our repeated humiliations at the hands of the voters were that
we were seen as a divided party, that it was all the fault of 'Cash and
his cronies'. I always disputed that this was the case, and I still do. The
bulk of ministers, the bulk of backbenchers, and the bulk of party
activists beyond were far more united over preserving Britain as a
nation state within Europe than they had ever been in the early 1980s
over Thatcherite economics. The real, and damaging, split was not
between backbenchers and the Government, but within the Cabinet
itself. The pattern of competing forces that was allowed to tie Major's
hands until the election became apparent from January 1995, when

Chancellor Clarke began to push quite openly a policy towards Europe that was very different from Major's. Thus the more sceptical lead given by Major in his Frost interview was followed a fortnight later by Clarke proclaiming on the same programme his support for joining a single currency, saying this was necessary if Britain was to be 'at the heart of Europe'. Major decided to use his invitation to speak at CWF's annual president's dinner at the start of February to spell out his new approach further, in which he conceded that joining a single currency would have profound constitutional consequences, and that the Government was setting further conditions over and above those agreed at Maastricht. Yet only a week later, Clarke, in a speech to the European Movement, flatly contradicted him, saying amazingly that it was possible to have monetary union without political union – and commending both. Thus whatever moves Major made to bring his Government's policy more in line with that desired by the bulk of his party, Clarke was ready to jump in and contradict. This deadlock never allowed Major to develop the European policy which he seemed to want and certainly needed.

I and many others spoke with John Ward, who at least seemed to have Major's ear, only to see him spread his hands in despair. 'Yes, George, I'm sure that's what John would like to do, but how do you get round Clarke? He's made it clear he'd resign rather than see your policy pushed any further. Do you really think we can stand the loss of a Chancellor?' So long as Clarke was at the Treasury he had a crippling veto over any development of policy. It was sheer frustration over this veto, sustained over several months, which largely explains the critical and bad-tempered meeting Major had with the Fresh Start Group in the larger ministerial conference room on 13 June.

The invitation to Major to attend a special meeting with us was pressed by Peter Tapsell, one of the most erudite Euro-sceptics. But clearly he had neglected to tell Major that the Group had grown considerably over the past year, taking in many who had reluctantly obeyed the whip during the Maastricht Bill yet now realised they had been conned. When Major arrived, fifteen minutes late, he was taken aback to find some sixty of his backbenchers, by no means all from the right, waiting to press their anxieties on him.

The meeting began agreeably enough, with tables thumped as a leader would expect. Across the table sat Norman Lamont, widely tipped to challenge him for the leadership that autumn – their first meeting since Lamont's sacking. Michael Spicer, in the chair, thanked Major for coming, said we would confine ourselves to questions on the single currency and how powers could be reclaimed from Brussels, and invited him to bat first. Major, aware of the nature of his audience, sought to adopt a sceptic stance: he doubted the practicalities of a single currency, which might never happen, but there was no sense in setting ourselves against it now. We had heard it all before. Barry Legg then put the anti-single-currency case, but the meeting really sprang to life when John Townend, 1922 executive member and chairman of the back-bench finance committee, jumped in: 'As far as most people are concerned, Prime Minister, it's time for you to come off the fence. The vast majority in the party and in the country would welcome a statement by you that so long as you are Prime Minister you would not advise the Commons to accept a single currency.' Hearty cheers erupted all round the room, and after this Major never regained the initiative. Lamont told him that if a single currency was unacceptable in principle in 1999, then it was unacceptable now. I then disputed Major's point that businessmen wanted a single currency, and said people had the right to expect a clear lead from him. 'There is no way we can fight the next election on a wait-and-see platform,' I warned him.

Major, tight-lipped and pale, repeated his position, and made the mistake of telling Townend that the public were not interested in the European issue – a point often made by Heseltine, but which all of us knew from attending constituency meetings was not the case. Spicer then invited Iain Duncan-Smith to put the case for pulling some powers back from Brussels, but Major, getting tetchy, interrupted him before he had finished. To one of his assertions Bernard Jenkin shouted: 'That's not true'; Major snapped back: 'It is true.' Bill Cash then took him on, but Major's sole response was to tell Cash that he had 'always misrepresented what I achieved at Maastricht'. By now several were openly heckling the Prime Minister. Spicer tried to restore order, but failed. In desperation he called in Ivan Lawrence, distinguished silk, member of the 1922 executive and chairman of the Home Affairs Select Committee – but Lawrence only made matters worse. 'You say Europe is not top of people's agendas. It's up to us to put it at the top. Just as you're arguing against devolution as a derogation of our sovereignty, so you must argue the same over a single currency. Just give a lead on this, Prime Minister, and you'll find a popular response. Without it we're done for.' Sir Nicholas Bonsor, who the previous autumn came close to wresting Marcus Fox from the 1922 Chairmanship, put a question, and when Major gave an evasive answer he accused the Prime Minister of distorting his question. By this time the meeting had become thoroughly bad-tempered, and after forty-five minutes Major stalked out with his entourage to only perfunctory applause. He had become the stag at bay. As he left I distinctly heard someone crack: 'I can see thirty-three names all right' – a reference to the number of signatures needed to force a leadership contest that autumn. Alan Clark, in his book *The Tories*, claims that I had already secured the thirty-three names. Not so; I made no effort to do so, though Clark's error is forgivable since he was not in the Commons at the time.

That meeting marked a watershed for me personally. Until then, as is the habit among politicians, I had persuaded myself that despite the current opinion polls we *could* still win the next election under Major's leadership. After that meeting I had to face the fact that so long as he remained leader, we could never win. But that bitter, acrimonious meeting had an even more telling effect on Major himself – for it was after this humiliating experience that he decided to lance the boil, resign as party leader and seek a renewed mandate from the parliamentary party.

After the showdown with Major, I left the Commons as soon as business was finished to reflect deeply on my own and try to analyse the situation in which the party was placed. There was no way we could win so long as he led us; he was deaf to party opinion, both inside the House and out, deaf to all the advice coming from the Tory press and the public at large. He was as obstinate as Ted Heath had ever been during his decline and fall. But would Tory MPs ever have the courage to ditch him, instead of preferring to shelter behind that self-deceptive optimism which had affected me too? There was much talk of a stalking horse to force a leadership election in the autumn; Norman Lamont, still keeping his cards close to his chest, was the favourite, though others were willing to volunteer if he did not. By then I was certain enough names would be forthcoming to activate a contest. The outcome would undoubtedly be damaging to Major, but would it be enough to topple him? Many on the right would love to see him go, yet feared that in an open contest too many in the centre would swing behind Heseltine rather than Portillo; equally, many on the left would prefer to keep Major, whom they felt they could control through Clarke, rather than see Portillo scrape home. Others would simply bury their heads in the sand, arguing that such a public squabble would put paid to our chances of winning the election that was looming ever closer. The myth propagated by the party Establishment and by Central Office – that the sole reason for the voters withdrawing support from the party was because it was split – was accepted by too many MPs who had little idea of the principles at stake.

My conclusion was that thirty-three plus names on a letter to Marcus Fox asking him to activate a leadership election would *not* be enough to secure the desired result. What was needed was some other development, another factor in the situation – such as some resignations from the Cabinet in protest that the lack of decisiveness at the top was leading to certain election defeat. Some Tory press commentators, most notably Simon Heffer, had long been berating the Euro-sceptics in the Cabinet for leaving it to backbenchers to make the points of principle while clinging cosily to their departments and salaries and ministerial perks, silent passengers as Major steered the Tory ship onto the rocks. Until then I had accepted the logic of their position, yet now it seemed all the logic pointed the other way. If Lilley and Portillo, joined possibly by Redwood, found a cause on which they could resign together before the new session in the autumn, then the thirty-three plus names would have real effect – not by opening the way for a stalking horse, but by enabling Portillo to challenge Major directly. No doubt others, like Heseltine and Clarke, would seize the opportunity to jump onto the bandwagon and into the fray. This seemed the obviously desirable outcome – yet I had my doubts whether it would ever come about. I also knew that I needed to watch my back – there were wolves in my Reigate association out to get me, plotting my deselection as candidate in the coming election (see Chapter Ten).

Two days later I was lunching with John Redwood at Pomegranates restaurant just around the corner from my flat in Dolphin Square, where at lunchtime at least we were unlikely to be gazed upon by fellow politicians. I gave him my account of the punch-up with Major, which confirmed all he had heard already. I then told him that in my view there would be more than thirty-three back-bench names to force a leadership poll in the autumn, but that this would be pointless unless some Euro-sceptics broke ranks within the Cabinet, forcing the rest to realise just how serious the situation was. He looked at me archly, then said: 'Don't ever assume that nothing will move on that front.' I smiled back, but deliberately did not press him. Clearly John Redwood was nearing the end of his tether.

Seven days later, on Thursday 22 June, Major announced to the world from the garden at 10 Downing Street that he was resigning at Tory leader in order to renew his mandate. 'It is in no-one's interest that this [leadership sniping] continues right through until November ... I am no longer prepared to tolerate the present situation.' Then, to his critics in the party: 'It is time to shut up, or put up.' Part of his package was a request that there be no further leadership contest till after the general election, which the 1922 committee later accepted. Later that afternoon Lamont sought my opinion; I suggested he hold back for a day or so – I could hardly tell him what I thought Redwood would do.

This was the most brilliant tactical move that Major ever made – certainly better even than his convenient wisdom-tooth trouble when his benefactor Margaret Thatcher needed his active support most. It took all but a few of his closest colleagues completely by surprise, and put the initiative squarely in his hands. Among those caught off guard was Redwood, who consulted friends over what he should do. Following our lunch the previous week, I had little doubt that he would resign and run, and indeed in a phone conversation I encouraged him to do so. But he knew that my support extended only to the first ballot in the hope that, by denying Major the 50-plus-15-per-cent majority required by the rules for a clear win, this would open up the field for a second ballot, which I was sure Portillo would enter. All my planning for an HQ and for a skeleton campaign team that could swing into immediate action had been designed to meet such an eventuality.

I was constrained in my public statements by the fact that I was chairman of the 92 group, which I knew would be split down the middle by this contest – as it had been by the last. Once nominations had closed it was our habit to invite the contestants to address the group in succession and answer questions, and as chairman of these meetings I had to be scrupulous in not declaring my own preference in advance. For that reason I did not do so, though that did not stop the likes of Tony Durant and Jim Spicer, passionate Major loyalists, from suggesting that I should hand the task over the a more 'neutral' chairman. The candidates' meeting with the 92 took place on the Monday evening, on the eve of the poll. Major presented his case well, though without great inspiration, and unfortunately many present were able to recall his Euro-sceptic assurances when he was seeking their votes in 1990. He now stuck firmly to his 'wait-and-see' line on joining a European single currency. His supporters cheered loudly as he left, while the rest gave polite applause. Redwood, by contrast, seized all the opportunities open to him, appealing to the ideals shared by most other members of the 92, and pledging a firm stand against the single currency. He spoke with real passion and commitment; his was by far the better performance of the two, though I suppose that, as the challenger, he had it made.

With that meeting over I was free to declare my allegiance. I had consulted all the officers, branch officers, councillors and recent councillors in my Reigate seat by confidential postal ballot, and found a majority of only 10 per cent in favour of continuing under Major's leadership. I had made clear I would be influenced by their views but not bound by them, and the fact that the margin was so narrow encouraged me to exercise my own judgement as to what was best for the party. John Townend, the 92's secretary, left it till after the meeting to declare his support for Redwood too – in his case, backed by his local party's executive council. Before the 92's meeting I had written an article for the *Daily Mail,* which appeared on polling day, arguing that the party desperately needed a ballot open to *all* likely contenders; that meant voting for Redwood in the first instance, if only to force a second ballot by denying Major the margin he needed to win outright. The argument seemed simple to me, yet I was amazed how obtuse some of my colleagues were in comprehending it; even two who at my Upstairs Club lunches had been most vitriolic in their criticism of Major argued that they could not vote for Redwood 'because he's not yet Prime Minister material'. 'But that's not the point,' I stormed. 'It's whether you want a second ballot with an open field, or not.' But no, they were scuttling to hide under nanny's apron.

In the event, Major carried the day, thanks to a pact, hinted at earlier but confirmed at the last minute, with Heseltine, under which Heseltine would become Deputy Prime Minister, thus bringing the latter's regimented supporters out to vote during the afternoon – but even then Major had a close shave. The figures were Major 218, Redwood 89, abstentions or spoiled papers 22. If but 16 of Major's voters had abstained instead, or just eight defected straight to Redwood, then Major would have been denied his 50-plus-15-per-cent majority, and a second ballot would have been necessary. More than one third of the parliamentary party had refused to endorse him, though you would never have thought this from the triumphalist display by his close supporters during interviews outside St Stephen's Entrance and on College Green. But the party was exhausted, and Major's lead was enough to be accepted. Redwood conceded defeat and congratulated Major, and when I saw the Prime Minister later that evening I did the same. In thanking me he said he hoped everyone could now work together for the sake of the party.

Many were branded by this experience. Redwood, despite conceding defeat gracefully, was never forgiven even by his former right-wing cabinet colleagues, though at least his hands were freed to argue for his own policies. Portillo, I thought, suffered worst. His friends, including me, had advised him not to declare his hand, but to keep his head down in the first ballot, ready to stand in the second if there was one. But the chance never came, and he became almost a shadow of his former self; many of his friends cringed to hear him declaiming a meaningless plea for 'Unity – Unity – Unity' from the platform at the next party conference; he was worthy of much more than this. He was not the only one whose reputation suffered from continuing to be part of such a putrid Cabinet.

Looking back, it was the pact with Heseltine that put paid to all hope of flexibility right up to the election. During the election Major was to plead eloquently in support of his 'wait-and-see' European policy: 'Whether you agree with me or disagree with me, like me or loathe me, don't bind my hands.' In fact, his hands were bound on the morning of 4 July, 1995, when he agreed to make Heseltine Deputy Prime Minister, in overall charge of a range of government policies, in return for Heseltine delivering his own supporters' votes. For months Major had been afraid of upsetting Chancellor Clarke on European policy; now the combined pressure of Clarke and a new Deputy Prime Minister would rob him of any freedom to develop that policy in the direction which he himself would probably have preferred. He had thrown down the gauntlet, yet in order to secure victory had made himself a prisoner.

Major's victory presented a golden opportunity to reconstruct his Cabinet and thus make it more representative of party opinion; the expected departure of Hurd, Hunt, Ryder and Aitken gave him ample scope, and no-one expected him to continue with the accident-prone Jeremy Hanley as Party Chairman. But he let the opportunity slip in quite spectacular manner. He still blamed the right for making it impossible for him to carry on without needing to renew his mandate, and in reconstructing his Cabinet he took his revenge, even though many of the right's leading figures had been foremost in his campaign team. True, Portillo was given the senior post of Defence Secretary, leading right-winger Michael Forsyth was elevated to Scottish Secretary as reward for his active support in the leadership election, and William Hague, still not clearly identifiable as coming from the right, was made Welsh Secretary. Hague was in fact as strongly Euro-sceptic as his predecessor, though as a new boy in Cabinet was far more cautious about sticking his neck out. But all this in no way compensated for the greatly increased power given to Heseltine, or the promotion to Cabinet of the ultra-Wet, Euro-enthusiast Sir George Young – yesterday's man if ever there was one – or of the hapless Douglas Hogg to Agriculture. John Gummer, who did nothing to bolster the party's reputation for anything except petulance and whose sole purpose appeared to be to further the aims of the European Movement, was retained as were a couple of other deadbeats. But worst of all was that not one Tory radical was left in any of the economic departments; all were controlled by the left, committed to welfarism and the high taxes needed to sustain it. As an election-winning team it looked a recipe for disaster, only slightly relieved by the appointment of Brian Mawhinney, by no means from the right but a tough realist with his feet on the ground, as party chairman.

The morning after the leadership ballot, before these cabinet dispositions were known, the 92's steering committee met in my room to assess the situation. I knew that all bar one had voted for Redwood, though not all had announced that publicly. Though the result had gone against our wishes, we decided to do all we could to ensure that the 92 gave Major active support and encouragement. After Mawhinney was made Party Chairman, I invited him to be guest speaker at our next St Stephen's Club dinner, which he gladly accepted. Despite the disappointment of the cabinet reconstruction we bit our tongues and said nothing. The agony of the leadership election had left backbenchers emotionally drained, and a general desire to show unity before the party conference was evident. Major had an easy run when he spoke to the full 1922 committee before rising. 'If you're worried about anything, my door is always open' he assured us, but many of us knew that was not so. Ever since the 92 steering committee's abortive gathering with him some eighteen months earlier, we had been seeking the promised resumed meeting, but to us Major's door was always closed. Not until that November was it pushed ajar for us. Meanwhile Michael Spicer called no further meetings of the Fresh Start Group, and in the European argument there was an effective truce. We suffered a further trouncing in the Littleborough and Saddleworth by-election at the end of July, showing that the new cabinet line-up hardly inspired the voters, but as the Commons broke up for the summer our ambitions extended little further than seeing the conference through without further trouble.

Through our various discussions within the Steering Committee, at the Upstairs Club and among CWF activists, we decided to switch our pressure to securing meaningful cuts in government spending in the autumn Budget, to make way for tax cuts. This had been a long-running theme from the right, though with little practical response from the Chancellor. Six days after Major's re-election, the 92's policy group – open to all members except ministers and whips – agreed the strategy, and at the end of July the steering committee members saw Clarke to present our pre-Budget submission. The line agreed by the group that the priority was not to cut 2 pence off the basic rate, but rather to target relief on 'those who naturally look to a Conservative Government for protection' like the elderly, home owners, those who save and those who provide a secure environment for their children. We argued that if he was prepared to be ruthless, he could prune £10 million from public spending, and reminded him that this would be the last Budget whose benefits would be felt by voters in their pockets before early May 1997. Clarke listened patiently, though in the end we might as well have been talking to a brick wall. But a full report of our meeting led the front page of the *Daily Telegraph,* and we knew from the flood of letters that followed how closely we represented Tory grassroots opinion. The pressure was renewed on the eve of October's conference, when CWF's *Forward* magazine carried an article by Redwood on how we could start delivering on our tax promises, while the editorial argued that 'there can be no argument that significant tax cuts, in one form or another, are essential'. The same message came through at Conference fringe meetings and indeed in the economic debate itself.

The damaging single currency disagreement was put on the back burner. In September many of us were invited to a delightful party given by Major at Number Ten to honour Baroness Thatcher's birthday, as well as Sir Denis reaching the age of eighty, at which old hatchets seemed to be well and truly buried. At the conference, even Norman Lamont's speech to the CWF fringe was under the mollifying title: 'We are all Euro-sceptics now.' So how did the truce break down?

The conference at Blackpool got off to a shaky start with the news that a Tory MP, Alan Howarth, was defecting straight to Labour. I knew Howarth well. Once a convinced Thatcherite and a 92 Group member, he confided to me earlier that year that he felt uncomfortable with us on a number of 'social conscience' issues. Could he remain a member of the 92 while joining up with Peter Temple-Morris's Mainstream Group? I advised him he had to choose one or the other, and he chose Mainstream – but that proved only a temporary resting place till he moved over to Labour completely. Most Tory MPs were shaken to the core, and were vitriolic in denouncing Howarth's 'treachery'. I could not regard it this way; if that was where his conscience took him, then so be it. Besides, there was no guarantee that Labour's leadership could find him a safe seat for the election. But party stability was hardly helped by some of the Euro-enthusiasts briefing the press anonymously that unless the Government took a 'more positive' stand on Europe, there would be other Tory MPs following Howarth. The briefing almost certainly came from Temple-Morris or Hugh Dykes, and the threat had often been used in the past to try to strengthen their position. But this one left a nasty aftertaste, and gave many on the right the chance to point out that, for all Major's apparent detestation of the right, it was the left who seemed willing to turn traitor.

The effect on the conference was predictably to pull it together, but sure enough the pro-Europeans would soon do their best to pull it apart. Portillo, winding up the defence debate, gave a brilliant speech, pledging that a Tory Government would never allow European institutions to get control over Britain's defence forces, and ending somewhat histrionically by adapting the SAS motto, declaring 'We dare! And we will win!' The conference loved it, the cheers lifting to the ceiling of the Winter Gardens Ballroom, and Major joined in the standing ovation. He had read the speech earlier, and liked it. But all this was too much for the acolytes of Clarke and Heseltine, who immediately briefed the press on how 'vulgar and tasteless' Portillo's performance was. They also claimed Portillo was attacking a European bogeyman which did not exist, obviously ignorant of all that continental politicians were saying about a European common defence policy. I saw this as the first sign that the truce over Europe was starting to crumble. But the conference ended successfully, with Major delivering his best rally speech ever.

The party returned for the spill-over from the 1995–96 session in good humour, but the lack of control from the top was soon apparent. Vacillation over the Nolan Committee's proposals for public disclosure of Members' outside earnings led to a free vote on the matter, but with the payroll vote whipped – never a happy arrangement – and the outcome was a defeat for Major's recommendation by fifty-one votes. The Queen's Speech in mid-November contained some promises of good legislation on criminal-law reform, but there was no central theme. It also contained a commitment to Lord Chancellor Mackay's Divorce Bill – an extraordinary decision for the last full session of a Parliament, given that Mackay's proposals split the party down the middle over 'family values'. I was admitted to Chelsea and Westminster Hospital the next day for some treatment where I remained for ten days, and was surprised to receive a personal note from Major wishing me a speedy recovery; Prime Ministers do not always make this kind of gesture, which I took as proof that our personal relations were on the mend. I came out in time for Clarke's Budget – an ultra-cautious affair with a paltry 1p off standard-rate tax, which was a great disappointment to everyone. We were buoyed up with the promise that 'this will leave room for something more generous just before the election', but we knew that a vital opportunity to start political recovery had been lost. Clarke was too enamoured of the welfare state to start tinkering with it himself.

Soon after Christmas Emma Nicholson defected to the Liberal Democrats – no real loss, having always been a Euro-enthusiast and a Wet, though I recalled with amusement her attack on me and her paean of praise for Major after the 92 steering committee's aborted meeting with him. She claimed it was the whipping on Nolan that pushed her over, though others thought she was jumping ship with an eye on a Lib-Dem peerage or possibly being a Lib-Dem MEP. Clearly she saw no hope of the Tories winning the election, and in fact a growing number of Tory MPs were coming to agree with her. Her defection brought our overall majority down to three. Another Tory, Peter Thurnham, followed her later.

In January I decided the time was ripe for me to retire as chairman of the 92; I had already made clear, when beating off a whips' office challenge in the form of Anthony Durant, that I wanted to see another chairman in place before the coming general election. Nominations were opened, and two contenders came forward: John Townend, who had served diligently as secretary and treasurer, and Neil Hamilton, seeking a fuller parliamentary role following his removal from the Government. His tortuous legal saga with the *Guardian* had not yet begun. I had always been very close to Hamilton since the days when we shared an office, and had known his wife Christine for far longer, but I thought it unwise of him to put his name forward. However, he had considerable support, partly based on sympathy from those who thought Major had given him a raw deal, and from others who wondered whether Townend was too much the hard man. In fact there was no doctrinal difference between them, and Townend was elected. A few days later the *Guardian* printed its allegations that Hamilton had taken money from Mohammed Fayed to table questions in the Commons. When I handed the chairmanship over to Townend at the next 92 group dinner, I was presented with a handsome port decanter and glasses to mark my years building up the group's influence.

The Government's drift continued on through 1996, as I was fighting my battle against deselection in Reigate. Sir Richard Scott's report on the Arms-to-Iraq affair put ministers on the defensive, and in the Commons debate at the end of February the Government scraped home by one vote. Major refused to countenance any ministerial resignations, though the consensus on the backbenches was that Attorney-General Nick Lyell should have gone, given the nature of the advice which he had given ministers.

The big European issue did not stay off centre stage for long, as preparations were made for the Inter-Governmental Conference (IGC) to update the Maastricht Treaty. At first the Government line was that this would be a simple matter of reviewing progress with no major decisions being taken, but the dangers were obvious. Accordingly, with my encouragement, Bill Cash established a new IGC monitoring group in January, though many still referred to this loosely as 'Fresh Start'. Apart from Michael Spicer, who had retired hurt and wished to concentrate on chairing his European Research Group, which had very useful contacts with anti-EMU politicians throughout Europe, and Roger Knapman, who had been made a junior whip, its members were much the same as before. Among former ministers, Norman Lamont was joined by John Redwood, while Iain Duncan-Smith, Peter Tapsell, John Biffen, Barry Legg and Bernard Jenkin played leading roles under Cash's chairmanship. Over the next twelve months, many who had once supported the Maastricht Bill, like Charles Wardle, David Wilshire and Anthony Steen, swelled our ranks. As before, the group was backed up by good research documents from Cash's European Foundation. We were ready for the next battle. Meanwhile the Staffordshire South East by-election saw a 22 per cent swing to Labour, while the May local elections cost the Tories 567 seats – the second worst result for thirty years. Ministers, led by Heseltine, simply whistled in the dark to keep their spirits up: 'Just wait for the "feel-good factor" to take effect.' But party morale in the constituencies was at rock bottom.

Opinion in the party, amongst the public and still more in the press was moving strongly against any deeper involvement in the European Union. What was happening to the British fishing fleet, the stupid confrontation between the Commission and Canada over fishing, where British opinion was overwhelmingly behind the Canadians, and soon the BSE debacle all played their part, together with a slow public realisation that all manner of British laws were now determined from Brussels or Strasbourg, leaving their own democratic Parliament powerless. As the BSE crisis unfolded, many Tory MPs were shocked to discover that the European Commission had the power not simply to ban our beef exports to the continent, but to the rest of the world as well. The message that came back from constituency speaking engagements was even stronger than when the Maastricht Bill was going through; party activists wanted to be loyal to Major, yet could not understand why he was paying no heed to their opinion. Soon after he became party chairman, Mawhinney initiated a massive consultation exercise covering every constituency association to establish the policy priorities of party members; he called it 'the most extensive consultation in the party's history'. The results that came back were totally consistent and predictable: lower taxation, tighter law and order, reform of welfare and above all no further entanglement in the European Union. The same message was delivered at area meetings. Mawhinney duly reported this to the Cabinet, while the advertising guru, Maurice Saatchi, whom he had engaged, saw a critical stance over further European involvement as a vital element in pre-election strategy. However, rumours filtered through that Heseltine and Clarke would have none of this. Whatever the rank and file might want, it was just never going to happen.

One by-product of this was a growing feeling that, if cabinet opinion was too divided to rule out Britain joining a single currency in the first wave, there was merit at least in promising a national referendum before any binding decision was taken. Sir James Goldsmith had set up his Referendum Party, and had highlighted the issue by promising to field candidates against all MPs who were not themselves committed to seeking a referendum on Britain's future in the EU. A single-currency referendum was seen as a defence against this, and was pushed by Euro-sceptics in the Cabinet (though oddly not by Portillo) in March; later, in Prime Minister's Questions, Major revealed that the Cabinet was considering this. Clarke, who was adamantly opposed, saw this as an attempt to bounce him and made his fury public. But the Tory back benches saw great merit in the idea, and the following month Clarke relented, claiming there could be 'no more concessions' to the Euro-sceptics. Meanwhile more Tories were flocking to join the IGC monitoring group, and we kept up pressure to reform our relations with the EU by use of the ten-minute rule procedure under which a back-bencher can use a ten-minute speech to seek permission to introduce his own bill to achieve a specific purpose, taking priority over the orders of the day. Since there is very rarely any time to consider such bills after they are introduced, the vote (in which the payroll vote does not take part) is largely propagandist and symbolic. In April Duncan-Smith sought to introduce a bill to make any decisions by the European Court subject to confirmation by the House of Commons; sixty-six Tories voted in favour, watched by sympathetic cabinet ministers Portillo and Forsyth. In June Bill Cash sought to introduce a bill to allow a national referendum on our future relationship with Europe – and this time eighty-six Tories voted for it. Major was livid, and retaliated by telling Cash he could no longer accept funds from Sir James Goldsmith to help run the European Foundation. This step marked the depth of Major's Stalinist instincts; such a totalitarian injunction was clearly unacceptable, and Baroness Thatcher jumped in to promise to make good whatever funding gap was left by the forcible exclusion of Goldsmith from the funds of Thatcher Foundation – and by then Goldsmith provided less than 25 per cent of the foundation's funding anyway. So Major ended up with egg all over his face.

When Major was a small child he must have learned and admired
the nursery jingle 'The Grand Old Duke of York, he had 10,000 men;
he marched them up to the top of the hill, then he marched them down
again', for periodically in his premiership he did his level best to emu-
late that military hero. The first obvious example was in 1994, when he
decided to take a stand over amending the procedures in the European
Council for qualified majority voting (QMV) to allow for the growth in
EC membership. On party platforms and in the Commons he made it
a great point of principle to resist change; Britain would exercise its
veto if necessary. He even derided John Smith, then Labour leader, as
'Monsieur Oui, the Poodle of Brussels'. This won him applause for
standing up for Britain, helped his MPs to win back waverers in their
constituencies, and no doubt made him feel good. But it turned out to
be an unsustainable position, and Douglas Hurd had to negotiate his
retreat at the EC Foreign Ministers meeting at Ionnina. It was the
same again when a European Summit had to find a successor to
Jacques Delors, president of the Commission and the supreme architect of European federalism. The European consensus favoured Jean-
Luc Dehaene, the Belgian Foreign Minister and an undoubted federalist. But Major would have none of it; Britain had a veto and was prepared to use it. He had obviously not worked out that there was no
non-federalist available; he tried to push the British Commissioner Sir
Leon Brittan (who more federalist than he?), but in vain. In the end,
after a month of huffing and puffing, he had to accept Jacques Santer,
no less a federalist that Delors – who the moment he was voted into
office delivered a swingeing attack on Britain!

So by the time the European Commission imposed a ban on all
exports of British beef (with little scientific justification), there were
several precedents for employing the Grand Duke's strategy. True to
form, Major announced a new policy of 'non co-operation' with the EU
until a timetable was fixed for the lifting of the ban on exports of beef
and beef products. 'Major digs his heels in for Britain', ran the headlines, while party activists were loud in their praise: he was showing
some fight at last. But the policy lasted barely one month, and at the
Florence Summit he was forced into a humiliating climb-down. Even
the publicity smokescreen could not hide the fact that he had agreed to
the slaughter of an *extra* 67,000 cattle, with *no* agreed timetable for lifting the ban. Small wonder that the party and the whole country were
becoming totally disillusioned with Europe. Word also reached us of a
bunker mentality starting to set in at Downing Street, with Major
believing stories of all kinds of back-bench plots to oust him. There
were no such plots; if there had been, I would have known about them.

Instead, the feeling was one of powerlessness to prevent the party being dragged towards oblivion.

Friday 28 June marked the culmination of the first attempt by a dissident faction in my Reigate association to deselect me as prospective candidate for the coming election (see Chapter Ten). I had booked the Jubilee Room off Westminster Hall for a press conference the following Monday in the event of my defeat to announce that I was applying for the Chiltern Hundreds – this is the way an MP resigns his or her seat to bring about a by-election. But this was never necessary, since I survived the 'shoot-out' by 311 votes to 206. The biggest cheer came when I pledged that so long as I lived, I would *never* vote to sell a Briton's birthright by joining a European single currency, and would campaign accordingly.

Though I was no longer chairman of the 92, I still organised my quite separate Upstairs Club at the Gran Paradiso restaurant. Alan Duncan had been a founder member, and though he was now PPS to Party Chairman Mawhinney I encouraged him to stay, provided he felt that no conflict of interest was involved. Even if Duncan did feel it to be his duty to report back, nothing said at these lunches was of a nature I would have wished to keep from Mawhinney; it was important that the Party Chairman should be aware of feeling in our section of the party. I was also still on the 92 steering committee, which met fortnightly in Townend's room (though without wine – odd since Townend was a wine merchant) and continued to get the feedback from the CWF network. 'By autumn 1996 it was accepted at meetings of the Upstairs Club and the 92 that under Major's style of leadership there was no way the party could possibly win the coming election. All discussion was of what we could do to limit the losses; the fear was that we faced near wipeout, as had been the fate of the Conservative Party in Canada.

Clearly Major was not going to move from his 'wait-and-see' position on the single currency so long as Clarke remained Chancellor and Heseltine retained his grip as Deputy Prime Minister over government policy. This was confirmed in private discussions with Portillo, and with other Euro-sceptic ministers. So an alternative strategy began to form in my mind: if only a way could be found to make clear to the electorate that the likely composition of the Conservative benches in the next Parliament would never even *allow* a Conservative Government to recommend joining a single currency, whatever the likes of Clarke,

Heseltine and Gummer might say. Soon after taking over as 92 chairman, Townend had written to all 92 backbenchers planning to stand in
the election. He asked whether they intended to commit themselves in
their personal election address to a national referendum before joining
a single currency (this was before the Cabinet became committed
itself), but also, more to the point, whether they intended to make a
personal election-address commitment to vote against a single currency in principle. The returns revealed that 90 per cent of 92 backbenchers standing again intended to make such a personal commitment. So, I reasoned, why not extend the survey to take in *all* prospective Tory candidates, and then analyse them according to the safety of
their seats to find out what the Tory Party in the next Parliament would
actually do, regardless of what meaningless formula appeared in the
national manifesto? If the result of the survey was as I suspected, then
an assurance could be offered to the voting public that might at least
save a few seats which would otherwise be lost.

I consulted with Townend, and we agreed to write in our joint names
to all prospective parliamentary candidates; I had obtained a full list of
candidates' home addresses from a source outside Central Office. The
text of our letter was as follows:

> You are doubtless aware of the widespread anxiety within the
> Conservative Party that we will go into the coming general election *with-
> out* a commitment to oppose UK entry into a European single currency
> in the lifetime of the next Parliament.
>
> We will not dwell on the differences between cabinet ministers that
> have brought this situation about. However, we are conscious that con-
> tinued ambivalence on an issue so crucial to the future of this country
> will be impossible to defend during the election campaign, especially
> since a decision on this will have to be made very soon afterwards. We
> will all be asked where we stand, and rightly so.
>
> A few months ago the 92 Group, which is the largest party grouping
> at Westminster, conducted a survey of those of its back-bench members
> who will contest the coming election, asking whether in their *personal*
> election addresses they intended to commit themselves on the single cur-
> rency issue. More than 90 per cent replied that it *was* their intention to
> pledge themselves to oppose entry. If a majority of prospective candi-
> dates were to do the same, it would be obvious to the voting public that,
> whatever equivocations were in our national manifesto, there would be
> no chance whatsoever that a Conservative Cabinet could ever recom-
> mend to Parliament that we join a single currency. May we therefore ask
> whether you, as a prospective candidate, are prepared to make the same
> commitment in your election address?'

A confidential tear-off slip, addressed to me, was at the foot of the letter.

Word of our initiative reached the whips' office and a worried whip, Derek Conway, rang me. He was a good chum, a member of the 92 and a Euro-sceptic himself. He thought a pre-emptive press release before our letter landed on doormats might save causing any embarrassment to Central Office. I accordingly drafted one and sent an advance copy to Charles Lewington, director of publicity at CCO – a former top-notch political correspondent who had turned from poacher to game-keeper. Thus there was nothing underhand about our inquiry.

However, as our letters were being delivered to prospective candidates' homes, Central Office went into panic mode. Several area agents rang their candidates, telling them not to answer our inquiry, which they described as deeply divisive. Several National Union area officers, clearly Europhiles, got into the act too. I received interesting feedback on the short shrift many of them had been given. One candidate told them he would consult the local party's executive council before reply-ing; his council endorsed his wish to reply positively, and went on to pass a motion deploring such Central Office interference; what a pity, they said, that CCO did not listen to what the grassroots were saying instead. Thankfully most of our candidates were made of sterner stuff, and despite this pressure well over half replied, giving their honest views. A couple of days later I received an angry phone call from Mawhinney: 'What on earth do you and Townend think you're up to? I'm working my guts out to present a united front for the conference, yet you're wrecking everything.' I replied that our letter was only seek-ing to establish what he must know already, but he would have none of it. Whatever our candidates thought on the matter, it had to be kept from the press at all costs. It was from that point that I lost Mawhinney's support in fighting off any further challenge to my posi-tion in Reigate.

The resulting figures were most revealing. Of those who replied, 85 per cent said they did intend to commit themselves against a single cur-rency in their personal election addresses, regardless of what the national manifesto had to say on the matter. But even more interesting was the analysis of replies from those candidates in seats we could expect to win if the voting pattern of 1992 were repeated. Here no fewer that 93 per cent promised to make such a commitment. This, taken together with the results of my own and Townend's inquiries among sitting MPs who were standing again, established beyond doubt that whatever the composition of the parliamentary party after the coming election, a clear majority would be against a single currency.

This, we felt, should go a long way to persuade the electorate that a Conservative Cabinet – unlike a Labour one – could be trusted never to recommend that Britain should hand the running of its economy over to an unelected European central bank. Townend and I had made it possible for the Tory grassroots effectively to impose upon divided cabinet ministers *their* priorities on how the single-currency issue should be handled in the election. It gave our activists some hope, and was a good week's work.

The build-up to the 1996 party conference in Bournemouth was not promising. There were rumours that Major would use his rally speech to toughen the Cabinet's stance against European integration, which in September prompted leading Tory Euro-enthusiast grandees – Commissioner Leon Brittan, Heath, Hurd and Lords Carrington, Howe and Whitelaw – to write a letter to the *Independent* asserting that Britain's future lay in 'accepting the European Union as an opportunity, not a threat'. Lamont responded tartly by labelling them 'dinosaurs, not grandees'. Lord Tebbit said that if the resignation of Clarke and Heseltine were necessary to get a cabinet commitment against joining a single currency, then that would be a 'price worth paying.' In an eve-of-conference article in the *Sunday Times* I wrote that 'faced with the choice of losing the next election through [Clarke's] effective veto or winning it without him, I would rather he went. And so, I fancy, would large numbers of conference delegates.' However, the Euro-sceptics knew that this could prove a very difficult conference, and did not want to attract any of the blame if it went wrong. For that reason our public calls for a change of cabinet tack were muted. In fact, the conference turned out a lot better than the Government deserved, owing much to the careful preparations of Mawhinney. It was as if the delegates arrived determined to forget the appalling opinion-poll figures and ministerial incompetence in fending off Labour attacks from the handling of Nolan through to the BSE crisis, and instead convince themselves that the feel-good factor – whenever that might come – would see us through. Hopes for significant tax cuts in the coming Budget ran high.

By November, the time had come to test whether Central Office accepted what Townend and I had demonstrated: that a majority of Tory candidates were determined to commit themselves against joining a single currency in their personal election addresses. As Party Chairman, Mawhinney was offering a good election printing package to candidates, covering the design and production of all the election

material needed. I had persuaded the Reigate association to sign up for
this, and I was among the first to present CCO with my draft election
address, complete with total personal commitment to keep Britain a
nation state by never agreeing to a single currency. We saw this as a test
case; if CCO refused to accept it, or tried to insist on different wording, then I and many more would move our printing elsewhere. But
despite great pressure from Heseltine, who wanted to impose the 'wait-
and-see' policy on every candidate, Mawhinney wisely decided it was
not up to him to dictate what appeared in candidates' personal mes-
sages. He knew that if he did and countless candidates withdrew their
orders, the resulting publicity would be immensely damaging.

But the upbeat mood of the conference was soon dissipated when
the Commons returned and the Government allowed itself to be tossed
like driftwood on the tide of events. No-one expected much from
a Queen's Speech for the fag end of a Parliament, but two developments – one a Government attempt to be less than honest with the
Commons, and the other a disappointing Budget – brought morale
back down to rock bottom. The debate among right-wingers turned to
how the party could be restored after defeat and the consequent resignation of Major; some feared the right would find itself disastrously
split in a leadership election between Portillo and Redwood. Townend
thought we might be able to broker a deal and so organised a lunch for
the 92's steering committee in his flat, which both Portillo and
Redwood agreed to attend. My own view was that the first ballot would
sort things out anyway, but there was no doubting the undercurrent of
excitement among Steering Committee members that we might avoid
a damaging conflict. Townend began by acknowledging that both
would want to put their names forward in the first ballot, but that we
wanted to avoid mutual accusations, and get an understanding that,
whoever of them scored more votes, the other would withdraw and
throw his influence behind him. Redwood agreed, and said that if he
ended up behind Portillo then he would support him. But Portillo was
far more cautious, refusing to commit himself to anything. There was
an unmistakeable gulf between the two, which came as a great disappointment to the others present; some, indeed, afterwards wondered
what it was that Portillo was about. Of course, when Major did
eventually stand down Portillo was not there to challenge anyway – the
voters of Enfield Southgate saw to that. But our lunch gave advance
indication of how little rapport there was between Redwood and his
former Right-wing colleagues in the Cabinet, which became evident
when the contest finally took place.

On 2 December Clarke was due to attend a meeting of EU Finance

Ministers to agree a 'stability pact' between those members who joined a single currency and those who did not. Official documents suggested that Britain's hands would be tied even if our Government decided not to join, and the Commons committee that monitored EU documents recommended that this be debated on the floor of the House – a perfectly normal procedure. But the Government was scared of allowing a debate at all, lest it give Labour the chance to exploit Tory differences in order to defeat the Government, whose overall majority was then down to one. However much Clarke protested, most Tory backbenchers suspected he had something to hide and 150 signed a demand for a debate. Clarke made a statement and gave all kinds of assurances, yet still resisted full parliamentary scrutiny. As soon as the Finance Ministers' meeting was out of the way, the furore died down, yet the Government's arrogant handling of the Commons left a nasty taste. Immediately after this came a mouse of a Budget, which destroyed any remaining hope of a feel-good factor being felt by the voters before the election.

By this time the mood on the back benches was one of grim foreboding, reflected by many junior and middle-ranking ministers who simply kept their heads down to wait for the crash they could see coming all too clearly. Colleagues with seats that in normal times would be counted as safe were casting round for outside jobs after the election. Those on the 92's steering committee predicted we would be lucky to save 200 Tory seats without a major shift in policy, and that had been ruled out. My Upstairs Club at the Gran Paradiso stopped meeting; what was the point, when the leadership was determined never to listen to its parliamentary party, or to those outside?

All this was bad enough, but worse disappointment was to come – developments which swept away any remaining respect I had for Major, and which effectively ended communication between us. On Monday 2 December, the Tory Party was taken aback to read a front-page exclusive in the *Daily Telegraph*, under the headline 'Major plans to hold out against Euro'. The first paragraph was music to most Tory MPs' ears: 'John Major has concluded that it would be against Britain's interest to join a single currency in the next Parliament – and is seeking a way to persuade Kenneth Clarke, the Chancellor, to agree to ditch the 'wait-and-see' policy in time for the election. He is understood to have the backing of eighteen of his twenty-two-strong Cabinet for a historic policy shift in favour of fighting the election on a pledge to keep the pound.' The report also noted: 'Apart from Mr Major's own change of heart, almost two thirds of Tory backbenchers contesting the election have indicated that they will issue personal manifestos stating their opposition to a single currency' – which was certainly true. He also recorded that Heseltine, a strong supporter of the 'wait-and-see' policy, was thought to be 'persuadable'. If the report was accurate, here was proof that the message we and the party at large had been pushing on Major had at last been heeded – and that, though this might be too late to save the Tories in Government, at least our election losses could be contained. Things were on the move.

The big question was, how accurate was the report? It appeared under the by-line of the paper's political editor, George Jones, a highly regarded correspondent who never ran speculative stories without having strong authoritative guidance. The report would also never have appeared without the clear support of the editor, Charles Moore, also an experienced judge of political developments. It bore all the hallmarks of an authoritative briefing from Downing Street itself, and also squared with Major's own political instinct. Rumour soon spread of a breakfast meeting between Major and Moore, and of a subsequent green light given by a senior Downing Street source. At the time this was thought to be Norman Blackwell, head of the policy unit, through this has since been denied. Major's biographer, Anthony Seldon, confirms there was a breakfast meeting, but that the Prime Minister was 'taken aback' when he read the *Telegraph*'s report. Yet Seldon concedes that Major 'was wont to muse on the politically difficult in private in order to tease out reactions, only to be drawn up short when his comments appeared in public as hard fact'. Maybe, though there was no need to 'tease out' Moore's opinion on a single currency, since it had been stated frequently. I am convinced that Major *was* the source of the report. So what was his motive? He was correct that eighteen of his twenty-two cabinet ministers favoured such a shift, so did he hope that the report would steel those eighteen to override the remaining four – or was this another example of his Walter Mitty syndrome, dreaming that obstacles in his path would simply disappear?

The effect of the report on Tory backbenchers as well as junior ministers was palpable; a new heady optimism took the place of deep despair. All looked forward to going to their constituencies the following weekend to spread the good news to their dispirited supporters: we were back in with a chance. Alas, it was not to be. When Clarke, in Paris for a meeting of Finance Ministers, had the report faxed to him he was livid, and suspected he was being stampeded into agreeing to a change of policy which was total anathema to him. He therefore seized the chance of a Monday-morning interview on the BBC's *Today* programme to knock down any possible change in cabinet policy. Downing Street's press office also issued a denial, though in somewhat ambiguous terms – perhaps because they knew Major's true feelings on the matter. For this reason the story kept running, and so Heseltine determined to crush it once and for all. He brusquely told the BBC's *World at One* programme that there could be no question of changing the Cabinet's 'wait-and-see' policy – not before the election, nor during the election campaign. This latter commitment certainly went beyond the Cabinet's deal the previous April. This resulted in an exceedingly uncomfortable Prime Minister's Questions for Major, who was forced to grovel and claim that Heseltine's comments reflected his own position while sullen-faced Tory backbenchers sat in silence. They knew he had been well and truly stitched up. The following day, at a private lunch with a couple of BBC journalists, Clarke made 'off-the-record' comments which, when reported, made him appear to be glorying in Major's discomfort. But by then, there was no doubt who was really running the Government.

My own feelings are not hard to describe. I felt a deep personal shame that my party should be 'led' by a man who, by his appointments of Clarke and Heseltine, had so boxed himself in as to rob himself of all freedom of manoeuvre, and in so doing was dragging the party down with him. But worse than this, I felt an anger which is most unusual for me. Of course I should have known; it was but a repeat of the Grand Old Duke of York's strategy, marching troops to the top of the hill over breakfast with Moore only to march them down again as soon as Clarke's and Heseltine's bugles sounded his retreat. But I felt a deep anger just the same, and when I got back to my flat late on Tuesday night I sat at my laptop and poured out my contempt in an article, which the *Sunday Express* were delighted to use the following weekend.

Last Tuesday will surely be recorded as Black Tuesday in the annals of the Conservative Party. It was the day when our leader and Prime Minister stood at the Commons' Dispatch Box and announced to the world his abject surrender to Chancellor Kenneth Clarke and Deputy Premier Michael Heseltine over European policy.

It was the day when, in obeyance to Clarke's orders, he threw away his party's strongest card in the coming election – a pledge that under a re-elected Conservative Government, Britain would keep out of a European single currency, the inevitable precursor to a United States of Europe, and that sterling would be safe.

It was the day when Clarke effectively became Prime Minister, ensuring that the key to 10 Downing Street was passed to Tony Blair by the outgoing tenant. Small wonder that Labour MPs were cock-a-hoop and there was gloom on countless Tory faces across our benches.'

But then came the real sting:

> On Tuesday afternoon [Major] stood at the Dispatch Box, playing the
> role of ventriloquist's dummy in response to probing from Blair. Yes, the
> 'wait-and-see' policy would stay. No hint, or lead, for the British people
> before or during the election. So in the campaign he ... will have to stand
> on platforms saying: 'So sorry, we can't say whether we're going to abol-
> ish the pound or not. You see the negotiations won't finish until June.
> Come back and ask us then.' The voters will fall about laughing, and
> rightly so.

The headline, 'We must not let Kenneth Clarke speak for Britain',
was relatively mild, but not so the illustration, which pulled out my
quote branding Major a ventriloquist's dummy, and was calculated to
give maximum offence. It was a computerised photo mock-up of a grin-
ning Clarke with a diminutive Major as the dummy on his knee – which
with monocle, dress tie and lantern jaw would be instantly recognisable
to any reader over the age of fifty-five as 'Archie Andrews', a music-hall
act popular in the early years of television. The use of the illustration
was a superb piece of journalism by the features editor – but it did me
no good at all! Indeed, it signalled the end of my political career, for all
my old opponents in Reigate (most of them over fifty-five) seized on it,
ran off copies and used them to drum up a motion of no confidence in
me as their MP, thus opening the door to another and even more bitter
deselection challenge. All this must be left to another chapter, as must
resigning the Tory whip to stand for the Referendum Party.

But did I ever regret writing that article? The answer is no.
Throughout my years in politics I never ceased to be a journalist, and
I still think this was among the most perceptive articles I have ever written. I may have paid dearly for the anger I felt over Major's ultimate
climb-down, but it can also be recorded that Major never recovered
from that self-inflicted humiliation either. For him and for the Tory
Party, it was then downhill all the way to the dreaded election.

The first two chapters of this book detail my role as a back-bench
activist in relation to Major as party leader and Prime Minister; the
account of my concurrent trouble with a section of my local association
because I was advocating what has since become official front-bench
policy over the single currency must wait till later. In only one marginal instance did this involve Major personally.

In the countdown to the end of the Parliament, morale on the Tory benches got steadily lower. Some who did not possess rock-solid Tory seats were consoled by the promise of an outside job when the inevitable happened; others did not have this cushion. The 92 still organised its St Stephen's Club dinners and the policy group still met, while the steering committee, seeing where power really lay, had occasional meetings with Heseltine in an effort to get him to understand what the situation really was. He was always courteous, but utterly deaf to our arguments. So far as he was concerned, none of the voters cared a fig about the European issue, so the less said about it the better; as soon as they understood how strong the economy was, and how Labour, even under Blair, would ruin it, then victory would be ours. Whether he actually believed this nonsense I will never know. He asked to come to a policy group meeting to argue his case that we should desist from opposing entry to a single currency in our personal election addresses; the steering committee called such a meeting, but Heseltine lost hands down. Meanwhile we had to suffer some appalling Central Office poster campaigns – demon eyes superimposed on Blair's face, and a roaring lion which gave way to tears.

It was Major's decision to make the 1997 election campaign a long one; a six-week campaign, he believed, would put Labour under pressure, and give the Tories time to get their economic case across. He was wrong again; it was the Tories who suffered from the long campaign, of which the first two weeks were dominated by 'sleaze'. When we were able to get down to the serious issues, everything of which we had warned Major came to pass. The electorate rightly demanded to know where our candidates stood on the single currency issue, and his 'wait-and-see' line was impossible to sustain. Even some ministers below cabinet level saw how implausible it was and broke ranks. Conflicting advice came from Downing Street, Heseltine, Mawhinney and the publicity gurus, while the Tory campaign was all over the place. Most pathetic of all was a man dressed up as a chicken, who followed Blair around flapping its wings. Finally, in desperation, without even consulting Clarke or Heseltine, Major tried to break free by promising a free vote for Tory MPs when the time came to recommend whether Britain should join a single currency or not – and this from the man who had doggedly refused a free vote at any stage of the Maastricht legislation, even on whether it should be subject to a national referendum! The resulting defeat on 1 May was even more humiliating than most Tories had feared in their worst nightmares. It was not just the right that was crucified, but the whole party. The nation was sick to death of us – not because of splits but because of perpetual incompetent fudge.

Not until after he subsequently resigned as leader and was no longer under Clarke's and Heseltine's thumbs did Major come out openly against the euro – at least two years too late to be of any use to his party. And only after that did Heseltine and Clarke come clean, revealing their 'wait-and-see' stance as the sham that it was; their agenda had always been to take Britain into the single currency regardless.

There are some who argue that it was all inevitable, that, after the debacle over our exit from the Exchange Rate Mechanism on 16 September 1992, the Tories – and Major in particular – could never recover. Certainly after that, in the words I quote from Robert Browning's poem at the start of this chapter, it was 'never glad confident morning again'. Yet I cannot accept this analysis. There were countless occasions when Major could have seized the initiative, but that would have meant apologising for Black (or rather Golden) Wednesday, it would have meant listening to the grassroots of Tory supporters, it would have meant not rejecting the advice of the Tory press in such cavalier fashion, and above all it would have meant accepting that the right, which made up the majority of his parliamentary party and to whom he owed his election as leader in 1990, wanted him to succeed and had useful advice to offer – yet all this would have required him to override his innate obstinacy, which he could not do. So instead we had a leader who responded to pressure by trying to appear all things to all men, who promoted ministers with stronger personalities than his who would not allow him to give the lead for which the country yearned. It is tempting to see Clarke and Heseltine as the ministers who screwed down the lid on the Tory coffin, yet it was Major who took the risk of making Clarke his Chancellor, and Major who gave Heseltine the powers of Deputy Prime Minister in order to buy his supporters in the 1995 leadership ballot. No, in determining who bore the ultimate responsibility for the 1997 election catastrophe, the buck has to stop with Major himself.

The true failure is revealed not by the tally of seats lost, though that was horrendous enough; never since 1905 had the Tory Party been brought so low. Neither does it lie in the numbers who voted for 'New Labour' – after all, Blair's share of the total vote was lower that Harold Wilson's in 1966, lower even than Hugh Gaitskell's in 1955. No, the true cost of Major's leadership is revealed by the fact that nearly one million votes went to the Referendum and UK Independence Parties (and my experience was that most Referendum supporters were former Tories who never could stomach Major's 'wait-and-see' policy on Europe), a million or so former Tory voters switched to Labour or Lib-Dem – anything to get rid of his Government – while the rest simply stayed at home. They did not see themselves as deserting the Conservative Party; rather, they felt that under Major's leadership the Conservative Party had deserted them.

Robert Browning's poem 'The Lost Leader' was inspired by his disgust over what he saw as William Wordsworth's betrayal of radical principles in taking a 'handful of silver' to become Poet Laureate. Browning uses 'lost' in the sense of being lost to him and his radical friends. Though lines in the poem are certainly relevant to Major, he was never 'lost' in that sense. In choosing 'The Lost Leader' as the title of this chapter, I use the word in the sense of having no sense of direction, of not knowing where he wanted to go. Though Major had one or two gut prejudices deriving from his early life, such as his yearning for a 'classless society', he had no deep convictions, and little conception of the kind of country he would like Britain to become. Leadership for him was essentially an exercise in manipulation to keep himself at the top of the greasy pole. But you can never be a leader if you have no clue where you are going – and that, alas, has to be Major's political epitaph.

CHAPTER THREE

The Roots of Conviction

'For in the case of nutrition and health, just as in the case of
education, the gentleman in Whitehall really does know better what is
good for the people than the people know themselves.'
Douglas Jay, *The Socialist Case* (1947)

THE YEAR IS 1948. A thirteen-year-old youngster with ears
standing out from cropped-back-and-sides hair, just into long
trousers as the convention then required, is carrying a tray of
Alexandra's Day roses and calling at doors in the streets near his home.
My mother had volunteered to help raise money for the blind, and I
was recruited to help. I am sure it is illegal today for a child to sell flags,
or Earl Haig poppies, or Alexandra roses, but nobody cared much then.
No-one refused to put a few big penny pieces or even an old threepen-
ny bit into my collecting tin, which was getting reassuringly heavy –
except one middle-aged couple. Fifty years on, I can remember them
clearly: not aggressive in their refusal to donate, simply smug and self-
satisfied.

'What are you collecting for then, sonny? The blind? Your mother
should know better: we don't need to do that sort of thing any more.
We've got a welfare state now that looks after everyone.'

'You mean ... you don't want to give to help the blind?' I was incredulous.

'Not necessary,' they replied. 'The Government does all that for us
now.'

I recounted the conversation to my mother when I got home, and
told her where the couple lived. 'Oh yes,' she sighed. 'They're *real*
Labour there.'

From experiences like this are political convictions born.

I was four and a half when World War II broke out. At that age, halves are very important. I was an only child and we were on a seaside holiday at the time. The moment the dreaded news came through, my father insisted we load up the car and return home straight away. He was manager of three village gasworks in West Sussex, and if Jerry was going to bomb one of his gasholders he had to be on hand. There was an air-raid warning even before we got back, but it was a false alarm – arranged, it was said, to test that the sirens were really working. For the rest of the war few enemy planes came within bombing distance of the gasholder at Storrington, the village under the South Downs where we lived.

The drama of war barely touched us in Sussex. A lot of people exempted from call-up became very important – air-raid wardens, Home Guard sergeants, even the local gas manager. My father was a sociable man, and spent many of his evenings playing darts with those manning the local ambulance HQ till my mother insisted he should stay at home to play darts with her instead. In 1943 he was promoted to manage a larger works at Maldon, Essex, and due to the housing situation it was some time before my mother and I were able to join him. While we waited, he fell for a local schoolteacher, and soon asked for a divorce.

My mother was devastated by the break-up of her marriage. Divorce was still quite uncommon outside the top flights of society, and even for the innocent party it carried a social stigma which she felt acutely. Her training had been as a book-keeper, but she had not worked since becoming pregnant with me. The gas company owned the house where we were living, so there was no marital capital to divide. Despite some alimony and maintenance payments for me, there was no disguising the fact that my mother had suddenly become poor.

We moved to Hythe, in Kent, where my mother had a sister, but the only job she could get was as a waitress in a tea room. Not until the war was over was she able to take up book-keeping again, for a local dairy.

Rationing of a whole range of foodstuffs and commodities had obviously been necessary during the war; imports of food by our Merchant Marines had to negotiate the submarine-infested waters of the Atlantic, while all resources had to be concentrated on the war effort. But after the war the Attlee Government preserved and indeed added to this emergency-control system so as to regulate all the basic goods which households needed to buy, while ministers placed bulk-buying contracts across the world. This was supposed to safeguard supplies and, through the sheer quantities involved, to secure cheaper prices than private importers, after taking their own profit, could have delivered.

Such stringent rationing brought particular hardship to a single mother with just one child. Larger families could at least pool their rations to buy a small joint of meat, but two small chops were the limit of our Sunday lunch. 1947, when I was twelve and into my second year at the grammar school, was the hardest year of all; even bread and potatoes, freely available during the war, were put on ration, and the meat ration, already meagre, was cut twice. Only small quantities of tea, butter and eggs were permitted, and our weekly ration of a few ounces of Cheddar looked lost in the middle of a tea plate. All tinned and bottled goods, even baked beans and an excruciating 'coffee' concentrate called 'Camp', were strictly rationed, as were sugar and children's sweets. Chicken was a luxury. Towards the end of the 1940s we knew that other countries, including some we had helped to liberate, had a higher standard of living than ours. But the natural aspirations of our own people had become victim to a doctrinaire egalitarianism; this was hardly a time for pride in the new Socialist Britain.

Even more galling were the justifications offered by Socialist ministers for this state of affairs. Rationing was turned from being an interim measure to deal with shortage to something supposedly of positive virtue in itself. 'Fair shares for all is Labour's call' was the slogan in the North Battersea by-election in 1946, and ministers could not conceive of any future situation where they would not control the nation's diet down to the last morsel. The gentleman in Whitehall really did know best. Douglas Jay is often misquoted, and in fairness I give his full quote at the head of this chapter. However, the doctrine that 'the gentleman in Whitehall really does know best' was applied far beyond nutrition, health and education. Cabinet committees decided how many cars should be produced, how many trucks, how many kitchen goods, while exchange controls stopped people wasting their time and the nation's money on holidays overseas. There was total denial of any market mechanism; a furious press campaign was whipped up against Argentina, who had dared to propose increasing the price of the frozen and corned beef sold to us under a bulk-buying agreement when they could get more by selling elsewhere.

The whole system came to be pervaded by an odious pseudo-morality. The gentleman in Whitehall would never permit nylon stockings to be made or imported – far too frivolous for the new Britain; women had worn thick lisle stockings or no stockings at all throughout the war, so they could do so still. Hitherto nylons had been the preserve of American servicemen, used to buy favours from their girlfriends, but when the Yanks went home their place was taken by men selling nylons from suitcases in pubs or on street corners. These were straightforward entrepreneurs who were selling women what they wanted, yet they were vilified by countless politicians and press cartoons as 'spivs' – usually pictured wearing large checked overcoats tapering down to their calves and looking decidedly shifty – who were corrupting the fibre of our nation.

While in the war years everyone had been willing to muck in and 'do their bit', a new meanness entered Socialist Britain. At the start of this chapter I referred to the middle-aged couple who refused to give to charity to help the blind on the grounds that 'the Government does all that for us now'. Many workmen applied to themselves Hartley Shawcross's observation that 'we are the masters'; it mattered little to them how long they took to do a job, or whether they completed it at all. Nye Bevan once allowed his oratory to get the better of him and described Conservatives as 'lower than vermin'. Immediately a 'Vermin Club' was established, selling blue plastic rats to pin to your lapel, with the proceeds going to cancer research. I wore my blue rat with pride.

It was in this environment that I developed a deep loathing for Socialism. At fifteen I joined the Hythe Young Conservatives, and in the election that year delivered leaflets for the Tory candidate. 'Set the people free' we chanted at election meetings. I wore a rosette of red, white and blue – the local Conservative colours – to school, Harvey Grammar in Folkestone, prompting some sarcasm from teachers, but I was not alone among pupils. In a discussion in the fifth form, only one boy confessed to being a Labour supporter; he did not know why, simply that his father was. I joined the debating society that met after school, and remember hearing Rab Butler, still in Opposition, speak to a packed audience in Folkestone's Leas Cliff Hall.

My academic performance was inconsistent. I resented the large amounts of homework set by the French master, and organised a petition signed by all my classmates asking him to ease up. His fury at being presented with it at the start of the lesson was indescribable. 'But ... but ... but ...' I protested, looking round to my classmates for support. But support came there none; they were all sniggering behind their hands, keeping their heads well down. So I learned a basic political lesson: that when the going gets rough, your supporters melt away like snow in the sun.

In the sixth form I studied History, Geography and Economics. The Economics tutor, brought in to teach just six of us, was a genial Socialist who saw John Maynard Keynes as the saviour of mankind. I argued for Beaverbrook's Imperial Preference, simply to promote something different.

It was the headmaster's idea that I should try for a place at Oxford to study Philosophy, Politics and Economics before taking my A-levels. One way of getting into Oxford was to try for a scholarship, on the basis of which ordinary places were also awarded. I opted for Balliol, sat the exam under supervision in a school storeroom, then to my surprise was invited to the college for interview, staying overnight. Before I returned, the tutors told me a place was ready for me either in Michaelmas term that year, or two years later after I had undertaken my military service. I chose to do my army service first. That summer, on the strength of my A-level performance I was awarded a state scholarship, which meant that all my tuition fees and maintenance were guaranteed. My mother was overjoyed, some of my teachers dumbfounded, while I looked forward to a sparkling future once I was through with the army.

My experience of Her Majesty's forces was much the same as any other male of my generation: a total suspension of rational judgement for six months while you concentrated on the need to defend the realm by carving your army number meticulously on a bar of soap; assembling a 'kit layout' in which every piece of heavily blancoed webbing was a precise number of inches from the next; polishing and burning the toecaps of your boots till you could see your face in them; and convincing yourself that the sight of a drill sergeant strutting across the square like a pregnant peacock was *not* the funniest thing you had ever seen. You got used to the insults and the language ('Yew fuckin' 'orrible li'l wanker yew'), though they became tedious with repetition.

I was conscripted to the Royal Army Service Corps, then earmarked as clerk. We were based in barracks, or lines, in Aldershot that dated from the Crimean War. It was a hard winter; the latrines froze regularly, and those on fatigues had to flush them twice a day with buckets of water. I went on to train as a tester, invigilating and marking a battery of intelligence and aptitude tests for all recruits to determine into which trade category they should be placed. This brought automatic promotion to sergeant, and better pay. Sergeant testers were posted away from their own corps or regiments; I was posted to serve the Royal Pioneer Corps' intake camp at Gresford in North Wales.

The Pioneers were not a corps anyone volunteered to join. By tradition they were the ones to dig trenches and field latrines, and were known to all other units as the 'Chunkies'. The derivation of this was unclear; I was told it was originally a reference to them having 'pine-apple bollocks', of which the Pioneers might conceivably have been proud. By the time I heard it, the term was used as an insult to mean 'pineapple head', which made the Pioneers see red. The military police had a hard job every Saturday night in nearby Wrexham keeping the Chunkies and the Royal Welsh Fusiliers apart. Handling such unpromising material was a challenge to any Sergeant tester; most were classified for general duties, some slightly brighter ones made store-men, while the lucky ones were trained as drivers. Most of our work with each fortnightly intake was to sift out those who should never have been called up at all, either because they were too dim to be of any use even to the army or on psychiatric grounds, and recommend their dis-charge. Then the slow bureaucracy of the army got to work, and many absconded while waiting for their discharge papers to come through. They were then brought back by the military police, while their dis-charge procedure had to start all over again. There were regular suicide attempts.

I never regretted spending two years of my youth in this pointless way. I managed to save £100 from my meagre pay – no small sum in those days – which cushioned me through my first year at university. And I went through the gates of Balliol a far more mature youth than I ever would have been had I gone there straight from school.

'Bliss was it in that dawn to be alive, but to be young was very heaven.' William Wordsworth's lines capture the sheer wonderment that thrilled through me on going up to Oxford. Never before or since have I been inspired by such innocent enthusiasm. The first freedom to lead your own life, and so many exciting things to do: traditional rituals to observe; finding romantic quadrangles and gardens hiding behind obscure entrances; the choice of hundreds of college or university soci-eties to join; different libraries waiting to be discovered; listening in awe to Oxford Union debates; cheering your college eight from the tow-path; greeting the dawn on May Morning from Magdalen Tower, while looking forward to lazy summer afternoons punting on the Cherwell.

Freshers at Balliol, in those days all men, underwent a spell of heavy indoctrination. We were divided into groups and lectured by the dean, a cleric who, as well as managing the college chapel, undertook some administrative duties. The message delivered was clear and strong. Balliol men were the cream of the university, which itself was the cream of academia. Benjamin Jowett's dictum when he was college master in the nineteenth century was drummed into us endlessly: that the essence of a Balliol man was 'a sublime consciousness of effortless superiority'. We were the elite of the elite. Many students, particularly those who had come straight from school without undertaking military service first, believed it fervently, but the more discerning of us knew it was utter crap. However, it was nice to pretend it was true, so we let the dean and master and senior tutors blather on about it if it made them feel good.

The Balliol tutors in PPE were most demanding; two tutorials and essays each week, and a long list of morning lectures recommended. I rarely went to lectures; I slept too late, and I found it far better to buy or get from libraries books the lecturers had written, and from which they invariably drew. I have lasting memories of one tutor, Dr Thomas Balogh, a strong Socialist economist who subsequently became economic adviser to Harold Wilson as Prime Minister, alongside another Hungarian, Nicholas Kaldor. Balogh worked in a room with the gas fire turned on full for most of the year, before which he frequently lay on the floor scratching his genitals with a ruler while sorting papers and pretending not to concentrate while you read your essay. When he got bored he interrupted, and your reading was never finished. His tutorials were often terminated by a phone call from Dom Mintoff, Prime Minister of Malta, whom Balogh advised.

Just below the surface of student life and its journalism, politics loomed large. When I came up in 1955, thirteen out of nineteen cabinet ministers were from Oxford, and several – like Harold Macmillan and Viscount Kilmuir – were Balliol men. Despite this, Balliol had a reputation of being left-wing and of taking more than a fair share of Africans and Indians. Over the wall in Trinity, its rowing club, when drunk, often stood chanting: 'Come on Balliol, bring out your black men.' Students joined a political club by buying a termly membership card which gave access to its meetings. Many, like me, joined the Conservative Association (OUCA) *and* the Labour Club so as to hear all the leading national politicians who paid regular visits. I heard countless Tory ministers and back-bench characters, as well as the likes of Anthony Crosland, Richard Crossman, Anthony Wedgwood Benn and even Konni Zilliacus. One memorable visit was by Enoch Powell, then Minister for Housing. The mechanics of OUCA meetings that term were under the supervision of the somewhat eccentric Adrian Berry, son of Michael Berry, owner of the *Daily Telegraph*, and the formidable Lady Pamela; Adrian was going through a Germanic phase, and Enoch came into the hall to marching songs from the Third Reich. The puzzled expression on Enoch's face I have never seen matched since.

I became OUCA's organiser in Balliol, where I set about building up a block vote for the OUCA elections that came towards the end of each term. I joined the Blue Ribbon Club, founded before me by Michael Heseltine in opposition to OUCA, but by this time simply a Tory discussion group that met on Sundays. I attended free classes for Tory students in public speaking, where I got to know other contemporaries who subsequently became MPs like Kenneth Baker, Tony Newton, Paul Channon, Toby Jessel and Alan Haselhurst. Female company was hard to find, but a small number from the women's colleges did join in Tory politics. That autumn four of us went to Bishop Auckland, a solid Labour seat in County Durham, at the invitation of local Conservatives to speak at factory gates and in market squares. I shared a lodging with Kenneth Baker, with whom I got on well. On that visit we gained some insight into the utter corruption of Socialist politics in County Durham, exposed long after to public gaze through the activities of T. Dan Smith. For example, no-one could be employed as a teacher or even get a garden allotment without being a paid-up member of the Labour Party.

Yet for a student in 1955, political involvement was a pretty shallow experience. It hardly seemed worth arguing that Marxism and the Soviet system were evil, that attempts to foment class war were deplorable, that Conservatives could run the economy better than Labour, but there was none of the *ideological* fire that young activists crave. We seemed to be in thrall to the Quintin Hogg (later Lord Hailsham) thesis: that social reform was achieved by bouts of Socialism with longer spells of Conservative paternalist consolidation in between. What Keith Joseph later described as the 'Socialist ratchet' was thought to be inevitable. So when we sat up late into the night disputing politics over wine, as students will, what did we find to argue about? As often as not, unbelievably, it was which side we would have supported in the Spanish Civil War! It was almost twenty years ago, yet that was the nearest we could get to ideological commitment; British politics of the day were conducted in an ideological vacuum.

All this came to an abrupt halt in November 1956 when Anthony Eden, in connivance with France and Israel, went to war with Nasser's Egypt to regain control of the Suez Canal. Here was a *cause célèbre* that rocked student society to its foundations. The dons too were in ferment, writing angry letters to *The Times*. Normal university life was suspended while students organised protest marches and made banners protesting at this 'blatant imperialism'. A couple of ministers resigned, including Balliol man Sir Edward Boyle, who explained why to a packed meeting of OUCA, which itself was deeply split. Some resigned from the committee; others, like Tony Newton, himself strongly opposed to the Government's action, kept their heads down. But the invasion provided me with the ideological spur I sought; here was Britain again playing the role that it should in the world, 'standing up for justice against Middle East dictators'.

Oxford was swamped by student protest against the invasion, yet I gathered like-minded friends to organise a petition supporting the Government and urging it to see the operation through to the end. I had a fight on my hands with my Balliol tutors to get excused from tutorials for a week; other colleges were freeing students to organise the protests, so why could I not have the freedom to campaign the other way? In the end they agreed, though with marked reluctance. In fact, my petition established what is often the case: that those who make the most noise do not necessarily represent the community from which they come. Well over a thousand signed my petition from all the colleges – a very respectable number. We went to the House of Commons to present the petition to Oxford's Member, the right-wing Lawrence Turner, who fêted us in the Strangers' Bar before dashing with it to Downing Street, giving a statement to the Press Association on the way – 'Oxford students say stick it out.' But back at Balliol, I soon learned from Peter Brooke, whose father Henry was Financial Secretary to the Treasury, that the game was up. Britain was withdrawing. It had been a botched exercise from the start, and President Eisenhower blew the whistle by starting to off-load sterling on the world market. Eden's premiership was in tatters; he pleaded a nervous breakdown and fled to Jamaica, while the party was left to pick up the pieces. Humphry Berkeley, then an ambitious Tory backbencher, was dispatched to OUCA to explain what a marvellous success the invasion had been, 'restoring peace to the Middle East'. William Deedes also came down; he was too old a hand to accept that kind of claptrap, but argued instead that the party had to come together to stand any chance of winning the next election. We also heard from Angus Maude, John Biggs-Davison and Patrick Maitland – backbenchers who had resigned the Tory whip in protest at withdrawal.

The Suez fiasco put the right doubly on the defensive, for it coincided with Soviet tanks moving into Budapest to suppress the rebellious regime of Imre Nagy. His pathetic plea to the West for help went unanswered; there was no way NATO would take on the might of the Soviet Union so far east of the Iron Curtain. Yet naïve dons and students blamed the Government for this too, the fashionable argument being that if Britain had not been fouling its own nest it could have applied moral pressure on the Red Army to withdraw its tanks. Some hope!

The suppression in Hungary had its ripples in Balliol. The Junior Common Room committee was controlled by a precious Establishment clique based on the Brackenbury, then a somewhat effete college dining and debating society. The only popular member of this group was Peter Brooke, JCR president. When the committee learned what was happening in Budapest they decided to pin their hearts to their sleeves; they obtained an old ambulance for two of them to drive to Hungary bringing 'humanitarian help'. It was not long before the JCR was asked to cough up the money, and the result was a riot. The venture had never been authorised by a JCR meeting anyway, support had simply been presumed; the pair with the ambulance had no medical experience whatsoever, and it was doubtful whether those chumps would ever find Hungary anyway. So the ludicrous venture was aborted fast – but it gave me and my closest friends a golden opportunity to conspire to defeat the Establishment nominee for the next JCR President. We found the ideal candidate in my friend Peter Davidson: a Canadian (and hence classless), a rowing man (so appealing to the sporting interest, who regarded the Brackenbury with contempt), and a practising Christian – even better, the son of a deacon. Balliol was a large college, but we organised cleverly so that every student was approached through a personal friend. Our campaign worked a treat, and a pretentious Establishment was overthrown. Innocent pleasures – and for me a foretaste of things to come.

The real skulduggery came with the elections for OUCA's officers and committee towards the end of each term. These were battles in which no holds were barred, fought with a cynical enthusiasm out of all proportion to the prizes to be won. The OUCA presidency could be a stepping stone to the more prestigious presidency of the Oxford Union, but not necessarily. No sooner had we started a term than we were jockeying to form alliances that would be put to the test in six weeks. It cost two old shillings and sixpence to join OUCA for a term, and members received a postal ballot paper, delivered to their pigeonholes in the lodge at their colleges – though, given the organisational pressure, colleges tended to vote in blocs. The big blocs then made deals with leading figures from the smaller colleges. The competition was vicious, and totally unprincipled. It was scurrilously rumoured that Michael Heseltine, who preceded me at Oxford by a couple of years, used to pedal his cycle a respectable distance behind the polling officer as he distributed the ballot papers, then removed a selection of the identifiable envelopes from pigeonholes to fill in and return himself, though subsequently when I knew Michael I never checked whether the story was true. When I arrived on the scene, Christ Church had the biggest bloc vote; by the end of my first year I had built up Balliol's to second in size, while Magdalen came a poor third.

With the high profile I had gained through organising the pro-Suez petition, I judged the following term that I was in a reasonable position to bid for the OUCA presidency. That would mean challenging Kenneth Baker, a good political friend from Magdalen, but friendship counted for little in that rat race. It was all a great game, and the game was everything. I could organise Balliol, and Christ Church looked promising; most of its power-brokers – like Paul Channon and Adrian Berry – had agreed with my high line supporting the Suez invasion. A deal between the Balliol and Christ Church blocs, with a few smaller colleges brought in, could do the trick. One Christ Church Tory wanted to be in on my campaign planning, but I smelt a rat, which is what he turned out to be. Christ Church swung behind Baker, and I lost.

The subsequent inquest proved interesting, for it emerged that a hundred or more OUCA memberships had been 'sold' through the Christ Church machine to a number of classy girls at finishing schools around Oxford, who were not even members of the university. I do not know whether these girls ever saw their ballot papers; put crudely, their votes had simply been bought at two shillings and sixpence each. With my limited resources, there was no way I could join in that game. When I put this to my closest Balliol friends, the response from Philip, who was some fifteen years older than the rest of us, was immediate: 'Well, George, if you can't afford to buy ballot papers, you'd better print your own.' And so the basis of the scam was laid; we began preparations for me to fight Tony Newton from Trinity in the next OUCA elections by feeding in bogus ballot papers.

Kenneth Baker, as the new president, thought OUCA should invest in a machine to stamp successive numbers on the ballot papers and the committee agreed. The first thing was for me to obtain its details, then to order an identical machine from a stationers away from the university quarter. Next I had to find out which firm would be engaged to duplicate the papers, so that the watermark on my copies would be the same. When the ballot paper was finally produced, I obtained an unstamped copy, so the race was on to find a typewriter with identical typescript; this was not difficult. As a candidate I had the right to witness the stamping of the genuine papers, so I was able to make a note of the blocks of numbers allocated to predictably low-voting colleges. Next we typed an identical copy of the genuine paper onto a 'skin' for a Gestetner duplicating machine (this was long before the days of photocopiers); I had been used to typing skins listing every Pioneer Corps recruit's results when I was a tester. This skin was then taken to another branch of the same firm in Reading. Then we stamped the bogus papers with the numbers allocated to the low-voting colleges. Finally, my close friends, and a few others sworn to secrecy, spent the whole night in my room addressing in various handwritings a vast number of different envelopes to the polling officer, and over the next two days they were delivered in batches to her college. I addressed no envelopes myself, nor did I deliver any of them.

The polling officer was amazed by the high turnout, which was in danger of exceeding OUCA's actual membership. Then someone suddenly noticed a minor difference between the papers – I think the genuine one had missed a full stop, which I had unwittingly inserted. Baker immediately decided that the ballot papers should be sorted into numerical order – whereupon the scam was revealed. Naturally I was among the first to demand a full inquiry to trace the culprit. So Baker got to work, but had precious few leads to follow. I gather a handwriting expert was consulted, but could find no trace of my writing on the envelopes used. The national press loved the story – remember that most of the Cabinet then were products of OUCA too. I kept quiet, and it looked as though I and my friends could brazen it out.

However, I was not allowing for the master of Balliol, Sir David Lindsay-Kier, a distinguished constitutional historian and something of a stuffed shirt. Sir David, sitting in his first-class compartment on the train from Paddington, noticed a report in *The Times* that a Balliol student stood to benefit most from the scam, and on arrival asked the dean to investigate. Now this raised the stakes dangerously. I could happily risk lying to Baker, and to the press, but lying to the master of my college was a wholly different ball game. If guilt were to be pinned on me, then inevitably I would be sent down – no degree, nothing. I also noted that my close friends, though they never broke ranks, were getting decidedly jittery for the same reason. So I decided to come clean and salvage as much of my career as possible.

Each university society had to have a sponsoring don, and OUCA's senior member was Robert Blake, the distinguished nineteenth-century historian and a tutor at Christ Church. I arranged to see him and confessed all. He was surprisingly sympathetic; having steeped himself in the history of Disraeli, this sort of thing was probably nothing new to him. I think it was he who commented that with so many people puffing into a balloon it was certain to burst in the face of whoever gave the final puff. I agreed to resign quietly from OUCA, in return for not being named publicly as the culprit. He promised to see what he could do with Baker and the new committee. If they reneged on the deal, and put my name into the headlines, then I was ready to tell all, naming those who had indulged in previous malpractices. I had already been offered a good fee by a Sunday newspaper to do just that. I then confessed to my dean, who was rather more censorious (a 'sublime consciousness of effortless superiority' clearly did not cover rigging ballots) but who promised to urge charity upon the master. Belatedly I looked for vacation employment, but the only job I could get so late was as a waiter in a third-class hotel in Folkestone, where I earned the princely sum of £4 a week, plus £4 in tips if I was lucky.

(OUCA has had some turbulent periods since, most involving ballot corruption. During the early eighties an extremely effective 'Magdalen Machine' held sway. Its power-broker was William Hague.)

Outside OUCA, life in my third year was very different. I was in lodgings, but still got up late, and after gossiping with my landlady I cycled into college for a lunchtime beer, then worked in the library before taking dinner in hall. I followed my own intellectual interests, reading widely outside my prescribed themes in politics, political theory and international relations. I had long given up attending lectures. If essay deadlines were not looming I spent the evenings playing poker with close friends. Brian Walden, who had risen through the Labour Club to become president of the Oxford Union, gave me a paper speech in one of the debates, but my heart was no longer in it. The fact was that I had become tired of university life. The innocent wonderment that had thrilled through me at the start had gone; now all I saw was an introspective society immersed in its own frivolities and feuds, oblivious to the outside world. The sooner I could join that outside world the better. As I approached Finals in Trinity term, I often hired a punt from under Magdalen Bridge to glide up the Cherwell. I was usually alone; my friends were busy revising. My intention was to revise too; I always took a book to read while moored, but if it was sunny I invariably fell asleep. The poker school was ended now, so I read into the night instead.

Finals did not distress me too much; I felt confident of my performance in all the political papers, less so in philosophy and economics. There then followed an idyllic week in which all the talk was of unfolding careers; very few left Oxford then without a job awaiting. I had secured a graduate apprenticeship as a journalist with the *Bristol Evening Post*. I kept my books on politics and modern history, but sold all those on philosophy and economics to the college bookshop, and with the proceeds I bought a cheap overnight return flight to Rome. My friends were either too broke or starting work too soon to join me.

I fell in love with Rome, as I had with Oxford three years before. I hired a second-floor room for ten days in one of the poorer areas, walked everywhere, and survived by eating bowls of pasta every evening. I usually bought the air-mail edition of the *Daily Telegraph* when it arrived on the magazine stalls around midday, and read it during the siesta. It was quite by chance, as I lay naked on my bed, that I came upon a page listing the results of the PPE Finals – and I learned that I had got a First. My reaction was to lie back laughing; I do not think anyone, least of all my tutors, would say that I had worked hard enough to deserve it, yet here were colleagues who could never be torn away from their regular lectures and reading programmes getting Seconds or even Thirds. I knew I was not brilliant; I had simply been fortunate in being set some unusual questions on areas that allowed me to draw on my extensive reading well outside the conventional boundaries of those subjects. I began to feel that I was born lucky – and that good luck would never desert me.

CHAPTER FOUR

Dirty Raincoats and Political Suits

'*The first duty of journalists is to make trouble.*'
Max Hastings, tribute to Sir David English (1998)

'*All newspaper and journalistic activity is an intellectual brothel
from which there is no escape.*'
Leo Tolstoy, letter to Prince Meshchersky (1871)

THE *BRISTOL EVENING POST* was a paper with a proud history. It was founded between the wars through public subscription by Bristol's citizens, who wanted their own independent paper after Lord Northcliffe took over the *Bristol Evening World*. By the late 1950s the *Post* reigned supreme, though the *World* was still published, and employed some good journalists. The only other paper was the *Western Daily Press*, a morning broadsheet laid out like *The Times*, with minimal circulation mainly to farmers around Bristol who needed to know the latest prices for stock in the West Country's markets. Its only reporter of note was Tom Stoppard, who subsequently won fame as a playwright; it was always fun covering a story with him.

Soon after starting work in Bristol, I fell for a rebellious girl who did not return my ardour; she was living with an older man who scratched a living repairing clapped-out veteran cars then selling them on. It was with them and their friends that I explored the disreputable 'scrumpy houses' of old Bristol, and shook the unsteady hands of their regular drinkers.

The policy of the paper was to give its trainees experience in a branch office working beside an experienced journalist, and *Post* branch offices were springing up across the West Country, from Malmesbury in Wiltshire to Cirencester and then Stroud in Gloucestershire. Soon after Christmas I was posted to Stroud, where I worked with Hubert Tyler, an experienced reporter from the *Liverpool Post*, a photographer and a circulation manager whose main job was to print the afternoon's racing results in the stop-press column of the editions driven up from Bristol. The *Post* was editionised according to circulation areas; Hubert and I had to fill one inside page daily, and if the story was good enough the front page was changed to carry it. Our task was to cut into the circulation of the *Gloucester Citizen*, the rival evening paper owned by Northcliffe.

There then opened up a truly joyous season in my life. I was living rent free, driving my first car, a rusty 1930s Austin convertible. I covered every conceivable kind of story in the steep valleys round Stroud, a town with an interesting industrial history dating from woollen mills powered by the valley streams, in beautiful Cotswold villages like Painswick, Bisley, Sheepscombe and Slad, then across the Severn Valley below. Hubert and I shared covering the magistrates court, the urban district council, the rural district council, parish councils, even village flower shows and gymkhanas, as well as the usual run of happy events and tragedies. Almost invariably we came together at night in the bar of the Imperial, used by many of the town's leading citizens and a hive of gossip, then returned to the office to send our copy to Bristol by teleprinter. I usually worked a six-day week, sometimes seven, which left little time for sowing wild oats, but I enjoyed every minute. My posting to Stroud was supposed to last six months, yet I managed to extend it to eighteen. I saw through a hard winter, my old car skating down the steep hillsides, and a hot dry summer when its hood was not raised for weeks.

I enjoyed covering the 1959 general election, attending every meeting and writing assessments of the Stroud campaign. I got to know the elected Tory MP, Anthony Kershaw; when I became a political correspondent he remained a friend until he retired from the Commons in 1987. When the count was through I went to the home of Terry, our photographer, to watch the results on TV with his wife. I took a bottle of gin. Terry had to photograph the rival candidates shaking hands after the count, then develop his prints in his darkroom before driving them to the Bristol office. While he was away his wife, a young woman with a gorgeously curvaceous figure, and I tucked into the gin. Terry arrived back earlier than we expected to find us in rather compromising circumstances. I also cleaned up nicely on the election result, having secured odds in a head-office book of 8–1 against a Tory majority of more than eighty, on which I laid a few pounds. Harold Macmillan swept home with a hundred.

The other delight in my time working in Stroud was the 'lineage' business I built up; this is the system whereby provincial journalists make extra money selling stories to national newspapers, or by obtaining information requested by national newsdesks. In the days when newspapers carried interminably long reports, the journalist was paid by the number of lines he contributed, but nowadays the payment is according to the use made of the story. Every national newsdesk maintains a list of such contributors, called 'stringers', across the country. When I arrived in Stroud all the lineage was held by an elderly reporter on the *Gloucester Citizen*, but he had lost interest in selling general news stories; he made plenty of money every Saturday rounding up the local sports results for the Sundays to print on their regional sports pages. I was determined to get the general lineage for myself, and before long I got as much as I could cope with, selling stories to the *Daily Express*, *Daily Mail*, *Daily Sketch*, the *Empire News* (a Sunday paper), but especially to the *Sunday Express*. Some months I was earning more from lineage than from the *Evening Post*. But the *Post* benefited from this too; when a national figure was involved in a big story and he had a relative or home in the Stroud area, I would learn of this quickly from national newsdesks who wanted something checked out or a quote, which meant that the next day I could provide my own paper with a local news story that had a national angle.

My principal market was the *Sunday Express*, from whose legendary news editor, Bernard Drew, I had sought advice on entering journalism while at Oxford. They paid very good money for exclusive midweek tip-offs of scandal. They would send a staff reporter down to Stroud, whom I would help build up the story for Sunday. All this was immensely enjoyable. There was the story of the Vicar of Bisley, a married man and amateur artist, who formed a dubious relationship with a village girl who modelled for him. Even better, her mother was the village chimney sweep. I picked up the rumour by keeping my ears open, but when the *Sunday Express* reporter and I interviewed the mother, she spilled all the beans – how the vicar had bought her daughter gifts and promised to take her away for a weekend, but let her down. The *Sunday Express* was then a broadsheet, and the story handsomely led an inside page. The following day the vicar fled the parish, and I was signed up to help the staffers for the national dailies write follow-ups. Orders were then placed with me to keep an eye on the situation in case the vicar returned. I dug out other stories of vicars who had quarrelled with their organists or parishioners in peculiar circumstances, and the *Sunday Express* ran them all. Many national figures had retreats in the Cotswolds, and their disputes with neighbours or local councils were a good source of stories too. I formed a memorable drinking friendship with Laurie Lee, who had just published *Cider with Rosie*, and his wife in Slad, and any stories of what he was doing were in demand too.

I joined a country-house drinking club outside Stroud, owned by a former Polish cavalry officer who had come from London, where he had managed to build up some capital running a coffee bar. According to Stroud police the coffee bar had been a pick-up joint for prostitutes, and it was not till the owner faced the prospect of being charged with living on immoral earnings that he closed it down. I had my doubts about this tale; he was a complex yet likeable man, a confirmed romantic who fell in love with a local hairdresser rather younger than himself, and who on his wedding night organised bonfires on all the old beacon hills around Stroud. He bought the house, with paddock, to found a country club and to breed horses. This was before the reform of the licensing laws, which, if I remember rightly, meant he had to close the bar at 10.30 p.m. Not surprisingly, drinking went on there well into the night; I often arrived after 10 p.m. on a Saturday after I finished work. But I was not there when it was raided after midnight by the police. When the case came before Stroud magistrates I was there to report it, and the evidence was quite bizarre. The two police officers in civilian clothes had been there since halfway through the evening; they could not have been used to drinking, for they spent the hours treating one other to rounds of Benedictine! How two men could survive so long on such a drink hardly bore thinking about. The story, which I handled myself, of two burly PCs drinking countless Benedictines for five hours waiting for their uniformed colleagues to arrive made another splendid page lead in the *Sunday Express*. The following Tuesday the paper's newsdesk was on the phone again: could I confirm that the two had driven their car away after the raid? My Polish friend and another couple present at the time assured me they had, so a reader's letter was stimulated for the letters page asking why two police officers so obviously under the influence of alcohol had driven themselves away. This was why I was not exactly popular with the police superintendent at Stroud.

Being on call to national newsdesks involved some grubby journalism too. A local dentist, a respected citizen, was brought before a judge in Gloucester, outside my territory. I cannot remember the charge, but in the course of the evidence it came out that he was in the habit of having sexual intercourse with his receptionist between appointments, and up to three times a day. He was found guilty, and given a jail sentence. After a couple of months, the *Empire News* rang with a request for me to interview his wife, and send them a spicy story. This I did ('Faithful wife waits in hope' and all that), but I did feel when interviewing her that I should have been wearing the proverbial dirty raincoat. I have always had a soft spot for what used to be called 'yellow journalism'. I used my lineage earnings to buy a new Austin-Healey Sprite soft-top, a totally different experience from my old banger, and to get married in 1961.

I also enjoyed writing the occasional feature articles to appear in all editions of the *Post*. Once, when a travelling circus came to Stroud, I interviewed the liontamer from inside his cage, surrounded by three snarling lions. Terry took flash pictures from outside the bars. 'He was never in danger,' someone commented afterwards. 'Those beasts never touch bad meat.'

But nemesis was catching up with me in Stroud. Thanks to my lineage revelations, I had made enemies. I never quite matched the notoriety of my opposite number in Cirencester whose activities were denounced from the pulpit, but I found doors being closed against me. Meanwhile the *Post's* editor insisted his paper did not train graduates to stay as sidekicks in district offices; after I had used up all excuses for staying in Stroud I was dragged back to head office. There was no specialist niche available for me there; I was simply part of the newsroom, with little scope for digging out stories of my own.

I have recounted these experiences because I believe such broad involvement with the sordid and the sublime in society provides splendid training for a politician. In the 1950s, the *News of the World* used an advertising slogan: 'All human life is here.' And so it was – far better experience for a future politician than going straight from university into political research, which appears to have become the fashion since.

It was around this time that the *Evening Post* took over the *Western Daily Press* and its heavy debt liability. Its printing operation moved to the *Post's* plant in Silver Street, and the two papers were served by a joint newsroom. The decrepit morning broadsheet had to be rejuvenated and given a totally new look before the drive to build up its readership could begin. For this purpose Eric Price was recruited as editor from the sub-editors' desk of the *Daily Express*, and he proceeded to make it look like the *Express* some ten years earlier. However, he was desperately short of subs, and I saw the chance to be trained in this valuable aspect of journalism. Now, for the first time ever, I was tied to a desk, starting work at 5 p.m. and finishing as the paper came off the presses around 1.30 a.m. Never since have I found working hours so congenial; as at Oxford, I rose late, then breakfast and toast at a coffee bar in Clifton. It was during this period that I married Juliet.

But my ambitions lay in Fleet Street, not Bristol. I used my old connection with Bernard Drew on the *Sunday Express* and was taken on as a temporary reporter on Saturdays during the summer holidays. I left Bristol as soon as the paper was put to bed in the early hours of Saturday, then drove up the A4 (a tortuous journey – no motorway in those days) to begin a reporting stint late morning. This mainly involved making checks or interviewing by phone from the office, though of course we were available to go out in emergencies. Then, another night drive back to Bristol.

My employers got the message; I had completed my indenture, and it did not look as though I would stay with them long. It was then decided that the *Western Daily Press* should have its own political or lobby correspondent based at Westminster, and I was given the job. So I arrived where I had wanted to be from my first days at Oxford: at the heart of politics.

———————— ∾ ————————

Lobby correspondents have been institutionalised at the House of Commons since the growth of the popular press in the nineteenth century. They operate under licence from the Sergeant-at-Arms, whereby they are allowed to hang around in the Members' Lobby, and in other corridors normally reserved for MPs, in order to chat to anyone about the political news of the day. All such conversations are on 'lobby terms', which is to say the information gained from them can be used but not attributed unless the informant chooses to make a statement. In my day, at 11 a.m. each morning, those correspondents and agencies serving evening papers and the broadcasting media trooped up Whitehall for a briefing by the Prime Minister's press chief at 10 Downing Street, again all strictly 'off the record'. Then at 4 p.m. the press chief came across to a turret room at the Commons to brief the morning-paper correspondents and the 'round-the-clock' media on the same basis. Lobby correspondents are provided with a seat in the Reporters' Gallery, together with a desk and phone in the warren of rooms behind. Over the years there have been many criticisms of the 'lobby system', with correspondents accused of being too subservient to their 'off-the-record' sources. But in my experience the system works well; politicians try to use the journalists, just as journalists try to use the politicians, yet the love-hate relationship works to the advantage of readers. The system also enables correspondents to use a multiplicity of conflicting sources, which is not often the case, for example, among diplomatic correspondents.

The Press Gallery has its own library and bar. All its members elect a chairman and committee to manage their joint interests, while the lobby elects a chairman and committee of its own. The lobby chairman presided at the garret-room meetings, to which ministers often came as guests. Members of the lobby also received advance copies of government publications under embargo, so that reports could be written in a considered manner before publication. The lobby committee investigated any complaint that a correspondent had broken the rules of the lobby system.

I served as lobby correspondent for the *Western Daily Press* for three years, and worked as a one-man team. I made contacts among West Country MPs of all parties, together with Tory backbenchers I had come to know during OUCA days. A regular contact was Tony Benn (known then as Anthony Wedgwood Benn), banished from his Bristol South East seat after becoming Viscount Stansgate; I covered his epic battle to win the right to disclaim his peerage and sit again in the Commons. Little did he know he was paving the way for the 14th Earl of Home to become Tory party leader.

My first party conference was the Tories' at Llandudno, 1962. Earlier that year the Cabinet had decided to apply to take Britain into the European Economic Community, known then as the Common Market; this had prompted strong misgivings among Commonwealth governments, since Britain was a leading market for their products, and there was strong opposition among Tories whose Commonwealth loyalties ran deep. The Government's application was down for debate and two Tory MPs, Sir Derek Walker-Smith and Neil Marten, were heading the opposition. It was essential for Macmillan to secure backing for his policy. The night before the European debate, I was invited by an MP to attend a reception for members of the Tory trade unionists' group, where I had my first experience of how the Tory Establishment worked. Part way through the evening we were visited by two senior figures in the National Union (which ran the conference in every sense of the word), as part of their tour of all the social functions taking place. There was a call for silence for the most senior member to speak. After thanking everyone for their loyal service over the past year, he turned straight to the next day's debate on Europe. 'Of course, this isn't really about Europe or our beloved Commonwealth at all,' he told them. 'It's about whether we're for Macmillan, or against. I hope you'll all be loyal to Harold tomorrow.' Sage nods and 'hear, hears', as the pair left to impart their message at other receptions. I was taken aback by the brazenness of their approach, but they were behaving true to form for senior National Union officers. Issues as such are of little interest to them, if anything they are rather a nuisance; all judgement has to fall under the steamroller of blind loyalty to the leader. How many crimes in history have been committed by honest men seeking to please their leader. Needless to say, the vote next day went against Walker-Smith and Marten.

From my new position I was perfectly placed to observe the decline and fall of Harold Macmillan, despite his having won such a landslide victory in 1959. The Profumo scandal inflicted the greatest damage, making Macmillan appear hopelessly out of touch with the 'Swinging Sixties'. We all knew the details of the scandal as it developed; the lobby was kept well informed by the Labour MP George Wigg, while Fleet Street knew more than ever appeared in print. So we were flabbergasted when War Minister John Profumo made his personal statement to the Commons denying any improper association with Christine Keeler. Those who understood the conventions of Westminster could not conceive that he could possibly be lying through his teeth. The press revelations ceased for a time, yet still the rumours grew and appeared to have substance. When my editor came to London to drink with his old *Daily Express* chums he heard the whole story and, back in Bristol, he phoned me straight away. 'When are you going to start reporting some of this, George?' he would bark. 'I don't want our readers to be left behind. What do you think you're paid for? Just go as far as you possibly can.' Yet he knew I could go nowhere without exposing his paper to colossal libel damages. However, Profumo's pretence could not hold. A desultory lobby meeting sprang to life when Macmillan's press chief Harold Evans dropped the bombshell: Profumo had come clean and resigned. After that the rumour factory went into peak production. The masked man, naked save for a masonic apron, serving canapes at a party attended by Stephen Ward, Keeler's 'protector', and their louche friends was said to be transport minister Ernest Marples, no less, while numerous stories recounted how Keeler gave oral sex to John Hare, as upright a cabinet minister as you could ever find, on the back seat of his ministerial limousine. Macmillan appointed Lord Denning to conduct a special inquiry into all these rumours, and he reported they were totally groundless. But the damage was done. At the subsequent party conference in Blackpool I watched the Tory Party tearing itself apart over who should succeed Macmillan – Rab Butler or Lord Hailsham. 'Just watch Home,' some of my old OUCA contacts whispered. I did, and wrote up his chances early. I then had the satisfaction of reporting how aristocratic guile won through and almost saved the party from defeat in the 1964 general election.

For most of my life I have worked a six-day week, and I had not been in the lobby for long before I secured a Saturday job as a sub on the *Sunday Times*. The paper's political correspondent was Jimmy Margach, a canny Scot whose career at Westminster dated back to when Stanley Baldwin was Prime Minister. He enjoyed the confidence of many ministers, but on paper he was prone to ramble. My task was to sub all the political material and to tighten up Jimmy's copy. Since he often provided the front-page lead I would follow it through to the 'stone' in the composing room to 'cut it in' to the space available. Those were the days of hot-lead type, set in lines by compositors on linotype machines that had been discarded across the rest of the world. The printing operation of all national papers was completely under the control of the print unions, and restrictive practices were rife. The 'stone sub' was a journalist, but he was never allowed to touch the slugs of lead print. He had to indicate to the 'stone hand', a printer, which lines he wanted inserted and which lines should be reset. I had never worked on the stone at the *Western Daily Press*, so all this was new to me. As a beginner my natural inclination was to reach for the slugs of lead I wanted, but I was fortunate in working with a stone hand who simply raised a kindly finger to me. If I had even touched the type, every printer in the composing room would have downed tools and delayed the entire print run.

The *Sunday Times* at that time had no connection with *The Times*, and was owned by Roy Thomson, a Canadian. It was in the same stable as Thomson Regional Newspapers (TRN), which owned mornings like the *Western Mail*, *Newcastle Journal* and *Aberdeen Press and Journal*, plus a string of evenings. Thomson also owned the *Scotsman*, though that was separate from the rest. Working directly under the editor of the *Sunday Times* on Saturdays was Patrick Murphy, a journalist of long experience who for the rest of the week ran the London office of TRN, housed in the same building. My work must have caught his eye, for in 1964 he offered me a post on the political staff serving TRN's morning papers. I jumped at the chance.

Lobby passes were granted on the basis of the historic rights of individual papers, regardless of their ownership. Thus the *Western Mail*, *Newcastle Journal* and *Aberdeen Press and Journal* each had their entitlement to an accredited lobby correspondent. The man running the TRN team was Joe Tobin, who held the *Newcastle Journal's* pass. The vacant pass was for the Aberdeen paper, and so it came about that I, having never in my life set foot in Scotland, became lobby correspondent for one of Scotland's oldest newspapers. The editor of the *P&J*, as it was always called, did not object at all; he was no supporter of narrow nationalism. I was sent on a two-day visit to Aberdeen, of which I became deeply fond. The *P&J's* office was then in the centre of that granite city, with seagulls forever wheeling and crying overhead. The *P&J* had a large and loyal readership throughout the Highlands and north-east, and was much trusted; it was a broadsheet deliberately laid out in an old-fashioned way, distinguishing it from its nearest competitor in the region, the more flashy *Scottish Daily Express*. By comparison, the sales of the *Scotsman* and the *Glasgow Herald* were miniscule. The *P&J* was editionised to bring really local news, and refused to recognise that Scotland's central belt even existed. It would rather carry a Reuters 'situationer' from Peking than a report of anything happening in Glasgow, whose citizens were deeply distrusted. The 1964 general election was almost upon us, and it was agreed that, after taking a holiday in Scotland, I would spend most of the campaign preparing special features on the campaigns in the Highland seats of Caithness and Sutherland, Ross and Cromarty, and Inverness.

By the time I was appointed to TRN, Juliet was pregnant, and we decided to take our summer holiday touring Scotland from Royal Deeside to the Isle of Skye. On a Sunday afternoon in Portree we queued in a disused garage with a leaking roof while the Sunday newspapers were ferried in surreptitiously from the mainland. I noted that by far the most popular Sunday read on Wee-Free Skye was the *News of the World*, delivered through letterboxes after dark.

Electioneering in the Highlands was like nothing I had seen before. The distances were immense; with roads as they were then, it took a full day to drive from one end of Caithness and Sutherland to the other, and candidates were out of reach for days on end. Election meetings in those towns and villages were different too; these Highlanders had time to think, and asked deeply serious questions that touched on philosophical matters. The three seats I covered had been Tory strongholds, though in 1959 the Member for Caithness resigned the Tory whip over his Government's handling of Highland affairs. The same issue loomed large in this election; Highlanders were badly shaken by Lord Beeching's proposal to close miles of railway track, thus making the area even more remote. In Caithness I caught up with the Tory Patrick Maitland, whom I had met through OUCA, and his daughter Olga, then barely twenty, in the middle of a heather moor. His opponent George Mackie, who looked much more like a Tory brewer than a Liberal, had his base at the best country hotel in Caithness, where I quickly booked a room. When the votes were counted he slipped through to win, and the story was the same in the other Highland seats I visited: Liberals routing former Tory MPs, who were seen as representing a southern party who cared little for the Highlands. This was the start of the long Tory retreat from Scotland, which took thirty-three years to complete. Liberals were the first beneficiaries; the SNP challenge was yet to come.

The election brought Harold Wilson to Number Ten, though with an overall majority of only four, which conferred deadly power on two of his foremost critics in the parliamentary Labour party, Woodrow Wyatt and Desmond Donnelly. It was an object lesson to see how they used this power to prevent the nationalisation of the steel industry. The 14th Earl of Home had served his party far better than many Tories had dared to think. But Ted Heath's supporters on the 1922 Committee executive had their knives out, so Home stepped down, decreeing that for the first time ever his successor would be chosen by a ballot of all Tory MPs. The old 'Magic Circle' was broken, and Heath became opposition leader. Soon after the election I was promoted to be TRN's chief political correspondent, with Roy Lilley, from Ulster, as my deputy.

After arriving in Downing Street, Wilson milked the lobby system for all it was worth; almost every day there was a story designed to reflect the dynamism of his leadership. He met us frequently, quizzing us from his apparently phenomenal memory. 'Who can tell me the Liverpool Rangers team for the Cup in . . . ?' he would tease, then rattle the players' names off to us. One lobby correspondent well versed in such arcane matters might hit back: 'OK, Prime Minister, but you tell us who won the Cup in . . . ?' Wilson told him, spot on. I was as guilty as any other lobby correspondent; we simply ate out of his hand. It was of course a decidedly unhealthy relationship, and bound not to last, but Wilson worked the system shamelessly till he called an election, hoping to increase his majority, in 1966. The message that it was safe to do this came from the North Hull by-election. I made a point of spending three or four days at significant by-elections, leaving Roy to manage the shop at Westminster. The serious contenders at Hull were my Balliol friend Toby Jessel and Kevin McNamara, defending a slender Labour majority of 1,181. Judging by the publicity battle and all signs visible on the surface Jessel was winning hands down. I wrote a feature for Thomson Newspapers that appeared under the headline: 'Only a miracle can save this seat for Labour.' What I never saw was Labour's streamlined organisation on the shop floor. The result was a majority for McNamara of 5,351 – a colossal swing since 1974. When teased by Labour MPs back at Westminster for getting it so wrong I could only suggest that, clearly, God intervened to help Roman Catholics. But Wilson saw the signal, and accordingly went to the country.

Covering a general election campaign from London is relatively easy for a political correspondent serving regional papers; all the parties' press conferences have to be covered, then a round-up story written at the end of the day. The task can easily be handled by one correspondent, not two. I arranged to spend the first part of the 1966 campaign back in Aberdeen, while Roy spent the latter part with the paper to which he was assigned, the *Newcastle Journal*. I was away when Ted Heath gave his first press conference, but I heard later of his blunder. When it came to questions, Roy piped up with his strong Ulster intonation; Heath mistook this for a Canadian accent, and replied: 'Perhaps we can take questions from the overseas press at the end.' All the lobby, who knew Roy well, could hardly suppress their mirth. This made me wonder whether Heath had ever spent much time Northern Ireland, and the question subsequently became more relevant after his clumsy handling of the Ulster Unionists, then allied to the Tory Party. In North Scotland I chose to cover the most marginal seats, and I know Tory MPs viewed my arrival much as an injured traveller in the bush regards a vulture circling above his head. I returned to Caithness and Sutherland where my Balliol friend Bob Maclennan was the Labour candidate. He took exception to my article drawing attention to his feline appearance, saying you felt that if you stroked him between the ears he would start to purr, but that was all brushed aside when he took the seat from the Liberals. I covered Aberdeen South, where Donald Dewar sent the Tory minister, Lady Tweedsmuir, packing, and Aberdeenshire West, the Deeside seat where the Liberal, James Davidson, beat the doughty Tory, Forbes Hendry. In the end Tory representation in Scotland dropped even further, to just twenty seats.

At Westminster I was building up my contacts with Labour ministers, but the joy of lobby work lay in the camaraderie with back-benchers of all parties, often late at night in the Strangers' Bar. OUCA colleagues Kenneth Baker and Paul Channon were MPs, I still had friends there from Bristol days, and I regularly met the Highland and Aberdeen area MPs to write short reports on their activities for the *P&J*. One such was Hector Hughes, the veteran Member for Aberdeen North, who was just about the laziest MP I ever met. Apart from chipping in during Scottish or Prime Minister's Questions, much of his time was spent with his feet up in the Members' Library; he employed no secretary, nor did he reply personally to constituents' letters. Instead he sent bundles of them periodically to the relevant ministers, asking for their comments; on receiving their replies, he sent the top copy to the constituent concerned, enclosing a compliments slip, and kept the copy for himself. Then, about every two months, he sent me a vast bundle of the letters and copied replies, so that I could write about how hard he was working on behalf of the citizens of Aberdeen North. He made no effort to reserve letters of a personal nature which could not possibly appear in print. One bundle contained a letter from a constituent who had inflicted grave injury to his testicles by falling through a ladder, and who wanted compensation from the State for his loss. I organised a competition among lobby colleagues for the best headline for the story. It was won by Joe Haines, later to become Wilson's chief press officer. But most entertaining of all were the Geordie MPs, whose safe Labour seats were in the circulation area of the *Newcastle Journal*, which carried my reports. On evenings when they were not at the dog track, they sank pint after pint in the Strangers' Bar, often accompanied by their mistresses, or 'London wives', as they were called. 'The secret of survival, George,' one of them sagely advised me, 'is always to keep a shot in your locker for the missus at weekends.' Those were days when journalists observed total discretion.

After 1966 I again became involved in active politics. Our Blackheath home was in the Greenwich constituency, a safe Labour seat held by my Westminster friend Richard Marsh. John Gummer, whom I knew from party conferences, was selected as Tory candidate, and he persuaded me to join his local executive as press officer. I also sensed the time was coming when I would tire of simply reporting political events and instead would want to help shape them, so I applied to be put on Central Office's list of prospective candidates. My loathing of Socialism and my belief that private enterprise was the best way to harness human endeavour were as deep as they had ever been. The system at CCO at that time meant being interviewed by two Tory MPs before being accepted by the vice-chairman in charge of candidates. Tony Kershaw, from Stroud, proposed me, but I was amazed to find the two MPs interviewing me were Paul Channon, an old associate from OUCA, and Martin McLaren, from Bristol North West, whom I knew well since my days as lobby correspondent for the *Western Daily Press*. We spent half an hour in jovial conversation, and in a matter of days I was on the list. Most of my friends and contacts among Labour and Liberal MPs at Westminster knew I was a Tory at heart, but since I always tried to deal with them on a fair and objective basis, I found this made no difference.

Even before Wilson secured his comfortable majority of ninety-eight in 1966, the magical power which he exercised over the lobby began to wane; we became distrustful of his briefings, and the press generally adopted a more critical tone. We found that some of his accounts to us did not match up with those from other members of his Cabinet, and such discrepancies came to a head in his fight to save Barbara Castle's 'In Place of Strife' industrial relations proposals, opposed behind the scenes by Chancellor Jim Callaghan. Forming a backdrop to all this were his persistent quarrels with George Brown, his Foreign Secretary, who, when he took to the bottle – a frequent occurrence, made his distrust of Wilson only too clear to all who cared to listen. Wilson realised he could manipulate the lobby no more, so resorted to secret briefings with a few trusties, who were derided by the rest of us as 'The White Commonwealth'. His other exclusive channel to the press was through his political secretary, Marcia Williams, who was romantically involved with Walter Terry, political editor of the *Daily Mail*, father of her two children.

I decided to try for a marginal seat in the next election, fastening on the Midlands as my area of interest purely because TRN had no newspapers in that region, enabling me to keep my two roles as separate as I could. Obviously I consulted Patrick Murphy first, since I needed his permission to be away from my duties during an election campaign. He was very generous and gave me every encouragement; there were not many Fleet Street managements who would agree to losing their chief political correspondent for the duration of a general election campaign! I got as far as the short lists in three or four seats before reaching the short list for Coventry South – held for Labour by William Wilson with a 5,540 majority. The seat had been held by the Tories from 1959 until 1964. My opponents on the short list were Ian Gow (subsequently to represent Eastbourne) and Michael Marshall (Arundel). Marshall then had a reputation of turning up for interviews with his fiancée, the only trouble being that the lucky girl was always a different person. Despite that, and despite the fact that Gow had previously fought Coventry East, I was the one selected. I later arranged to meet William Wilson in the Strangers' Tea Room at the Commons. He was a pleasant fellow, a Coventry solicitor with a conspicuous hearing aid, who bore no rancour towards me; he was on the left of his party, with close connections with the Communist regime in East Germany.

I was still working on Saturdays as political sub on the *Sunday Times*, and now that I was on the TRN staff, I was made deputy political correspondent to Jimmy Margach. This meant that I fed him any stories or ideas from the lobby he might find useful, and when he was sick or on holiday I moved from the subs desk to writing the political stories. I remember the occasion when I was handed the Press Association advance of Enoch Powell's famous 'Rivers of Blood' speech. I phoned Ted Heath to get his reaction, and was fortunate to get him soon after he returned home. Had he approved the contents of Powell's speech? I asked. 'What speech?' was his reply. When I read him sections from it he was incredulous: 'Did he say that?' So was I right in assuming he did not agree? He replied: 'It's preposterous.' So what did this mean for Powell's future as a member of his shadow team? 'We'll have to see about that,' he replied ominously. I was the first to write that Powell might face the sack, and it was not till Monday's papers that other correspondents had a field day following that one through.

After I was selected to fight Coventry South, I incurred the wrath of a small number of north-east Labour MPs over a story I wrote about shadow minister Keith Joseph and his plans for the regions. I believed their move against me was instigated by Ted Short, Member for Newcastle Central and Education Secretary. The plot was relayed to me by the Geordie mafia in the Strangers' Bar, who remained good friends. Apparently a petition was being circulated among north-east Labour MPs, to be sent to Lord Thomson asking him to remove me as a political correspondent for TRN. When they secured a few names they took it to show Bob Mellish, Government Chief Whip, a blunt-speaking Cockney and old political war horse who controlled the London Labour Party with a rod of iron. I soon secured a good account of that interview; as the MPs sat before him, Mellish looked at their document scornfully under his desk light, said 'Don't be so fucking stupid!', then tore it into little pieces before dropping them in his waste-paper bin. A wise old bird was Mellish; he knew I was on the lobby committee and also the parliamentary branch committee of the National Union of Journalists, and the last thing he wanted in the run-up to a general election was a row accusing the Labour Party of trying to rob a journalist of his job for reporting facts as he saw them.

I worked hard on Coventry South. Roy Lilley had been whisked away from me to be editor of the *Belfast Evening Telegraph*; he was replaced by Gordon Leak, who later became political editor of the *News of the World*. He was a Tory councillor at Sevenoaks; I worked doubly hard to cover for him when he attended council meetings; and he in turn made sure I was able drive to Coventry for weekday or Friday evening events, always returning to London for my subbing duties on Saturday.

I had no previous experience of the industrial situation in car towns like Coventry, and what I saw appalled me. Managements were barely in control of their own production; everything had to be organised through the shop stewards, who had a vice-like grip over all the plants.

Demarcation disputes came up at regular intervals, usually culminating in a one-day strike; casual strikes were simply seen as supplementing public holidays. The Wilson Government might imagine it was imposing a pay freeze, but this was avoided by the car workers of Coventry: their pay was governed by the 'Coventry toolroom rate' – a hangover from the war years – which was outside the pay policy and adjusted monthly. My deep hatred of trade union power dates from that experience. Coventry had little cultural climate, and its blue-collar workers were the prototype for what subsequently came to be called 'Essex man'.

A large number of Asian immigrants had settled in Coventry, the first having arrived to work in the man-made textile factories. Many of them, particularly the Sikhs, lived in Coventry South, and were deemed to be in William Wilson's pocket, since he would represent them if they came before the magistrates' court. But the Asian communities were riven by faction, which meant many were declared enemies of Wilson's henchmen and were eager for recognition from the Tory Party. I worked hard on these individuals, often returning to meet them on a Sunday. Their politics were without scruple; one supporter was Gurdev Singh, who employed a number of Asian women stitching anoraks; he had two lively sons who would follow Labour canvassers round the mean streets and remove all their literature from letter boxes. I also received much useful advice from Dr 'Paul' Bedi, a learned man whose father was a holy man in the Punjab; I once arranged to meet him in a pub patronised entirely by Asians, and as he entered a hush fell and everyone stood up. This community feared the possible consequences of Enoch Powell's 'Rivers of Blood' speech, and I did my best to distance myself from it. Racial prejudice was high in Coventry; many working whites regarded Powell as their Messiah, and the unions were rigorous in keeping Asians out of the car plants except, *in extremis,* as cleaners. I witnessed an uncomfortable celebration at a working men's club where some tarted-up scrubber belted out patriotic songs, interspersed with the crudest racist jokes. Once, after midnight, Gurdev Singh drove me to meet the night shift at a foundry in Nuneaton where he had first got work; most were Asians under an Irish foreman. The scene was positively Dickensian; big vats of molten metal on the floor, with men dipping in ladles and pouring metal into casts to make engine casings. There were no protective guards, and most of the workers had discarded their clumsy safety gloves; Gurdev still had the scars on his hands from burns inflicted while working long hours through the night – this was before he saved enough to strike out on his own. Throughout the West Midlands there existed a substratum of industry apparently beyond regulation or control.

The 1970 election campaign is etched deeply in my mind. Ted Heath was not popular with many Midlands Tories; Enoch Powell was their real hero, but I stuck to the official line. The June campaign was fought in baking heat; Quintin Hogg made a supportive walkabout in a shopping mall, dressed in a heavy country suit, waistcoat and lace-up boots, standing out conspicuously against everyone else in shirtsleeves. Robert Carr, then shadow employment minister, spoke on a sweltering evening in a community hall on a council estate. All but two of the twenty-five-strong audience were Labour supporters, yet they listened in silent fascination as he unfolded the Tories' proposed trade union reforms; questions were incisive and informed. Anthony Barber, the Party Chairman, spoke at an open-air meeting in support of all three Coventry candidates. Michael Heseltine, who had been the candidate for Coventry North in 1964, gave a quick press conference on his way elsewhere. Angus Maude spoke in my support too. Central Office rated Coventry South a marginal seat. Juliet came to join me for part of each week while our au pair took care of the children.

The real enemy for the Tories in 1970 was not so much the Labour Party but the opinion polls, which were consistently against us and getting worse. At the end of the first week, Gallup reported a 5.5 per cent lead for Labour. Later in the campaign I rang Gordon Leak, who was managing TRN's political team back in London. 'I don't want to kick you in the balls, George,' he said, 'but NOP's about to give Labour a 12.4 per cent lead.' That would give Wilson a majority of around 150. 'I don't believe it,' I said. 'No,' he replied, 'and if it's any comfort to you, Transport House [then Labour's HQ] don't believe it either.' I had a good band of campaigners, but in such circumstances I had to work hard to keep their spirits up. Some bold initiative was needed. I confided this need to a friend after closing time one night in the Conservative Club. 'Don't worry,' he replied, 'I know just the man for you.' Early the following evening, before I set off for another round of canvassing, a rough diamond who ran a fruit and vegetable stall in the market presented himself and invited me out to look inside his large van. Sitting on fruit cases in the back were two of his chums surrounded by some 300 of my large posters (an arresting design in black and day-glo orange), a large bucket of wallpaper paste with brush, another full of three-inch nails, a heavy hammer and a ladder. I grinned at them: 'I don't think I'd better know about this.' After midnight they set off to fly-post almost every flat surface they could find in the city-centre area of Coventry South; tramps dossing down in derelict houses awaiting clearance for road schemes were given cigarettes while the trio set about their task; the posters still remaining by 3 a.m. were nailed high on the trunks of the City Corporation's trees. A furious official was on the phone as soon as our office opened; my agent and I professed ignorance, but promised to get the posters removed from the trees. However, the sheer effrontery of the exercise worked wonders in raising the morale of my troops.

Heath and party chairman Barber kept their nerve throughout, and were rewarded with a workable majority of thirty. On polling day itself the Opinion Research Centre actually gave the Tories a 1 per cent lead, but collectively the opinion polls could not have been more wrong. I came in 2,194 votes behind William Wilson.

Back at Westminster the defeated Harold Wilson became a very embittered Leader of the Opposition, and his earlier courtship of the lobby degenerated into the petty jealousies and spite of a dead romance. His old 'kitchen cabinet' had broken up, and later one of its former members, Lord Wigg, published memoirs in which he bitterly criticised the role played by Marcia Williams in flattering Wilson and shielding him from reality. I reviewed the book for TRN, in which I said many of his assertions had the ring of truth: 'I can personally recall how, after his 1970 defeat, Wilson refused to attend a reception for political leaders from both sides of the House because the hosts declined to invite Marcia too.' The hosts concerned were the lobby committee, who held a small annual reception for regular guests at their collective meetings: leaders of parties, the Leader of the House and his shadow, Downing Street and party press officers. Wilson was invited because he came to lobby meetings occasionally, though never with Mrs Williams. However, he refused to come unless she were invited too; the committee replied that whether he accepted or not was up to him. Wilson claimed that the reference in my book review constituted a breach of lobby confidentiality, and informed the lobby that he would never come to its meetings again unless I were barred from those he attended. The lobby committee refused to bow to such pressure, and it was not until the run-up to the 1974 election that Wilson wisely decided to eat humble pie and attend collective briefings again.

Much of our reporting in the early part of that Parliament was of Heath's efforts to secure British entry into the European Economic Community, with Geoffrey Rippon as chief negotiator. The senior foreign office official involved was Sir Con O'Neill, and at lobby meetings we were frequently told that 'Sir Con's assessment is this ... ' or 'Sir Con thinks that ... ' (Once, a puzzled Wilfred Sendall, the *Daily Express's* urbane political editor, asked why the Government could not choose an official whose name showed more understanding for the French language – '*con*' in French means vagina. No doubt Sendall knew, as I did, that all French correspondents in London regularly called the poor man 'Sir Cunt'.) I was a fervent supporter of Britain joining the Common Market, and at Sir Tufton Beamish's invitation became a founder member of the Conservative Group for Europe. What an innocent I was!

In the early 1970s I began a weekly political diary, called 'Commons Confidential', which was syndicated to TRN papers under my by-line. The style was acerbic, heavily personalised, and exposed the ups and downs, the foibles and the ironies of the political scene. It was printed regularly by the *Newcastle Journal* and a string of Thomson evenings, including the *South Wales Echo*. The lead item was always of a serious nature, but the aim was to end up with a humorous item, which on one occasion landed me and TRN in serious trouble. When the EEC negotiations had been completed successfully, it became known that Heath wanted to make George Thomson, Labour MP for Dundee East and a fervent European, one of Britain's first Brussels Commissioners. Thomson had agreed to speak at the afternoon session of the Labour Party's north-east region rally, but two Labour MPs who were strongly anti-Market objected to his presence. The result was that, as he rose to speak, Tom Urwin and Bobby Woof ostentatiously left the platform. This prompted much hilarity and gossip in the Strangers' Bar the following week, and I wrote in my diary that the real reason for them leaving the platform was not anti-Market principle at all. Several beers had been consumed during the lunch break, and the pair found it necessary to leave the platform to attend to an urgent call of nature. Within days, notice of a libel writ arrived at TRN. I had broken one of the golden rules of safe journalism – never question a man's motive. A grovelling apology was printed the following week, and the pair collected several hundred pounds each in an out-of-court settlement. One spent the money buying himself a caravan, the other was said to have taken his 'London wife' on a Mediterranean holiday. Both were good friends of mine from that point onwards, often encouraging me to write scurrilous items about them again.

With the experience of fighting Coventry South under my belt, from 1971 onwards I was being invited to selection interviews for prospective candidates in safe Tory seats throughout south and south-east England where the sitting MP had announced his retirement. In some I was encouraged to find myself short-listed, but never did I encounter such a bizarre selection process as in Reigate. Sir Geoffrey Howe, whom I knew reasonably well, was its MP, but in the coming boundaries revision the seat was to be divided. Howe had opted to stay with the more rural part, which was to become East Surrey, while Reigate and Redhill would be merged with Banstead and other wards above the North Downs escarpment, served at that time by a senior backbencher called Captain Walter Elliot. Representatives from both parts of the new constituency made up the selection committee, charged under the association's rules with presenting five names to the executive council, who would then choose two to appear before a meeting open to all paid-up members of the association. To vest the final selection with all association members is standard practice now, but then it certainly was not. The Reigate association had gone to town when choosing their candidate for the 1970 election, even calling in the television cameras to film Geoffrey Howe and Christoper Chattaway slogging it out. They also subjected the applicants' wives to detailed political questioning – a practice which earned much criticism and was subsequently dropped.

Members of the new Reigate selection committee obviously enjoyed their role, narrowing their list only slowly and calling the successful applicants at each stage back for further interviews. I learned that I was running neck and neck with Norman Fowler, sometimes scoring more votes than him, sometimes less. Former MP Fred Sylvester was doing well too, while newcomers Patrick Mayhew and Peter Temple-Morris were eliminated towards the final stages. I did well at all my interviews, except finally with the executive council, when I came third behind Fowler and Sylvester, and so had to drop out. However, within days Fowler told me in the Members' Lobby that he had just been selected at Sutton Coldfield, and soon afterwards Reigate's chairman Derek Hene was on the phone asking me to rejoin the list, which I did. Then another bombshell burst over the heads of the Reigate selectors: Captain Elliot, who still served part of the new seat but who hitherto had shown no interest in fighting it, asked to be included on the short list. This put the association in a dilemma; under their rules they could put only two names before the full meeting of members; two had already been agreed, so after a further interview with Elliot they told him somewhat cavalierly that he was too late. This was unwise, since Elliot had many loyal supporters in the northern part of the new constituency. It must also have been hard for Hene, who was a personal friend of the Elliots. The date was fixed for the final selection meeting, open to all paid-up members, in Redhill's old Market Hall.

John Lacy was the Central Office agent for the south-east area, which meant he had to keep an eye on the candidate selections in his domain. I had known him since he was agent for the northern area, based in Newcastle, and he was a good friend. South-east area was covered from party headquarters in Smith Square. Lacy had always offered constructive advice when I failed to get beyond the short-list stage in other seats ('George, why did you come in that suit, looking like a band-leader?'). I knew he was following my Reigate progress with interest, though the very worst thing he could have done would be to try to swing the selection in my favour, even assuming that had been his desire. Local associations generally take a dim view of any pressure from Central Office. I had taken a day off work for Reigate's final selection, and by 10 a.m. Lacy was on the phone. He thought I might like to know that association members in Banstead and other wards to the north of the Downs were organising coaches to the selection meeting, with a view to getting Captain Elliot's name added to the list and then, presumably, voting him in. Elliot would be in a hotel nearby, waiting for the call. With two factions north and south of the Downs at loggerheads, and the local press invited to witness the carnage, clearly we were in for a fascinating evening!

The Market Hall, built soon after Redhill's emergence as a railway town on the Brighton line, was near the end of its life and awaiting demolition to make way for a modern shopping centre. It was constructed rather like a Victorian music hall, with dressing rooms either side of a stage. These rooms were linked by a rear corridor, and those immediately adjacent to the stage also had a door which opened on to it. When Fred Sylvester and I arrived with our wives, we were each ushered into one of these rooms, complete with make-up mirror and surrounding circle of bare light bulbs. As members checked in at the door, the association's officers were in a panic. Lady Ashdown, a small, dynamic silver-haired lady representing the National Union, came into our dressing room, wringing her hands. 'It's all Robert Carr's fault,' she wailed. 'He could have had this seat for the asking.' Home Secretary Carr had probably sensed the danger in Reigate; he had gone for the more marginal Mitcham.

Hene, obviously nervous, called the meeting to order – and immediately an emergency resolution was moved that Capt Walter Elliot's name be added to the list. 'But that would be against our rules,' poor Hene pleaded. It fell to Lacy to advise that in the circumstances the relevant rules were to be waived; had he recommended otherwise there would have been a riot. So the motion was accepted for debate, whereupon bitter recriminations ensued. All the dirty linen of the new association, itself the product of a shotgun marriage, was washed before the eyes and ears of an astonished *Surrey Mirror* reporter. I discovered that the door between our dressing room and the stage could be eased open, so Sylvester and I sat by the crack listening to the battle that was raging on the other side. I later learned that members from Reigate and Redhill were taking pass-out tickets to commandeer all the phone booths within reach to call absent friends to come quickly to stop 'that Banstead lot' getting their way. After a while it was judged that enough insulting words had been exchanged and the vote was taken: 236 to add Elliot's name to the list, 232 against; the association was split almost exactly down the middle. It had to be assumed the 236 had come from the northern wards, rooting for Elliot, though it was quite possible that some from the south had voted for him in the hope of healing the rift. But there were 232 members who almost certainly would never vote for him, so either Sylvester or I was in with a chance.

Elliot was summoned from a lounge bar nearby, while I was ushered onto the stage first. We were each allotted ten minutes for our speech and twenty minutes to answer questions. I was a right-winger and I delivered an unashamedly right-wing speech. I weighed in against monopoly trade unions in all the state industries and spoke in defence of quality and freedom of choice in education – Surrey County Council, supposedly Tory, was then intent on abolishing all grammar schools in the county. The audience seemed reasonably receptive, but they really came alive when I urged much tougher penalties for violent criminals and restoration of the death penalty for murder – this prompted loud cheers. The questions caused me no difficulty. It had been agreed beforehand that our wives would be asked just one question: 'Mrs X, how do you envisage being able to help your husband if he becomes our MP?' Juliet's answer met with general satisfaction: yes, she would do all she could to help me, but of course her young family had to come first.

I then made way for Sylvester, who made much of Heath's prices and incomes policy ('fair to all'), but ran into choppy water responding to questions when he declared he was opposed to capital punishment. He and I then sat together with our ears to the door while Elliot and his wife were brought on from the dressing room at the other side of the stage.

Boos greeted them from parts of the hall, promising trouble. Elliot made a reasonable presentation in difficult circumstances, explaining his strong opposition to Communism and his service to his constituents. He was heard in silence, but when it came to questions the Reigate and Redhill element erupted; never have I heard a Tory Member of Parliament submitted to such hostile questioning from a Conservative audience.

'How old are you, Captain Elliot?'

'Sixty-two, sir,' he replied.

'So when *are* you going to retire, then? Don't you think you've done enough?'

'Captain Elliot, do you believe in upholding the rule of law?'

'Most certainly.'

'So why are you conniving in breaking our rules here this evening?'

Then came the standard question to Mrs Elliot from the women's chairman, who as it happened came from Elliot's part of the new constituency. She duly put her question, whereupon Mrs Elliot, who was clearly on a pretty short fuse, turned on her: 'Mrs Pearce, I'm shocked that you could even ask that question. Surely you of all people know the support I've given to my husband and to our association!' Sylvester grinned at me. 'Own goal!' he muttered. As Elliot left the stage to a mixture of claps and boos I judged that he had done nothing to add to the 236 who had supported him on the first motion and might well have lost some; the way was open for either Sylvester or me to come through in a second ballot. He and I came from different wings of the party, and I suspected that, if only the personal factor of Elliot could be removed, most of the audience would be of my persuasion.

The first ballot gave Elliot 208, myself 132 and Sylvester 117, so Sylvester had to drop out; he took it stoically, knowing he had lost during his question session. The second ballot, between Elliot and myself, resulted in 229 votes for me, and 215 for him. My tally was just three votes short of the 232 who had voted against allowing Elliot's name to be added to the list at the beginning. My twenty-three-year marriage to the safe Tory seat of Reigate had begun.

Elliot took defeat well, and appealed to his supporters to unite behind their new candidate: 'You have the chance to start afresh.' He was a dignified man, and through our talks over coffee at the Commons in the following months I became convinced he was secretly glad to be relieved of the task of winning over 'that troublesome lot' in Reigate and Redhill. Two days after my selection I received a letter from Neil Wilson, who had organised the coaches to bring in Elliot's supporters. He expressed his personal loyalty to Elliot, but acknowledged he had been beaten in a fair ballot, and pledged me his full support. He was as good as his word; that was how the Tory Party worked in those days.

The combination of being a political correspondent while also prospective Tory candidate in a less-than-marginal seat had proved manageable; it became a joking matter with my Labour MP friends, who accepted that I did my best to avoid political bias in my reporting of their activities. I was soon to discover that being the candidate for a safe Tory seat was very different. My weekly 'Commons Confidential' column was popular among the TRN titles, and early in February 1973 my first item was a devastating assessment of the ineffectiveness of Maurice Macmillan, Heath's Employment Secretary. In truth, the young Macmillan had been dealt a bad hand in politics; his father, when Prime Minister, had denied him promotion for fear of being charged with nepotism, and now Heath had saddled him with the impossible task of making sense of the convoluted Industrial Relations Act as well as steering through standing committee the totally un-Conservative Counter-Inflation [better described as Prices and Incomes] Bill. John Biffen, a strong Tory critic of the bill, was on the committee, and at its next session circulated photocopies of my article, to sniggers all round.

The following week I arrived in the Press Gallery just before lunch to find an early day motion on the order paper under the name of Neil Kinnock, then a cheeky backbencher. It read: 'That this House congratulates Mr George Gardiner, the Conservative prospective candidate for Reigate, for his perspicacious article in the *South Wales Echo* of 6 February headed 'Son of Supermac – The Flop of the Freeze', in which he describes the Secretary of State for Employment as 'hapless', 'disastrous', 'limping through his Civil Service brief', 'totally unsure of his material' and HM Government's 'Achilles heel'; and, while noting the implied criticism of the Prime Minister's capacity for choosing ministers, eagerly anticipates further and similar examinations of his future honourable and right honourable friends in the Conservative Party.' It was a deft swipe by Kinnock, whom I often met downing beer in the Strangers' Bar, but it made it impossible for me to continue writing a political column. 'Commons Confidential' had to be killed off immediately.

Some time before, during 1972, I had been contracted by Conservative Central Office on a freelance basis to edit and revamp a somewhat turgid party publication called *Monthly News*. The first priority was to change its name; it was already jokingly referred to by CCO staff as the *Menstruation Herald*. It swiftly became *Conservative News*, professionally laid out as a tabloid by an agency in Fleet Street, and sold in bulk at subsidised rates to Conservative associations, with a far greater circulation than Transport House's *Labour Weekly*. I was given my own office in Smith Square and a shared secretary, where I worked about ten mornings each month before taking up my TRN duties at the Commons. I thus came to know many of the CCO apparatchiks well, and developed good relations with the party's deputy chairman, Jim Prior; my differences with him did not begin until after I had been elected an MP.

The publication was obviously heavily propagandist, though I endeavoured to give it a panache that at least made it readable, occasionally attracting notice in the national press. We boasted of the high (and of course unsustainable) growth rate of Chancellor Tony Barber's boom, we justified Heath's U-turn from the principles upon which he had won the election to a shameless adoption of collectivist policies, we trumpeted the 'fairness' of stages 1, 2 and 3 of his policy for controlling prices and pay. I soon realised there were grave flaws in all these policies, but I was paid to make the best case for them and that is what I did, much as a lawyer will protest the innocence of his client, knowing full well he will go down in the end. And by the end of 1973 the Tory Government was certainly going down, lost in a wilderness of collectivist policies far outside its own traditions, including a prices and incomes policy which predictably could not cope with rapidly changing conditions, such as the hike in international oil prices as a result of the Arab–Israeli War and the high pay rise demanded by the National Union of Mineworkers (NUM), upon whose product we were increasingly dependent.

In the third week in January I went back to Central Office to prepare the next issue. By that time we were into the sixth week of a three-day working week, thanks to a ban on overtime working by the miners, though the full effect of this had been slightly masked by the Christmas holiday. But the new austerity was biting hard: rationing of power supplies, much higher petrol prices, and no TV after 10.30 p.m. There were growing calls for a general election to show just who ran the country – the Government, or the NUM. Everyone in Central Office was in a state of high excitement; no need to prepare a February edition of *Conservative News*, I was told, they were geared up to fight an election on 7 February. And so they were; that evening, their preparations complete, the senior officers and directors gathered together over a bottle of whisky to wait for the message from 10 Downing Street to start firing on all cylinders. The message duly came – but it was to stand them down. Heath had flinched at the last minute and decided to make a final effort to do a deal with the NUM. Party officers to whom I talked afterwards were bitterly critical that such an opportunity had been missed.

Heath and the Tory Party were to regret that decision. In the end, the election was called on 28 February, but by then the issue of who governed Britain had been running too long to be sustained through a further three weeks' campaigning. I had a good campaign machine running in Reigate, but most of my workers regretted that the Prime Minister had not gone to the country three weeks earlier. Had Heath chosen the earlier date he might just have won – though what he would have done with victory, not even he knew.

CHAPTER FIVE

The Joseph Years

'Incomes policy alone as a way to abate inflation caused by excessive money supply is like trying to stop water coming out of a leaky hose without turning off the tap ...We knew all the arguments [against it]. We had used them in Opposition in 1966–70. Why then did we try incomes policy again? I suppose that we desperately wanted to believe in it because we were so apprehensive about the alternative: sound money policies.'

Sir Keith Joseph, speech at Preston (1974)

'[Keith Joseph] was so impressive because his intellectual self-confidence was the fruit of continuous self-questioning ... one after another [in his Preston speech] he led the sacred cows to the slaughter.'

Margaret Thatcher, *The Path to Power* (1995)

FEBRUARY 3, 1975. Margaret Thatcher's campaign committee was meeting in a subterranean committee room at the Commons. As always the mood was good-humoured, even jocular, but this time there was a nervous edge to the laughter, for this was our final meeting before the fateful first ballot to decide the Tory leadership, due to take place the next day. Under the direction of Airey Neave, the senior back-bencher most known to the outside world as a war hero who escaped from Colditz, we had all been canvassing our colleagues on how they would vote – for Thatcher, for the present leader, Ted Heath, or for the maverick outsider, Hugh Fraser? Every Tory MP available had been canvassed from at least two different directions. Throughout the two-week campaign the results had been recorded by Neave's deputy, Bill Shelton, working from a desk in the Members' Library. At this meeting we reported our latest findings. Shelton scribbled, then passed his notes to Neave. We all knew the figures were encouraging, but the final tally was not revealed to us, and the faces of both men were inscrutable. Then Neave spoke.

'Tomorrow's vote looks like it will be very close,' he told us. 'Maggie's certainly there with a real chance, but any show of jubilation by any of us would be unwarranted – and counter-productive.' Under the new leadership ballot rules, whoever won had to secure 50 per cent of the vote plus a further 15 per cent to avoid a second ballot – and all Neave would say was that Heath was unlikely to get that. Neave and Shelton then left to report the final results of the canvass to Margaret and her closest adviser, Sir Keith Joseph.

I cannot remember all who were at that meeting. There were back-bench worthies like Julian Ridsdale, Michael Alison, John Stokes, Angus Maude, Jill Knight and Jack Page; more junior hard-hitters like Norman Tebbit; some from my own 1974 intake like Dr Rhodes Boyson, Peter Morrison, Michael Morris and John Corrie; and the unforgettable rogue barrister Billy Rees-Davies, severely war-wounded with one shoulder higher than the other and without one arm, who when he moved appeared to have been bolted together by some mad scientist. After the meeting was over he shambled to a phone booth to place another, even heavier, heavy bet with his bookie on Thatcher becoming the next leader of the Conservative Party. An example of insider dealing?

How did I come to be there? Even after the election in February 1974 I was still a Heath supporter, accepting the inevitability of the need for the Government to control pay and prices and the consequent electoral defeat at the hands of the National Union of Mineworkers. It was not until after I had 'fallen from grace' from the Press Gallery to the floor of the House that I realised the number of critics I had on my own benches who resented what I had written about them at various times. My efforts to press Prime Minister Harold Wilson on the 'slag heaps scandal' did not find universal favour with my new colleagues. The press had discovered that Marcia Williams' brother had been speculating in derelict slag heaps, in which he appeared to have received active support from Wilson's private office. The only element of 'scandal' was that this conflicted with all Wilson had said in attacking property speculators, and in my view showed up Labour hypocrisy. My efforts were helped by the investigative journalist Chapman ('Harry') Pincher, until his employers, the *Daily Express*, tired of the story. Wilson, predictably, told a press gallery lunch that the press lobby was 'a cleaner place' following my departure from it.

That short Parliament, from February to October 1974, was for me

the most miserable I have ever known – far worse than the decline and
fall of 1992–97. It was not simply that we were in Opposition; after all,
I had no experience of being anywhere else. No, it was the fact that we
were utterly leaderless. After the February defeat Heath had tried to
cling to power by offering a coalition to the Liberals, who rejected it.
Yet he decreed that the eleven Ulster Unionists, who before the election had been a constituent part of the Conservative and Unionist
Party, could not be regarded as such any more, and spurned their offers
to support him in a minority government. Had he accepted their offer
he could have remained Prime Minister, but so deep was his hatred of
Ulster Unionism that he spurned it. However, the Ulster Unionist offer
was concealed from the 1922 Committee, and it was left to Wilson to
form a minority government instead.

After defeat Heath went into a sulk. He took little interest even in
meeting his new backbenchers. He was never comfortable in the smoking room, but worse still he gave no steer to his shadow cabinet or to
the rest of us on the line of attack we should be taking. He was interested only in defending his previous policy position. I took my seat
below the gangway, frequently finding myself next to Jeffrey Archer,
then MP for Louth, and almost the only encouragement I got to join in
proceedings came from him. I remember Archer intervening in Heath's
occasional speeches from the front bench in order to give him good
leads, yet rarely did Heath seize the chance offered to him. He came to
take the view that the only government which would stand a chance of
success would be a coalition of 'moderate men and women' from all
parties, and by the October election this had become a fixation. After
virtually no consultation with his shadow cabinet colleagues he made
the need for a 'Government of National Unity' central to his platform,
on the amazing assumption that leading figures in other parties would
agree to serve under him. His plea went down like a lead balloon with
most Tory MPs and party workers in the country, who could see little
point in working to elect a Conservative Government if they could not
guarantee Conservative policies. Providentially, the country avoided
the coalition trap by returning Labour, this time with a majority of
around twenty.

However, Heath remained convinced that his old policies would be
proved right before long. A friendly whip gave me a graphic account of
Heath's reflections late into the night with his whips in their office – the
only place in the Commons where he seemed completely comfortable
– when he lapsed into monologue. Apparently the predictions poured
out from his heart – how within months inflation would take off, the
pound would face a crisis that not even devaluation could solve, how

the Wilson Government would disintegrate and the likes of Roy Jenkins, Harold Lever, Shirley Williams and possibly Anthony Crosland would press for a coalition government 'of all the talents' to impose pay and price controls to get the country out of the mess. The unstated assumption was that he, Heath, would be there to lead the coalition. The whips listened sympathetically, and Heath went home to his bed feeling a great deal better.

But the important point, so far as many Tories were concerned, was that Heath did not believe that he had got anything wrong. There was no need to rethink Conservative policy; his policies, which had dragged us down, did not require any improvement. It was this refusal to learn lessons or contemplate new directions which led many on the Tory back benches to believe that there just had to be a change of leadership. I was invited to a party given by Alan Clark, a new backbencher like me, where countless of my new colleagues were complaining of the 'abysmal' election campaign that Heath had just fought. Also present was Airey Neave, gently sounding out opinions in a voice you had to strain to hear.

On top of this was the message coming from Keith Joseph. There is good reason for calling this chapter on our spell in opposition 'The Joseph Years', for it was his thinking that showed us all why the Heath recipe for controlling inflation was futile, and he who shaped the new economic policy which was successfully applied by Thatcher after 1979. It was Joseph who established the Centre for Policy Studies in March 1974 as an alternative research institute to the Conservative Research Department (then under Heath's control), its objective to rethink Tory policy from first principles, before Thatcher joined him as vice-chairman; and it was Joseph who in a succession of speeches – in Upminster where he highlighted the policy faults of previous Labour and Tory Governments, in Leith and above all in Preston in September – offered an alternative way forward. As Thatcher acknowledged in *The Path to Power*, his Preston speech was 'one of the few speeches which have fundamentally affected a political generation's way of thinking'. But that October, speaking in Edgbaston in uncharacteristically care-less language, he appeared to condone eugenic controls over young mothers in 'social classes four and five ... least fitted to bring children into the world' – and all hell broke loose around his head, to the delight of Heath's acolytes. Joseph was besieged by the press and labelled 'the mad monk'. Many of us had expected him to challenge Heath for the leadership, but that one speech put paid to his chances. He told Thatcher he could not do it, and straight away she decided that if he would not stand then she would have to. But without Joseph's earlier speeches, and the inspiration they gave to many thinking Tories, her successful challenge to Heath would never have been possible.

One evening, as we left the division lobby, I told her that although I was a fledgling MP I was willing to do all I could to help. She accepted my offer with enthusiasm; she knew that only a year before I had been a member of the press lobby, where she lacked friends, as well as having experience of Conservative Central Office through editing *Conservative News*. 'You can help me with my press work,' she said. 'I'll ask Airey to have a word with you.' And so I was drafted onto Neave's team. Heath, in a letter to *The Times* on 2 November, 1998, claimed that her team 'was led from Central Office by George Gardiner, and outside by Airey Neave'. The notion that a newly elected MP could lead any successful campaign is of course ludicrous, and the idea that I could somehow use Central Office for this purpose is even more far-fetched; many of the most influential men and women there were out-and-out Heathites, while Maurice Trowbridge, Heath's personal press officer on the Central Office payroll, was a first-generation spin doctor, carefully feeding to the press any story that might put Thatcher in a poor light. Most of CCO's apparatchiks probably shared the view of Tony Garner, later to become CCO's director of organisation; when, in the mid-1950s, he encountered her as guest speaker in a northern constituency, he wrote to a National Union friend describing this 'awful woman', adding that on no account should she be allowed near any short list of prospective candidates!

A few days after my encounter with her she was invited to speak at the Guinea Club, a luncheon club restricted to twenty-one senior lobby correspondents, each with one guest, often an editor of a national newspaper. The lunch was in a private room at St Stephen's Tavern in Bridge Street, opposite the House of Commons, and the club worked under lobby rules of non-attribution. I was invited by Jack Warden, an old friend who was political editor of the *Glasgow Herald*. Thatcher gave a short and lively speech, indicating her political beliefs and reason for challenging, but when it came to questions she positively sparkled. She used all her skill to condense a complicated economic argument into plain man's language in less than two minutes; as I wrote in my biography of her later that year, 'journalists present would dearly have loved to be able to explain the concept of negative fiscal drag to their readers in five hundred words as clearly as Margaret did to them that day'. Though most of the press thought she had no chance whatsoever of becoming leader, from that day on they took her a good deal more seriously.

There was a marked contrast in style between the two campaign teams (Fraser had no team worth speaking of). Most of Thatcher's time was taken up leading the Tory team on the finance bill committee, but when her team discovered colleagues who were doubtful over their support, she saw them in small groups in Robin Cook's room, where she answered their questions in the same concise style she had used to such good effect at the Guinea Club. Joseph took her to a private meeting of the 92 Group, where she won majority support, but as I was not yet a member I knew nothing of this. She met her full campaign committee only once before polling, when we were fired again by her enthusiasm.

Heath's campaign was run by Sir Tim Kitson and Kenneth Baker, with considerable help from Peter Walker, who had managed Heath's successful campaign in 1965. From the beginning they assured the press that Heath would win the contest outright, and I have no doubt their confidence sprang from their own optimistic and, in the event, extremely unreliable canvass figures. There was also an assumption, shared by many in the press, that Heath represented 'the modern wing' of the party and so would have the support of the fifty plus new Members elected to safe Tory seats in the two elections of 1974. This I knew to be wrong. Those his team identified as 'don't knows' were invited to lunch or dinner at the London homes of his supporters, like Anthony Berry (later killed in the IRA bombing of Brighton's Grand Hotel) and Nicholas Scott (the only new-generation MP promoted by Heath to ministerial office). In my biography of Thatcher I recorded a telling account of such an occasion I heard from another Member of the February 1974 intake:

> I met my leader for the first time over lunch yesterday. He seemed slightly uncomfortable, and spoke for twenty minutes justifying the way he handled the miners' strike a year ago. He seemed convinced he had been totally right, both then and in October. Any doubts I'd had about whether to support him were certainly dispelled. I came away determined to vote for Margaret.

I did not identify that backbencher, but I can now. He was John Corrie, MP for North Ayrshire and a past president of the Scottish Young Conservatives.

In this campaign there were no 'manifesto' documents as such, but obviously both contenders wanted the press, and through them Tory activists, but above all the MP-voters themselves, to be fully aware of the platforms on which they were standing. On 30 January Thatcher published an article on 'My kind of Tory Party' in the *Daily Telegraph*, which I believe she drafted herself. 'To deny that we failed the people is futile, as well as arrogant,' she wrote. 'Successful governments win elections. So do parties with broadly acceptable policies. We lost.' She then spelt out the middle-class values she was committed to promote.

The weekend before the ballot was obviously crucial, and at this point her 'manifesto', circulated to all the newspapers, fell into two parts. The first was set out in a speech to her own association officers in Finchley on Friday 31 January, in which she explained why it was necessary for the party to change its leadership. I suspect that Angus Maude, a very experienced journalist, provided the first draft of this, and it was featured prominently in all Saturday's papers. But I drafted the second part of this manifesto, a letter to her association chairman portraying the different style of leadership that she was offering. The Tories, she wrote, must provide for the people 'leadership that listens. Perhaps our greatest fault in office was that we did not listen enough to what our supporters and sympathisers were saying. We allowed ourselves to become detached from the many who had given us their support and trust ... Ours is a national party, and it must be an *open* party ... To listen and to lead – that is our role.' This was also well featured in Sunday's papers.

'To listen and to lead' – what an irony that this passage could be lifted word for word and used again as an indictment of the kind of 'leadership' John Major provided for the party from 1992 until 1997!

Finally there was a short press statement, which I also drafted, released on Sunday, showing how unity in the party could be restored, and then short letters with different wording drafted by Neave were sent to appear in *The Times* and the *Daily Telegraph* before MPs cast their votes, as a final appeal. Both letters concluded: 'A majority of Conservative MPs know in their hearts that we cannot go on as we are.' But the old fogeys of the National Union, predictably, came down in support of Heath.

Right up until the morning of the vote the Heath camp were boasting to the press that their candidate would win outright – that is to say, secure more than a forty-two-vote lead. They were emboldened by their excessively optimistic canvass figures. But when the press approached Neave, he was far more cautious; that the result would be close was all he would say. The political correspondents drew their own conclusions. 'Ted Forges Ahead' proclaimed the *Evening Standard* – exactly what Neave had hoped it would say. He knew a small number of backbenchers were intending to abstain on the first ballot, in the hope of opening up a second when they would be able to vote for a different candidate; when they read the *Standard's* headline they would realise that if Heath got his forty-two-vote lead, their purpose would be frustrated. Their only means of bringing his reported bandwagon to a halt was to vote for Thatcher – which they did. Neave's cunning had paid off.

The result declared on Tuesday 4 February was:

Margaret Thatcher	130
Edward Heath	119
Hugh Fraser	16

There was a gasp of astonishment when the 1922 chairman, Edward du Cann, read out the result, then cheering. It was not an outright win for Thatcher, but the figures meant that more than half the party had voted against Heath. He was done for, and announced his resignation soon after. When Kitson reported the disastrous figures to him, his sole reported comment was: 'So we got it all wrong.'

The second leg of the campaign to the second ballot, where a 50 per cent majority would suffice, was a far more congenial affair. There was no rancour between the contestants – Thatcher, William Whitelaw, Geoffrey Howe, James Prior and John Peyton. When Thatcher and Whitelaw spoke from the same platform at a Young Conservatives conference three days before polling, they were pictured outside embracing and Whitelaw planted a kiss on her cheek. When her campaign committee met in buoyant mood the evening after her first victory, the numbers were swollen by several who had been reluctant Heath supporters. There was cheers for Norman St John-Stevas, who as a member of the shadow cabinet had felt obliged to stay loyal to Heath, and for Keith Joseph, who had always left Neave to run these meetings. A completely new canvass was ordered. Neave and Shelton knew that some forty voting for Thatcher in the first ballot had done so to keep the door open for a different candidate – usually Whitelaw – in the second. Heath's old team were also urging his voters to support Whitelaw, but it was among those former Heath voters that Margaret had to look to offset any losses. Yet she had a head start on the new challengers, and many MPs wanted to see the issue settled conclusively in the second ballot six days later. On Tuesday 11 February she romped home:

Margaret Thatcher	146
William Whitelaw	79
Geoffrey Howe	19
James Prior	19
John Peyton	11

It is worth recording how accurate Shelton's final canvass figures were: Thatcher 137 with a further nine marked down as 'doubtful-plus'; Whitelaw 78; Howe 19; Prior 11; Peyton 9; doubtful or uncanvassed

13. No canvassing team could ever get closer to the final result than that.

Julian Critchley, an obvious Heathite, called it 'The Peasants' Revolt;' I called it, I think more accurately, 'The Back-bench Revolution'. The like of this had never been seen before. Under the old 'magic circle' system of consultations, it was the party grandees who decided on the new leader. When, in 1955, Anthony Eden followed Winston Churchill, it was a natural Establishment succession. When Eden had to go following the Suez debacle, it was the party's elder statesmen, Churchill and Lord Salisbury, who advised the Queen to send for Harold Macmillan. When Macmillan stood down, the test that would decide if Lord Home could succeed was whether he could form a Cabinet from the existing one, and whether Rab Butler would agree to serve in it. Of course there were consultations, over drinks and by phone, with Tory backbenchers, but it was at the top of the party that the final decisions were made. Even when a formal balloting process was introduced in 1965 (through which Heath was elected), it was not comparable with the style of the leadership election ten years later; rather it marked a stage in the transition to it. 1975 saw the first manifestos issued by the candidates, and the first meetings with doubters to try to win them over. The result was an undoubted defeat for the party Establishment.

This could never have happened with the 'magic circle'. If the National Union, sycophants to a man and woman, had been given much influence it would not have happened in 1975 either; Heath would have been saved, and if he had then decided to stand down, the mantle would have passed to Whitelaw. Nor could it have happened under the leadership voting system introduced by William Hague in 1998. But in 1975 it was the backbenchers, with their closer knowledge of the issues at stake, who seized control – and it was the backbenchers who got it right. Few of us then understood the full implications of what we had set in motion, but for more than twenty years the party and country were the beneficiaries.

The experience of being on the Thatcher campaign committee almost from the beginning taught me a great deal, and I learned much through watching Neave and Shelton at work. Remember that at the time I was a pretty raw backbencher of just one year's standing, even though thirteen years in the press lobby had given me a nose for politics. Now I saw how it was possible for Tory backbenchers to impose their will on the party's Establishment. But most of all, I learned that for this to happen required thorough and determined organisation by highly motivated individuals. These were lessons that I applied for the rest of my parliamentary life.

The selection of the first woman to lead a British political party in history, especially a woman who had found the temerity to take on the Tory Establishment and win, immediately captured the public's imagination, and Margaret Thatcher's popularity soared. It was not to last, of course, as Chancellor Denis Healey eased open the public purse strings to indulge countless sectional interests, yet already it seemed she had earned her place in history. Even before she had settled into her new role I was approached by the publisher William Kimber to write her biography. I liked the idea, but would undertake it only with her active co-operation. When I put the idea to her, Thatcher was honestly amazed that anyone should want to publish her biography so soon, but agreed to help. Whether she would have done so had I not been a member of her campaign team I rather doubt. So I signed a contract with William Kimber, and arranged to see Thatcher every Saturday in her Chelsea home to ask my questions and record her replies on my tape recorder. At first she was suspicious of the machine, but soon became at ease with my way of working. I was the first to learn all the fascinating details of her Methodist upbringing, which later formed such a vivid part of her memoirs *The Path to Power*.

Before I completed the interviews I began writing the initial chapters at my home in Dorking, where we moved soon after I became prospective Conservative candidate. It was five miles outside the Reigate constituency; after the rancour shown between the two area factions at my adoption meeting I judged it wiser to live a short distance away from either of them. But at the start of 1974's Easter recess, disaster struck; I began suffering severe cramps and perspiration, and when in the passage of one hour I asked my wife seven times which day of the week it was, she sent for the doctor. Straight away I was admitted to Dorking General Hospital – I was suffering from sub-acute bacterial endocarditis: a malfunctioning heart valve was allowing poison to build up before it coursed through my blood. The cure was heavy injections of penicillin over three to four weeks. As I began to feel better, I had a telephone installed at my bedside so that I could continue my book inquiries, leaving the final interviews to my former colleague Gordon Leak to complete. With my portable typewriter and tape recorder installed on my bed table I continued the work. This was essential because there was now a race on between two publishers to bring out the first biography of this new political phenomenon – William Kimber with mine, and Routledge & Kegan Paul with a book by my old friend Russell Lewis, a former director of the Conservative Political Centre.

Lewis's biography was drawn from press cuttings and his own experience, but I had the advantage of taped interviews with the subject herself. Eventually, long after I had left hospital, the two were published on the same day – my *Margaret Thatcher: From Childhood to Leadership*, and Lewis's *Margaret Thatcher: A Personal and Political Biography*. The fact that the two appeared together was an open invitation to leader-page articles throughout the press.

Thatcher had the opportunity to prove her mettle twice a week in Prime Minister's Questions, pitting her wits against her opposite number for fifteen minutes each Tuesday and Thursday. Wilson was a very wily character at the dispatch box, and his mastery of the House was then at its peak. Thatcher respected this, yet when the event was broadcast she saw this as a opportunity to extend her appeal to a much wider audience. To make sure she was properly briefed beforehand, she assembled a small team of 'ideas men' in her office over sandwiches to help her work out her first question and possible follow-ups, and I was invited to join this team. Her two PPSs were generally there, plus a man from the political department at the Research Department, Norman Tebbit, Geoffrey Pattie and myself. Occasionally a member of the shadow cabinet – perhaps Nigel Lawson or Nicholas Ridley – was invited to give specific advice, but our role was essentially that of tacticians helping her to target Wilson's weak spots. Tebbit was in his element here, and he generally contributed as much as the rest of us put together. Later we did our best to get called upon to put our own supplementary questions to the Prime Minister, to back Thatcher up. When, in April 1976, James Callaghan succeeded Wilson we had to rethink our tactics; Callaghan was not as nimble as Wilson, but I always thought his straightforward manner gave him an authority which the shifty Wilson rarely achieved.

My membership of this briefing team had the added advantage of giving me great insight into Thatcher's thinking as it developed; as editor of Central Office's *Conservative News* I was able to communicate her ideas directly to our grassroots workers in the constituencies. The Thatcherite message I conveyed was thus clear and unambiguous, and was occasionally noted in the national press.

Madam Mao, or Jiang Qing, the wife of Chairman Mao Zedong, has a notorious place in history for furthering China's cruel Cultural Revolution of 1965–69; she was also responsible for introducing 'The Gang of Four' into political terminology. After Mao's death in 1976, she and three other Chinese leaders attempted to regain their power by organising coups in Shanghai and Beijing; they failed, and in 1980 she was tried and found guilty of subversion. As a result 'The Gang of

Four' acquired a sinister meaning – so you can imagine my surprise when I read on the front page of *Labour Weekly*, early in 1978, that I was one of a new 'Gang of Four' that was 'dragging to Tory Party to the right'. It was a brilliant propaganda invention by Julia Langdon, then *Labour Weekly's* political correspondent. According to her front-page splash, the 'Gang of Four' was made up first of Thatcher, the British equivalent of Madame Mao, and the remaining three were Neave, Tebbit and myself. Langdon's justification for this theory relied on three recent news events: Neave was there because he had just said that power-sharing in Ulster was dead (not such an outlandish statement as it might appear now; see Chapter Six); I was included because, as editor of the most recent *Conservative News*, I had splashed on Thatcher's remarks in a *World in Action* interview about the need to reassure our citizens that they were not being 'swamped' by immigrants (hardly an extreme right-wing statement), while Tebbit was included simply for being his usual 'semi-house-trained polecat' self in the Commons.

Langdon's joke – for it could hardly be taken seriously – was at least enjoyed by Neave, Tebbit and myself. Neave, as he passed me in the Commons corridors, would mutter in his quiet voice 'Good morning, four', while I would reply 'Good morning, two.' But like most inspired propaganda the British 'Gang of Four' soon passed into general usage, and the term was also adopted by the press to describe the regular pre-Questions briefing in Thatcher's office, which was most inaccurate; Neave was never part of that group, which in any event numbered more than four. The next 'Gang of Four' to be identified was in 1980, when four former Labour cabinet ministers – Roy Jenkins, Shirley Williams, David Owen and William Rodgers – were preparing to break away to form the Social Democratic Party. Since Madam Mao, the name has at least become respectable.

Once the party leadership had been placed in Thatcher's sure and inspirational hands, the next back-bench challenge, not long in coming, was in the shape of devolution legislation. One can understand why, in the 1974 Tory manifestos, Harold Wilson made the pledge to establish a Scottish assembly or Parliament in Edinburgh; he was under great pressure from his party in Scotland, who saw it as a means to undercut the Scottish Nationalists. Why he thought the same formula could be applied to Wales remains a mystery, though doubtless the influence of Jim Callaghan had much to do with it. However, his Cabinet's decision in 1975 to bulldoze such radical constitutional changes through the

Commons on a tiny majority of three verged on political insanity. For the rest of Wilson's term and the whole of Jim Callaghan's, devolution was the Government's exposed flank which, in the end, brought about its downfall.

It was at the Scottish Tory conference at Perth in 1968 that an astounded audience learned that Ted Heath had bounced the party into a commitment to establish a Scottish assembly. The vibrant Winnie Ewing had won a by-election at Hamilton for the Scottish National Party in spectacular fashion in 1967, and Heath saw his pledge as a means of cutting off the SNP's appeal at its roots. He had consulted no-one beyond a tight clique of Scottish left-wing Tories – not the 1922 Committee, and certainly not the still substantial number of Scottish MPs at Westminster. The following year Wilson kicked the issue into touch by appointing a Royal Commission under Lord Crowther, succeeded later by Lord Kilbrandon, which did not report till October 1973. Heath then insisted on putting an Edinburgh assembly, together with a Scottish Development Fund financed by North Sea oil, at the heart of his Scottish manifesto in October 1974. It did the Scottish Tories little good in the election, and in 1975 Heath's promise still hung like a dead albatross round the Tory Party's neck.

I knew all the arguments over Scottish independence, and over devolution as a halfway house towards independence, from my days serving the *Aberdeen Press and Journal*. Its editor was a canny Scot, suspicious of anyone from the central belt of Scotland, conservative with a small 'c' and emotionally opposed to Scottish nationalism. 'Once you allow a separate assembly in Edinburgh you'll have Scottish independence before you know where you are,' he once told me, and neither could I see what future there would be for Scottish MPs at Westminster once an Edinburgh assembly took over most of their functions. I was deeply opposed to devolution long before I became a southern English MP, and the Wilson Government's plans posed a challenge I could not resist. Whatever Heath's past commitment, devolution must be resisted to the end.

The Opposition's dilemma was revealed in the debate on the Government's White Paper in January 1976. Sir David Renton, from our front bench, moved an amendment which 'affirms the need for an assembly in Scotland, but rejects the Government's particular proposals for Scotland and Wales which will lead to confusion and conflict, and which will threaten the unity if the United Kingdom'. The two halves of the amendment were of course totally contradictory. Strong speeches attacking the principle of devolution were made by Enoch Powell (by that time returned to the Commons as Ulster Unionist

Member for Down South), Maurice Macmillan, Julian Amery and Betty Harvie-Anderson, formerly a Deputy Speaker and as tough a Scot as they come. I voted for our meaningless amendment with a heavy heart, but Macmillan, Amery and Iain Sproat (recently elected for North Aberdeen) abstained.

By this time it was quite obvious that, with Heath's albatross round its neck, our front bench were going to keep as low a profile as they could in attacking the Scotland and Wales Bill, so a group of Tory back-benchers came together to take the initiative. The group had three joint presidents: Macmillan, Amery and Harvie-Anderson, all Privy Councillors. Three secretaries were appointed: Iain Sproat (Scotland), Ian Grist (Wales) and myself (England). I was given the task of arranging meetings to co-ordinate tactics, and so effectively became the organising secretary. Our meetings were generally chaired by Macmillan. I grew to have a deep affection for Maurice; his political brain was as sharp as any, leaving me to wonder how he had come to perform so badly as Heath's Employment Secretary. I deeply regretted having savaged him with such reckless abandon in my old 'Commons Confidential' column, but he was a kind man and never reminded me of it.

It was at our second meeting that Michael Clark Hutchison, a wise old owl from Edinburgh South, brought with him a small Union Jack on a stand – the kind that are often placed with others on tables at international conferences. 'This is just to remind us what we're about,' he said, as he placed it on the desk in front of Macmillan. From then on I brought it to every meeting, and my circulars advertising group meetings took the form: 'The Union Flag will fly again in committee room 10, Tuesday, 6.00 p.m. Please make every effort to attend.' So we came to be called the 'Union Flag Group'. Up to forty back-bench Tories attended our regular weekly meetings throughout the time that the devolution bills were before the House.

The Union Flag was not a secretive group. The opposition whip shadowing the bill was John Stradling Thomas, who sat for Monmouth, and he came to our meetings regularly to give advice and serve as a conduit between us and the shadow cabinet. Teddy Taylor (then sitting for Glasgow Cathcart) was shadow Scottish secretary, and did all he could to encourage us.

Since the bill was a constitutional measure, its committee stage had to be taken on the floor of the House, so the best chance for impeding it was to organise a filibuster in the hope that, over long days and nights, time would run out for further discussion. Filibustering is of course contrary to the Rules of Order, yet it can never be strictly defined; providing a back-bench speech can be shown to be even vaguely relevant to the matter under discussion, the only limit to its length is the stamina of the speaker. True, when two or three hours has been spent discussing just one amendment or group of amendments it is possible for the Government to move a 'closure motion', but even if the Deputy Speaker (always a Deputy during committee-stage discussion) accepts the motion, it can still be tested in a division, which spins the proceedings out for a further fifteen minutes. It was my task to organise this filibuster from the Tory benches.

Straight away I sought advice from Marcus Kimball, farmer, landowner and a veteran organiser of filibusters against any measures seeking to curtail hunting or field sports, affecting Lloyd's underwriters or much else. He was totally sympathetic to our cause, though declined to take part himself. However, he gave very sound advice. 'A successful filibuster,' he told me, 'depends on having an active "floor manager". If you're the floor manager it's your job to organise the speeches – not to speak yourself. You must be party to the strategic design, you must ensure plenty of amendments to swallow up time, providing briefing notes if necessary, and you must be constantly available whatever the time of night.' Later, Neil Marten, the old anti-Common Market campaigner whom Heath had tried unsuccessfully to get deselected, told me much the same. I heeded that advice – and never looked back.

The first task was to establish a small amendment-drafting committee. The principal members I chose were Peter Rees, a brilliant tax lawyer who later became Chief Secretary at the Treasury, and former minister Graham Page, a solicitor who had sat on more standing committees on bills than he cared to remember. Whether our amendments were of the nit-picking variety or raised substantial points of principle, these Members knew the correct legislative language in which they should be phrased. Also on the committee was Joe Egerton, Macmillan's research assistant, and later Adam Fergusson, representing the pressure group Scotland is British. Often we devised amendments that were totally contradictory in their effects. It hardly mattered, so long as discussing them took up more time; I just had to be careful to list separate names as the proposers of the contradictory amendments. It most cases the final name on the list of proposers was my own, purely to identify it as a Union Flag amendment on the Order Paper. As expected, the shadow cabinet were sparing in the amendments they tabled. Once we knew which amendments the Speaker had accepted for debate, and how they were grouped, I rang round to ensure that we were never short of speakers. Timothy Raison, Eldon

Griffiths, Ian Gow and Ian Percival stepped in regularly. Egerton often provided briefing notes to which our filibusterers could turn if they felt themselves flagging.

There were many committed opponents of devolution on the Labour benches too. Standing out above them all was Tam Dalyell, an independent-thinking Member first elected for West Lothian in 1962, who was quickly to become a 'House of Commons man' to his finger-tips. It was he who formulated the basic dilemma posed by devolution outside a fully federal system which came to be known as the 'West Lothian Question': with responsibilities for schools, health, transport and the environment transferred from Westminster to a Scottish assembly, Scottish MPs would have no voice in legislating on the matters that deeply affected their constituents; similarly, English MPs, robbed of power to share in legislating north of the border, would still find Scottish MPs still legislating on matters affecting their constituencies in England. Dalyell was able to personalise the argument to telling effect; once a Scottish assembly came into being, he told the House on 19 January:

> I can vote on policy and money to the Arts in Alnwick, but not in Armadale, West Lothian; I can vote on aerodromes at Heathrow and Gatwick but not at Edinburgh Turnhouse; I can vote on buildings in Bath but not in Bathgate in my constituency; I can vote on burial laws in Blackpool but not in Blackridge; I can vote on betting, bookies and gaming in Blackburn, Lancashire, but I cannot touch the bookies or the gaming laws in Blackburn, West Lothian; I can vote on building control in Bolton but not in Broxham, West Lothian; I can vote on bridges mainte-nance regulations in Bradford but not in Bo'ness; I can vote on land use in Leicester but not with regard to the new town – part of which I repre-sent – Livingstone; I can vote on the licensing laws in Liverpool but not in Linlithgow; I can vote on shop hours in Stratford-on-Avon but not in the village of Stoneyburn in West Lothian; I can vote on water supply in Wolverhampton, but not in Whitburn, West Lothian ...'

And so it went on, the endless yet fascinating stuff of good filibuster.

Dalyell was not alone on the Labour benches. George Cunningham, a Scot who sat for Islington South, was equally cogent, while many rep-resenting England's deprived regions were just as opposed – like Eric Heffer (Liverpool Walton), Ted Garrett (Wallsend) and Tom Urwin (Houghton-le-Spring). Welsh Labour MPs were bitterly divided; Leo Abse (Pontypool) could filibuster for an hour or more, taunting those Welsh Labour MPs who took the official line, goading them into mak-ing equally long speeches in reply. Neil Kinnock (Bedwellty) was also deeply critical. The BBC often invited Kinnock and me to be interviewed together on news programmes, expecting us to take different views; we often shared a taxi to and from the studio, and would speculate how much longer it would take BBC producers to realise there was nothing to separate us in our contempt for devolved assemblies.

Given that it was not long since Northern Ireland had its own subsidiary legislature at Stormont, one might have expected the Ulster Unionists to be tolerant towards devolution for Scotland and Wales, but not a bit. Enoch Powell was a formidable opponent of the Government's legislation; though he could not always guarantee the attendance of other Unionists, his speeches exposing the weaknesses of the proposed arrangement were, as always, a delight to hear.

Thus there came into being a most effective cross-party coalition of opponents of devolution – Labour dissidents, the Ulster Unionists and a majority of Tory backbenchers – and it was here that the real fun began for me as organising secretary for Union Flag. For as the bill proceeded tortuously through debate on the floor of the House, taking up to two days each week, I was in contact by phone each morning and sometimes over weekends with Tam Dalyell, George Cunningham, Enoch Powell and, less frequently, Eric Heffer and Leo Abse. We coordinated our strategy and our tactics supporting each others' amendments, to devastating effect.

The first victory was scored by Abse, who tabled an early day motion declaring that if the devolution bill were to be passed, its enactment should be subject to approval by separate referendums in Scotland and Wales; some 140 MPs signed it, Labour as well at Tory. Scenting the trouble that was clearly coming, Prime Minister Callaghan conceded the principle of referendums in December 1976 before his bill even received its second reading, thus minimising the likelihood of revolt within his own party's ranks. However, when the committee stage began on 19 January, the Government had still not yet tabled its promised amendment. In the course of the second reading debate, Leon Brittan, then Tory front-bench spokesman on devolution, confirmed that Heath's promise of an assembly in Edinburgh was still opposition policy, so strengthening the resolve of every member of the Union Flag Group.

The bulk of that first day's debate was taken up by a Union Flag amendment, moved by Harvie-Anderson, to exclude Shetland and the Orkneys from the proposed assembly. This had the support of the Shetland council, who could foresee an influx of money into the island from the promised North Sea oil terminal, and did not want Edinburgh politicians getting their sticky fingers involved. A small group of us had previously flown up to Shetland for talks with the council, and had spoken to a very full public meeting; they left us in no doubt that the Shetlanders were allies in our cause. Dalyell was with us; I remember him bursting in for breakfast the first morning dressed in tracksuit, purple-faced and gasping for breath following his early-morning jog. From the look of him I doubted whether he would survive even until the committee stage started! We lost the amendment by 189–170.

Later, the Government's amendments accepting confirmatory referendums were incorporated in the bill. As we neared the end of February, discussion was still lumbering on, taking up time and revealing deepening concern among backbenchers of all parties. Hordes of amendments were still on the Order Paper, awaiting discussion; our filibuster was succeeding beyond our wildest dreams. At this point the Callaghan Government ran out of patience, and tabled a guillotine motion to fix a limit to the time spent discussing the bill. At last our front bench came into action; any Opposition *had* to oppose a guillotine. Meanwhile the Labour rebels had to consolidate, and the Union Flag promised to do nothing to make their task more difficult. The debate was tense; Macmillan, Amery, Sproat, Raison, Powell, Dalyell and Abse made devastating speeches, and for once I ignored Kimball's advice and made a speech myself. I told ministers that 'by curbing debate they will increase the dangers implicit in the bill. They will increase the resentments which have been aroused by their proposals. By imposing a guillotine they will turn a bill which began as a deformed creature into a monster.'

When the division was put, the guillotine motion was lost by 312–283. Altogether, twenty-two Labour MPs voted against their Government, and a further twenty, including Kinnock, abstained. It was a textbook example of MPs asserting the interests of their country above the demands of party loyalty – and had no equal until the great Tory rebellion over the Maastricht Treaty in 1993. The immediate consequence was that the Opposition tabled a motion of censure on the Government, leading Callaghan to forge the 'Lib–Lab Pact' with David Steel to survive.

Yet still it seemed the Cabinet had not learned its lesson, for in November 1977 devolution was back on the agenda, this time in two separate bills, one for Scotland and the other for Wales. Provisions for referenda, agreed in the previous bill, were incorporated in both of these. As before, there was a high degree of co-operation between Union Flag, Ulster Unionists and the Labour rebels as our amendments flooded on to the Order Paper. The second-reading debates also showed that a few Labour MPs had changed sides, most notably Robin Cook, newly elected Member for Edinburgh Central, who now spoke strongly *against* creating a devolved assembly in Edinburgh. The Government realised from the start that their key test was to get a guillotine motion passed this time, which they managed to do in November; many of the Labour rebels were won round by appeals to party loyalty as a general election drew nearer.

However, the most crucial amendment of all was still to come from George Cunningham; his proposed amendment to the Scotland Bill – that unless 40 per cent of the Scottish electorate voted Yes in their referendum, then the provisions of the bill could not take effect – was intended to ensure that such a radical change to the constitution would not result from a narrow Yes verdict on a very low turn-out. We were in close touch with Cunningham throughout the drafting of the amendment, and were convinced that with shadow-cabinet backing it would be passed. Yet Francis Pym, by now our shadow spokesman on devolution, refused to be budged, and this was the only occasion on which he and I exchanged cross words; he did not like the idea of referenda in any case, and saw placing conditions on them as indirectly compromising Parliament's eventual right to decide. Several shadow ministers joined us in the vote, though Pym himself abstained. However, we knew by this time that the Union Flag campaigners had won over the shadow cabinet; never again would there by a Tory commitment to create a Scottish assembly.

Cunningham's speech from the back benches was one of the few in my Commons experience which actually influenced the outcome of the vote – undeniably brilliant and persuasive. John Smith, the Minister of State handling the bill, despite all his charm and lawyer's footwork, was unable to fault Cunningham's logic. After three hours of keen debate, in which I again joined, the amendment was carried against the Government by 166–151. From that moment the Edinburgh assembly was doomed. When the referenda finally took place, early in 1979, supporters of devolution in Scotland were marginally ahead, but totalled well short of the 40 per cent of the electorate required, while in Wales, devolution was rejected decisively. The Lib–Lab Pact had long come to an end, and with the death of devolution there was no remaining reason for the small band of Scottish and Welsh Nationalists to support the Government. On 28 March, 1979, Callaghan was defeated on a motion of confidence by one vote. Through its obsession with devolution, his Government brought about its own downfall.

Though of course one never ceases to learn in politics, you could say that my experience as organising secretary of Union Flag completed the first round of my political education in Parliament. The successful campaign to elect Margaret Thatcher as leader had taught me how, with good organisation, the back benches could overthrow an entrenched Establishment. Now, the experience of fighting devolution bills over two parliamentary sessions taught me how – again, with good organisation, – the back benches could reshape official party policy. The fact that, in this case, I was working in alliance with independent-minded MPs in other parties was an added bonus – and a joy I will never forget.

British politics has been enriched by a number of dynastic families. The Churchills are obvious examples, as well as the Macmillans, Channons and Soameses, Tory fathers and sons. Labour has had the Foots and the Lord Stansgate/Benn succession, the Liberals the Lloyd George clan. Being brought up in a constant background of political discussion, national and international politicians regular visitors to their homes, the offspring take to political involvement like ducks to water. They have an ingrained *instinct* for politics. One such Tory family were the Amerys.

No-one could avoid being deeply impressed by Julian Amery's understanding of political events throughout the world and of their place in history. I first met him at Oxford, and can remember his recollections of service as a special agent in Yugoslavia during the war. By 1975 he had worked in the old Air, Colonial and Civil Aviation Ministries, as well as a stint as Minister of State at the Foreign Office. Foreign affairs were his passion; someone once said he brought 'an oriental mind' to his assessment of British interests and how they could best be served.

One evening in late October 1978, I was invited to his home in Eaton Square. I was shown to his library on the first floor, which ran the full depth of the building. This was a room where you felt British history bearing down upon you from the long shelves of political works. It had been used by his father, Leo Amery, the great Tory imperialist who was in turn First Lord of the Admiralty, Colonial Secretary and finally wartime Secretary of State for India and Burma. He was also famous for shouting Cromwell's words to Prime Minister Neville Chamberlain in 1940: 'In the name of God, go!' How many plots in Tory politics must have been hatched in this library. That evening we were there to hatch another.

When I arrived I found the quixotic Hugh Fraser, who had thrown his doomed hat into the ring in the first leadership ballot in 1975, was already there. He asked in his usual laid-back manner whether it was

any coincidence that all present were products of Balliol. The real factor drawing us together was our experience as comrades in arms
against the Government's devolution bills, and our purpose now was to
exchange thoughts on the coming annual vote to renew economic sanctions against Rhodesia. There were a small number on the Tory benches who had forced a vote against renewal every year, but now the situation was different. No longer was Rhodesia's rebel Government made
up purely of white settlers; in an internal settlement earlier that year,
Bishop Muzorewa had joined the Ian Smith Government, though the
majority Patriotic Front of Robert Mugabe and Joshua Nkomo were
still excluded. Many Tories thought the time was ripe to seek a settlement. Economic sanctions were having little effect on the Rhodesian
economy in any case, since oil was easily imported, and were seen as a
hindrance to achieving a political rapprochement.

The shadow cabinet was split on the issue. Peter Carrington, who
led the party in the Lords, felt strongly that scrapping sanctions at that
juncture would make it more difficult to persuade the Patriotic Front
to compromise, while shadow foreign secretary John Davies was less
sure. So the decision was that the front bench would abstain on the
vote, and that the party would be whipped to abstain too – a quite ludicrous arrangement. Humphrey Atkins, the Chief Whip, advised that
only around forty backbenchers would rebel against the whip and force
a vote to reject sanctions.

Amery, Fraser and I decided at our meeting in Amery's library that
we would work to push the rebel numbers a good deal higher. We would
canvass all our friends to spread support, and find out through them
which other backbenchers might be persuaded to join us. My job was
again to serve as an unofficial whip, counting the numbers and assuring any fainthearts that there was safety in numbers. We knew we could
never win this vote, but by boosting our numbers we could send a signal to Mugabe and Nkomo, and to our front bench should we come
into Government, that the days of economic sanctions were numbered.
I was back in the business of organising rebellion. There was no danger
of this harming Margaret Thatcher, since I knew she intended to scrap
sanctions anyway if she were to become Prime Minister.

The rebellion extended on to the front bench. Winston Churchill,
then junior defence spokesman, intended to vote against renewing
sanctions, as did John Biggs-Davison. He at least was warned that if he
persisted in taking this course, he would be required to resign as junior
spokesman on Northern Ireland, but he was adamant that principle
had to come first. Knowing this, and aware that Ian Gow, who was also
deeply interested in Northern Ireland, was intending to join the rebels

too, Humphrey Atkins called in Gow and dangled the bait of being appointed in Biggs-Davison's place if only he would obey the whip and abstain. Gow too responded with contempt.

On the day of the vote I reported to Amery that I expected more than a hundred to defy the whip. 'That'll show them,' he chuckled. In the event the rebel numbers reached 114. As the figures were read out to the Speaker, I was standing at the Bar of the House, then caught the eye of Atkins as he strode out to the Members' Lobby; his expression was black as thunder. Until quite late in the day he had assured the shadow cabinet that the rebels were unlikely to number more than forty; we had made him look ridiculous. I do not think he ever forgave Amery or me.

A footnote to this story came the next day when I and Geoffrey Pattie, who was also among the rebels, turned up for Thatcher's pre-Questions briefing session. We wondered how she would receive us, and decided that perhaps the less we said the better. But she was in buoyant mood. 'What's the matter with you two?' she teased us. 'Have you lost your tongues?' She cared not a jot that we had defied the whip the night before. If only her successor as leader had shown the same respect for the conscience of his supporters!

———————— ⌒∞⌒ ·————————

These were exciting years to be in Tory politics. When Keith Joseph first questioned the Heath policy of seeking to abate inflation through pay controls, with all the corporate mechanisms this futile effort involved, he set off a flurry of intellectual activity throughout the party. Research papers came not just from his own think-tank, the Centre for Policy Studies, but from the Institute for Economic Affairs, the Adam Smith Institute, the Bow Group of Conservative graduates, not forgetting the so-called 'Black Papers' on future directions in education. Press commentators such as Paul Johnson joined in the quest for 'radical solutions'. From 1975 onwards, papers were published by all these bodies and more, springing up like fresh mountain streams and feeding into rivers flowing to swell the intellectual tide which came to be called 'Thatcherism'. Policy groups were set up involving both back-bench MPs with particular knowledge and outside experts. Joseph was in charge of policy formation, steering what was often a sceptical shadow cabinet in the right direction, though few of their policy decisions were made public; grave dangers face opposition parties who reveal too many of their policies in advance. But one exception was an idea that sprang from Michael Heseltine: giving council tenants the right to buy their homes at a discount proved to be immensely popular.

Within a few months of my re-election in October 1974 I felt the need to return to my natural habitat – journalism. I had been writing occasional pieces for Thomson Regional Newspapers, my former employers, but I knew I needed a national outlet. The motives for this were two-fold. Upon my 'fall from grace' from the press gallery on to the floor of the House, I suffered a severe drop in income – indeed, I had been obliged to cash in my pensions policies to continue paying my mortgage, though in those days this was by no means unique. My wife had academic skills but no secretarial ones, so could not be paid from my MP's allowance to be my secretary, nor did she wish to be. But second, I knew that I wrote reasonably well and wanted an outlet through which to popularise, especially to likely Conservative voters, the merits of the new radical Conservatism. I approached John Junor, renowned editor of the *Sunday Express* – and thus began a valued relationship which lasted nearly twenty years.

Junor was the old-fashioned kind of editor who read in galley proof (remember those were still the days of hot-lead typesetting) every word that appeared in his paper. Though once a Liberal parliamentary candidate, he had an intuitive feeling for politics and for the prejudices of his readers; those were the prejudices of his paper, and the recipe for its success. The leader-page articles and others, like his own sharp 'Current Affairs' column and the 'Crossbencher' political diary, not to mention the leaders themselves, had to reinforce those prejudices. It was not unusual at that time for voters of Conservative persuasion to take the *Daily Telegraph* for six days of the week and the *Sunday Express* on the seventh, so this was an ideal medium through which to popularise the party's new stance and policies. I am appalled to think what my first offerings must have been like, but Junor gave me every encouragement, and before long I found he was accepting my leader-page articles. The competition to get that slot was intense; Angus Maude was a regular writer under contract, though that stopped when he became a minister; other regular contributors included former Chancellor Reggie Maudling, Teddy Taylor, Norman St John-Stevas and, after a while, the former deputy leader of the Labour Party, George Brown – a particular favourite of Junor's. He would commission several pieces, then decide on Friday night or even Saturday morning which to use. At first, until I was on contract, I was paid half rate for pieces not used, but that still made all the difference to me paying my mortgage.

My first article appeared in the *Sunday Express* soon after Thatcher's election, but then there was a long gap while I was in hospital and completing her biography. It was in 1976 that the fun really began. I used my articles to attack mercilessly Labour's egalitarian policies and its crypto-Communist MPs, but particularly the trade unions, who had the Government and the entire economy in their grip. At this time the National Front were making a nuisance of themselves most summer weekends in the streets of London, and though supported by only a small minority they spawned another equally noxious movement called the Anti-Nazi League – in fact, a front for the Socialist Workers Party and other Trots – who tried to spread their influence in schools and the professions; they too were fair game for my campaigning. I also expressed my fervent desire to see capital punishment restored (see Chapter Eight). This caused trouble with Wet members of the 1922 executive when I suggested that readers who wanted capital punishment reintroduced should ask their prospective candidates (by implication Tory as well as Labour) whether they would support restoration, and then vote in the general election according to their answers. The stuffed shirts saw this as far too populist; 1922 chairman Edward du Cann never mentioned their complaint to me, though I learned of it indirectly through a journalist. In my experience the 1922 executive has never been secure from motivated leaks.

Despite the flurry of fresh radical thinking that was under way throughout the party, the shadow cabinet, made up largely of appointments from the Heath era, proved very hard to shift. I have already explained how it took eighteen months of campaigning by Union Flag to make the front bench change its stance on Scottish devolution, but the same battle took place over economic policy; not many of its members were willing to embrace outright the economic philosophy enunciated by Joseph in 1974–75. Shadow chancellor Geoffrey Howe was slowly weaning the others away from their faith in incomes policy as a means of controlling inflation, but still there was a yearning for some kind of concordat with both sides of industry. The publication in 1977 of *The Right Approach to the Economy*, seeking to establish a consensus between the pros and the antis, was a backward step. Even as late as October 1978 Heath was urging the Tory party conference to throw its support behind Callaghan's 'Stage Three' incomes policy with its 5 per cent maximum for pay rises. Throughout this period I used my articles to deride the fainthearts in the party, trying to prepare our potential supporters for more radical solutions.

It was the same over trade union reform; many in the party were scared stiff of facing this issue, believing the best the party could do in Government would be to mollify the trade unions and never antagonise them. Jim Prior epitomised this strain of thinking, and Thatcher, though disagreeing, continued to support him in his position as shadow employment minister. But a vicious industrial dispute at Grunwick, a small photo-processing business in north-west London, blew this compromise wide open. Its owner, a vigorous Asian businessman called George Ward, fell out with a section of his largely Asian workforce, and sacked them. They began to picket the plant, and their cause was taken up by the trade union APEX, looking to expand its membership. By June 1997 there were violent scenes daily as police tried to hold back mass demonstrators in order to let the buses carrying Grunwick's frightened workers through the picket lines. In support of the pickets the Post Office Workers' Union blacked all mail leaving Grunwick, which would have spelt death to a firm that developed and printed holiday snaps. The Freedom Association came to the rescue, smuggling out the mail to post in hundreds of boxes round London, but ministers refused to do anything to stop the illegal action of the pickets, which Sam Silkin, the Attorney-General, called 'lawful intimidation'. Some, like Shirley Williams, even joined the picket line! Neither Ward nor his law-abiding workers got much sympathy from Jim Prior, who clearly thought Ward should cut his losses and recognise the union, which would then make Grunwick a 'closed shop'. But, as before, it was Keith Joseph who in a speech in my own constituency raised the torch of human rights, going on to condemn the whole idea of closed shops, which were then the norm throughout state industries and in large privately owned ones too. As you might expect, my *Sunday Express* pieces were solidly behind Joseph, whose views echoed the gut feelings of most Tory supporters. Without doubt, these were the Joseph Years.

The excesses of the Grunwick picket line barely prepared the public for the horrors of the Winter of Discontent in 1978–79, as the unions turned against their Government's pay policy and wave after wave of strikes brought havoc to hospitals, ambulance services, schools, freight transport, refuse disposal, roads and even council mortuaries. The Transport and General Workers Union set up special strike committees to decide which essential supplies should be let through. 'Now We've Had Ten Days of Rule by Commissars' was the headline on my next article. I did not have to read the newspapers to find out how the whole social fabric of the country was being pulled down around us: hundreds of readers wrote in with detailed examples of abuse of union power in their own communities and workplaces. At last, the agony was over – though it took the country thirteen years to forget. Providentially, it was the rejection of devolution by Scotland and Wales that finally came back to finish off the Callaghan Government.

Before the general election my marriage with Juliet broke up; for a couple of years we had developed incompatible interests, not least in politics, and neither of us could see much point in continuing together. I never subscribed to the popular theory that the demands of being an MP put an impossible strain on married life; after all, the time spent away from home, especially in the evenings, is no worse than in many other professions, and for that matter no worse than endured by, for example, long-distance truck drivers. We were both concerned to protect our three children, and did our best to make the transition easier for them. For this reason our divorce was as 'amicable' as any divorce is likely to be. In 1980 I married Helen.

On the afternoon of 30 March I cleared from my Embankment office all the papers I thought I would need for the election, and was on my way to collect a few more from the main building of the Commons when there was an almighty explosion ahead of me; the smoke was so thick it was impossible to work out what had happened. I raced back to my car and drove away before Parliament Square was cordoned off, heading for my constituency. Only later did I learn that the gentle Airey Neave had been the victim of a car bomb planted by the Irish National Liberation Army, murdered because he was shadow minister for Northern Ireland. I had already written an article for the *Sunday Express*, but a quick call to Junor established that I would write another overnight. Neave had become a personal friend, and was due to speak in my constituency the following Friday; I bitterly recalled his intended subject: 'Defending our Freedom'. I poured all my grief and hatred into the article, declaring that if ever these murderers were apprehended they should be stood against a wall and shot; it has long been my belief that this is the only appropriate penalty for terrorists who murder. The presence of a Special Branch officer at my side throughout the election campaign was a constant reminder of a personal, and indeed the party's, loss.

CHAPTER SIX

———— ·◦◦◦ ————

Conspiracy Aborted

'The key to power [in government] is inside the party.'
Richard Crossman, *Diaries of a Cabinet Minister* (1975)

'Let our children grow tall, and some grow taller than others, if they have it in them to do so.'
Margaret Thatcher, speech in New York (1975)

'My experience is that people write well only when they write about the things in which they believe.'
John Junor, *Listening for a Midnight Tram* (1990)

FROM THE DAY Margaret Thatcher became Prime Minister on 4 May, 1979, there was a conspiracy within the Tory Party against her. It began in whispers, becoming bolder and louder as the effects of monetary discipline were felt and the unemployment figures grew ever higher. It held its breath for the duration of Falklands War, then when victory was ours on 14 June, 1982, it expired in a gasp of disbelief. Though there were still Wet rebellions, the conspiracy was not to revive as a serious force until the end of the decade.

The conspiracy took various forms. I smelt it first among the apparatchiks of Central Office almost immediately after our election victory. Thatcher's supremacy would be short-lived, they said; monetarism was Chicago-school voodoo, a ship that would surely founder on the hard rocks of reality before the new Government was obliged to return to the inevitable prices and incomes policy. Once ingrained in the mind, old orthodoxies are very slow to die.

The whispers became louder as press commentators, weaned on corporatist government, realised that the majority of Thatcher's first

Cabinet were not really Thatcherites at all. Somehow the myth has been created of a woman charging unthinking into situations, hand-bagging everyone in sight, but the reality was very different. Thatcher was in reality a very cautious Prime Minister; while she had a clear idea of the kind of society she wished to see – a vision shared with Keith Joseph but also with Geoffrey Howe – she knew that in order to achieve general acceptance this vision would have to evolve over a period of time. During the 1979 election Heath had put his bitter criticism behind him and campaigned vigorously across the country for a Tory victory, leading to press speculation that he would be offered a senior Cabinet post. Wisely, Thatcher saw that this would leave her a very vul-nerable hostage to fortune, but she over-compensated for his exclusion by surrounding herself in her first Cabinet with his former acolytes; even Peter Walker, who made no secret of his deep disagreement with her economic policies, was brought in at Agriculture, a non-economic ministry. She also judged it too risky to dispense with Prior at Employment, and though he did his best to be loyal to her personally there were many occasions when his aides made clear to back-bench MPs and to the press how much he disagreed with the thrust of her policies. For the rest of her junior appointments she relied more on the advice of Humphrey Atkins, her former Chief Whip, than on her own instincts, with the result that more Wets were given jobs than their tal-ents strictly merited. However, one appointment was solely hers, and it was brilliant: she made Ian Gow her PPS. A good right-winger with a wicked sense of humour, Gow was popular throughout the party; he was assiduous in attending back-bench committee meetings and chat-ting wherever MPs gathered, and kept his mistress better informed of all currents of opinion in the party than the whips' office ever did.

However, the fact remained that those in her Cabinet who support-ed the Thatcher–Joseph–Howe economic policy were outnumbered by Wets who did not: Lords Carrington and Soames, Prior, Walker, Sir Ian Gilmour, Norman St John-Stevas, Francis Pym and Mark Carlisle. The Prime Minister could always count on the loyalty of her deputy, Willie Whitelaw, who understood little about economics anyway, but even his heavyweight support might not be enough. Thatcher loyalists like myself who kept out ears to the ground knew we could expect trouble – and sure enough we got it.

When I was a member of the press lobby I got to know Barney Hayhoe, the MP for Heston and Isleworth, quite well. After I was elected he came up to congratulate me, then almost as an afterthought asked whether I would like to receive 'guidance' on the most 'forward-looking' colleagues to vote for in the immediate elections to the 1922 executive and the subsequent elections of officers to all the back-bench committees. I replied that I saw no reason why not, and so found myself a regular recipient of the 'Lollards' Slate' – or, as it was later known, the 'Wet Whip'.

I knew from my press days how important control of the 1922 and the subject committees was; after regular weekly meetings (also attended by a listening whip who reported back to his chief), the chairman could request (in effect, demand) an immediate meeting with the relevant minister to warn him of anxieties about emerging policies; often, in anticipation, a minister would ask to attend a meeting to explain a policy or to account for himself; and – especially in time of trouble – the relevant committee chairman would often be invited for interview on *Today*, *The World at One* or other similar BBC programmes. As for the 1922 executive, the reader will have appreciated from Chapters One and Two of this book how influential that could be. Though the structure is somewhat different, much the same applies within the parliamentary Labour Party, which is what Richard Crossman meant when he recorded in his diaries while Labour was in Government that 'the key to power is inside the party'.

I cannot remember how much notice I took of Hayhoe's slate, but it was astute of him to try to recruit me to his left-of-centre pressure group; after all, while working as a lobby correspondent I generally kept my own views to myself, and he was not to know that they were well to the right of his. During the Douglas-Home and then the Heath premierships this group had established an ascendancy in key back-bench committees, and thanks to superior organisation its influence extended after Thatcher's election. The Lollards was in fact an umbrella organisation embracing several small left dining clubs and individuals, and was so called because it met shortly before the annual back-bench elections in William van Straubenzee's apartment in the Lollards Tower, Lambeth Palace, to agree their slate. Van Straubenzee, for long a Commons spokesman for the Anglican Church, was a meticulous bachelor and seen as a kind of patron saint of the Young Conservatives – and very Wet. His distaste of Thatcher was personal as well as doctrinal, springing from his days as her Minister of State at Education.

It was not long before Hayhoe realised that I was not a suitable recipient of the Lollards Slate, and in 1979 I was elected a member of the 92 Group, whose chairman was Patrick Wall – there were no other officers at that time. The group had been established as a small dining club by anxious right-wingers after Heath was elected leader, with the declared purpose of 'keeping the Conservative Party Conservative'. The first chairman was John Hall, and the group's name came about because its periodic dinners were held in Wall's Chelsea home at 92 Cheyne Walk. I think Wall was the most right-wing MP I ever knew; with a distinguished military record from World War II, defence was his major (and certainly expert) interest; he was vehemently anti-Communist, strongly supporting the Anglo-American Alliance; he backed white rule in Rhodesia and indeed anywhere else, including South Africa; he took much further my antipathy towards trade unions, and advocated government spending cuts so long as they left the defence forces intact; and he believed capital punishment should return, along with tougher sentences. Yet he had an easy manner with the many colleagues with whom he disagreed – and was always as straight as a die. It was he who described the 92 as 'Maggie's Praetorian Guard'. He left me in no doubt why I had been elected to the 92: after my success as organising secretary of Union Flag (see Chapter Five), my task was to organise the 92 slate for back-bench elections, which until then had had only limited success against the Lollards.

The 92 generally held four dinners over the year; the first, after the summer recess, was to agree a slate for the coming elections to the back-bench committees, and ministers were generally invited as speakers to the rest. As some members eagerly availed themselves of the wine, the atmosphere often became raucous, which must have irritated Wall, himself a teetotaller, as he strove to keep order. I was soon able to analyse the group's weaknesses: some saw it as a club only for senior MPs; any new Member had to be given time to 'prove his mettle', and it was necessary for only one hand to be raised to blackball a proposal for membership. This explains why the 92 fared so badly in back-bench elections from 1974 to 1979, though a few from my intake had been admitted before me. There was also a dearth of women Members; one of its founders, Sir Ronald Bell, was a misogynist so far as women in politics were concerned, and would automatically blackball any woman proposed. That was why Thatcher was never in the 92 before she became a junior minister (appointments were always made from the back benches, though when members subsequently became ministers they were still encouraged to attend). Sir Ronald must have been absent on one occasion, otherwise its first woman member, Dame Jill Knight, would never have slipped in. The names on the group's back-bench election slate were drawn solely from its members; there was thus no whipping to support worthy candidates outside its ranks, which was a help to those on the Lollard slate. There were also occasions when the 92 slate was not available on the Members' message board till after the contest had taken place! As I saw it, the need was first to broaden the 92's membership to include more sound men *and* women who might not be so obviously 'clubbable'; second, to recruit Members of promise from new intakes much more quickly, and encourage them to stand for junior posts; third, always to back the candidate with the soundest views, regardless of whether he or she was a 92 member; and finally, to get our slate on the message board before lunch on the day of any contest.

Our first successes came in the autumn of 1980; old Heathite Geoffrey Rippon, who had become a strong back-bench critic of the new radical policies, was ousted from the chair of the foreign affairs committee, while I supplanted Hugh Dykes as chairman of European Affairs. I was a strong supporter of Britain's membership of the European Economic Community, though drew back from the kind of political union that was Dykes's ambition. My election probably marks the first Tory back-bench recognition of the distinction between pro-Europeans who simply wanted a single (or common) market, and those with straight European federalist ambitions. I remained chairman of the European committee for several years, and was often taken to Strasbourg or Luxembourg to see the European Parliament at work. I always tried to get to Strasbourg in mid-summer – sumptuous alfresco meals on verandas of renowned Michelin restaurants as my hosts explained how *civilised* European politics were; I was interested to see their Parliament at work, though it seemed totally ineffective in controlling Commission policy.

After the 1979 election I gave up editing Central Office's *Conservative News*, feeling I had served this role long enough, but strengthened my contract with the *Sunday Express*; with Angus Maude now a minister he was no longer able to be a regular contributor, but the competition between me, Teddy Taylor and Lord George Brown to fill the leader-page slot was intense, with other politicians muscling in when they could.

As the necessary curbs on public spending driven by Thatcher, Joseph and Howe began to hurt, the conspiracy among the Wets became more vocal. From their positions in Cabinet, Peter Walker and Sir Ian Gilmour, who served under Lord Carrington as the Foreign Office's voice in the Commons, made speeches in the country urging priorities very distinct from Thatcher's, and many Wets were predicting that before long the majority in Thatcher's Cabinet would turn on her, telling her that either she had to modify her policies or go. Their argument was that in time of recession a degree of inflation was desirable to

keep more people in work. In the summer of 1981 they used the rash
of race riots in some of our cities as evidence that social order was
breaking down under Thatcherite policies. Even her old friend Lord
Thorneycroft, still party chairman, was becoming decidedly wobbly –
though he was never part of the conspiracy. A group of old Heathites
who called themselves 'The Blue Chip' produced a booklet entitled
Changing Gear, largely written by William Waldegrave and Chris
Patten; its intellectual case was lightweight, arguing that though
reforms were needed, they should be undertaken with hesitation.
Meanwhile there was always Heath grumbling from the wings, still
believing the corporatist policies he had pursued in government were
the only ones to make sense in any conceivable circumstances. He
made no attempt to lead a faction against Thatcher – indeed, there
were times when leading Wets tried to restrain him lest his obvious bile
should reflect unfavourably on them too – yet still he constituted a conspiracy all of his own, bitter resentment bursting to get out of his
Buddha-like frame, and bristling to lend spice to any hostile press comment.

The conspiracy reached its peak with Howe's 1981 Budget, cutting
public spending while unemployment was running at 2.4 million, freez-
ing tax thresholds while inflation was still 13 per cent, and hiking up
petrol duties. That evening, Prior made his displeasure known in the
Members' Dining Room in tones that could be heard three tables away,
while close friends of Gilmour and Walker told every lobby journalist
with time to listen how appalled their masters were. But backbenchers
came to the rescue, as they so often did; an early day motion promoted by a senior MP, John Loveridge, collected plenty of signatures, and
there was strong support for Howe's measures at the subsequent 1922
Committee meeting; the following week the Budget was opposed by
only a handful of Wets. Yet it could so easily have worked out differently. We later discovered that the three dissident ministers, Carrington,
Prior and Walker, met over breakfast the day after the Budget to discuss
whether they should resign collectively in protest. This was the moment
of their greatest opportunity; had they seized it, Thatcher would have
had a real party crisis on her hands – but they funked it. If they did not
have the collective guts to strike out on principle then, it was unlikely
they never would.

However, the 92's objective was to do what we could to ensure
the conspirators never had such a chance again. I used a speech in my
constituency on Saturday 21 March to alert party supporters all over
the country to what was really happening. 'A determined effort is being
made by a minority of Tories at Westminster to undermine Margaret

Thatcher and secure her replacement as party leader – if possible before the next election.' My warning led the front page of the *Sunday Express* (in which I was not writing that week), and was well reported in other Sunday papers, given added weight by a simultaneous speech by Walker in his own constituency, in which he conspicuously avoided any endorsement of Howe's Budget, and made another of his coded calls for different policies. I said:

> When [Thatcher] became leader in 1975 her critics wisely kept silent. But now that the depth of recession puts her policies under greatest strain, they are reappearing to exploit every opportunity to weaken her position. Most frequently this takes the form of an attack on Geoffrey Howe's anti-inflation strategy, which she firmly supports. It is also there when certain Cabinet Ministers leak their criticism of policies for which they are collectively responsible. When so-called Tory voices urge a radical change of course, or that we should tear up election pledges [on curbing inflation], their real hope is that Margaret Thatcher will be discredited, then disowned.

The conspiracy was now out in the open.

As spring turned into summer, many of us wrote articles and gave speeches calling for a reconstruction of the Cabinet to make it more evidently Thatcherite and more representative of party feeling both inside and outside Westminster. We also made private submissions to the Prime Minister; she was cautious as ever, but by the time the House rose she became convinced that to protect her radical policies she needed a more supportive Cabinet. The long-awaited reconstruction came on 14 September. Gilmour was sacked, complaining as he left Downing Street that the Government was 'heading for the rocks', along with Wets Lord Soames and Mark Carlisle. Thatcher, still cautious, kept Walker, but made him Welsh Secretary, where it was thought he would cause least trouble; as for Prior, despite his public protestations that he would never accept Northern Ireland, he nevertheless did. Three right-wingers – Norman Tebbit, Nigel Lawson and Cecil Parkinson – moved up. The conspiracy rumbled on until the end of the Falklands War, but its back was broken. Heath, Gilmour and St John-Stevas tried to revive it at the Brighton Conference, but were shunned by the party. As usual I arrived in Brighton before most MPs, where over drinks in the lounge of the headquarters hotel I received the hoped-for invitations to help 'set the scene' in TV and radio interviews.

Back at Westminster for the 1981–82 session, the 92 made further modest gains in the back-bench committee elections, but the stage army of Wets – Peter Temple-Morris, Christopher Brocklebank-Fowler, Robert Hicks, David Knox, Hugh Dykes and others – in alliance with left-wing press commentators, refused to lie down. One right-wing whip tipped me off that their views were being taken seriously by the whips' office, which of course reported to Thatcher regularly. I quickly organised a round-robin letter to the Prime Minister urging her not to dilute her policies, and within twenty-four hours some hundred back-benchers had signed. Thatcher told me later that she used to keep it in the drawer of her desk: 'Whenever some whip or minister came to me saying backbenchers would not take much more, I slapped it under their noses and asked them how they explained that letter.' An essential part of our task was to give her the weapons with which to fight back.

----------·◦◦◦◦·----------

The most telling example of Richard Crossman's observation that the key to power in government lay within the structure of the governing party came early in Margaret Thatcher's premiership, over reform of the trade unions. As over economic policy, the Wet opposition within the Cabinet centred on Jim Prior, Employment Secretary. I felt it unfortunate that so often I found myself organising against him, for of all the opponents I have encountered within the Tory ranks he was by far the most likeable, arguing his case against you with no trace of mal-ice and with a generous disposition. But alas, all his political attitudes were set in concrete when he was a minister under Heath, and he could never bring himself to question his old assumptions. Thatcher, in *The Downing Street Years*, saw him as an example of the 'false squire', whom she defined as having 'all the outward show of a John Bull – ruddy face, white hair, bluff manner – but inwardly they are political calculators who see the task of Conservatives as one of retreating gracefully before the Left's inevitable advance'. Ralph Howell, the farming MP for Norfolk North and the first exponent of 'workfare' in Parliament, was more succinct when he told me: 'Prior's just like a Suffolk sow – when he wants to go in one direction you'll never turn him towards another.'

We saw in the last chapter how as shadow employment secretary he prioritised 'getting on with the trade unions' over the need to reform Britain's industrial relations structure, which exactly bore out Thatcher's subsequent description of him. It was only pressure from Joseph, Howe and especially Thatcher herself that brought him to accept the need for substantive legislation; even the lessons of the Winter of Discontent did not persuade him to change his position. But in our manifesto we *were* committed to a programme of trade union reform, so as Employment Secretary he had to bring forward reform proposals in his Employment Bill. These were quite good so far as they went, but that was not very far.

He proposed first that the unions should be obliged to hold secret ballots of their members for election to union office or to amend their rules, rather than have such matters decided by a show of hands at all-too-often rigged meetings, and that the costs of balloting would be borne by the Government. His second proposal was to confine picketing in support of a strike to a person's own place of work, so that mass picketing involving workers not directly involved in a dispute ('secondary picketing') would not enjoy legal protection. The third made limited changes to the 'closed shop' system, under which workers were forced to belong to a particular union if they were to be employed in certain occupations, proposing compensation for those who refused to sign up to a union on grounds of conscience, and giving new closed shops legal protection only where 80 per cent of the workforce gave their approval in a secret ballot.

But there were glaring gaps in his proposal package. Though secondary picketing was made more difficult, secondary blacking and blockades were allowed to continue under protection of the law; thus workers at one plant not involved in a dispute could refuse to supply components to another that was involved, the Post Office Union could still refuse to deliver or collect mail from a strike-bound factory, as had happened in the case of Grunwick, and countless more cases . All existing closed shops, which covered most manufacturing industry, nationalised industries and public services were left intact. Worst of all, he proposed no change in the very widely defined immunities which protected union funds against action by the courts. He defended his timid package by urging that in industrial relations the Government should proceed 'step by step' to avoid upsetting the union leaders too much, but the fact remained that his proposals fell far short of the public's expectations following their suffering in the Winter of Discontent.

Leaders of the CBI, who still appeared to be guided by the corporatist tenets of the Heath Government, were even more cautious than Prior, and expressed concern that even his modest proposals went too far. Even worse was the Industrial Society, a body dedicated to 'bringing the two sides of industry together', who sought to persuade Tory MPs that such industrial matters were best left to employers and unions to sort out between themselves.

Prior's mouse of a measure proceeded with little challenge though its second-reading and committee stages – but not so when it came back to the full House on report. This is when whole new clauses can be moved, and several groups of Tory backbenchers, many from the new intake, began tabling their own clauses to toughen the bill up. There was obviously a need for some co-ordination, so I invited all those backbenchers showing an interest to a meeting in my office in the Norman Shaw Building, just along the Thames Embankment. I also invited Walter Goldsmith, Director-General of the Institute of Directors (IoD), whose thrusting enterprise was fast putting the Institute on to the political map alongside the fuddy-duddy CBI, and who gave us a lot of sound advice. The first organised back-bench rebellion of the new Government was under way.

Experienced Members who played a significant part in the rebellion were Jock Bruce-Gardyne, Ralph Howell, Peter Fry and John Gorst (who had bitter experience of Prior's pusillanimity during the Grunwick dispute in his constituency), alongside newcomers like Gerrard Neale, John Browne, Vivian Bendall, Michael Brown, Michael Colvin, John Townend and myself. Though we knew we were flying in the face of a three-line whip, and that we had absolutely no hope of success against the combined forces of the Government's payroll vote and the Opposition, we knew we were staking out the ground for the next Employment Bill, to come after a further consultation paper which Prior had been forced to concede in Cabinet. We were also heartened to learn that the Prime Minister took a benign view of our rebellion, since it would strengthen her own hand and those of Joseph and Howe when that legislation came to be drawn up. I was also greatly encouraged when, after writing to demand a tougher bill in the *Sunday Express*, I received scores of letters from members of trade unions in closed shops saying how they looked to a Tory Government to free them from the grip of their union leaders and shop stewards.

So we pressed our rebel new clauses to bring all secondary action within the law, to undermine the closed shop in all workplaces, to give employees a right to demand a secret ballot before they were ordered out on strike, and for ballots to confirm all existing closed-shop agreements. In successive votes around fifty Tory backbenchers defied the whip. I know that many ministers voted against us with a heavy heart, but they knew we were simply blazing a trail in preparation for the next Employment Bill.

The battle continued into the Lords, where we had some strong supporters, notably Lord Orr-Ewing. Though some eccentric rulings by the Lords of Appeal made it necessary for Prior to seek to insert a new clause to limit some secondary action, it was still woefully short of our manifesto commitment, which promised protection to companies and workers 'not concerned in the dispute but who can suffer severely from secondary action (picketing, blacking and blockading)'. This woeful gap came under attack from the president of the Law Society and from the chairman of the Bar, but Prior would not listen. I organised some forty MPs to write to the 1922 chairman, Edward du Cann, asking if the 1922 executive could apply pressure to have the bill strengthened, but du Cann argued correctly that this was better left to the peers themselves. On the eve of the Lords' debate I wrote an article in the *Sunday Express* showing just how far Prior was betraying our election promises. Prior replied by issuing a public rebuttal, addressed to me, to strengthen the peers' resolve before the crucial vote, which predictably he won with ease.

We then had to prepare for the promised consultative paper on next steps, which caused several battles in Cabinet along predictable lines. Now the focus for more radical curbs on the unions shifted from the Commons to the headquarters of the IoD, masterminded by Walter Goldsmith. Seminars were held, often with John Hoskyns, head of the Downing Street policy unit, present. The MPs involved then pushed the emerging ideas through the back-bench employment committee and all other channels available. In this area the IoD was much more influential than the CBI and certainly the Industrial Society, both still hankering after corporatist cosiness. We were greatly encouraged by all the evidence that the public wanted more radical action – and that included vast numbers of the unions' own members.

All our efforts bore fruit after the Cabinet reconstruction in 1981, when Norman Tebbit was made Employment Secretary. His Employment Bill included a number of the proposals we had trailed, plus some of his own. Most important, the unions were to be exposed to damages claims in the courts for any actions that went beyond a legitimate 'trades dispute', which was to be much more strictly defined, thus removing a legal protection they had enjoyed since 1906. There would be no immunity for those organising industrial action in support of a closed shop, increased compensation from employers and unions for those who lost their jobs under closed-shop agreements, and contracts which specified union-only labour were rendered unenforceable. However, unions would still enjoy immunity for strikes called without approval in a secret ballot first; that had to wait till the next Employment Act in 1984.

Of all the statutes enacted in that Parliament, I remain convinced that Tebbit's was the most influential in pulling the country out of the union-induced paralysis that had afflicted us since World War II, enabling our industry and commerce to compete effectively in world markets, and freeing working men and women from an oppression they had come to resent. The Tory back-bench rebellion against Prior's timid legislation in 1980 staked out the ground for this monumental reform. Richard Crossman was right: the key to power lay within the governing party.

With the reader's tolerance I will briefly flash forward: to 15 December, 1983, when I was in the back of a limousine speeding towards Enniskillen in County Fermanagh. My companion was Chris Murphy, elected in 1979 for Welwyn and Hatfield, and we were part of a delegation of Tory MPs on a brief visit to Northern Ireland to inform ourselves of the security situation. The previous day we had been briefed by the top brass and by the Northern Ireland Office on the threat from the Provisionals, and in the evening had donned flak jackets to join an army patrol around the Falls Road. This was my first visit to the Province since August 1979, when, on my way to speak at a Unionist meeting in Armagh, I stopped off at Warrenpoint and to my horror watched the final scraps of flesh from British soldiers killed in the massacre there a couple of days before being removed from the trees and placed in sacks. On its second day the delegation had split up to visit local politicians in different parts of the Province, and Murphy and I were assigned to the district council at Enniskillen.

The interesting thing about this district council was that it was divided almost evenly between Unionists and Republicans. We were met by the council's clerk, who explained the councillors were in session discussing how best to promote further tourism to the beautiful lakes nearby, on which part of the prosperity of the town depended. The clerk tiptoed in to tell the chairman we had arrived, and through the half-open door we could hear a perfectly sensible discussion of their future tourist potential. This was one of the few matters left for local council decision following the imposition of direct rule from London. The chairman immediately adjourned the discussion and all the councillors trooped into a reception room nearby. We were seated, while they stood before us.

The chairman began by saying how honoured they were to be visited by MPs from Westminster, and invited us to ask any questions we wished. Since I was the senior I apologised for interrupting their important business, and began by asking an innocuous question about how they saw future constitutional developments in Ulster. That was the last word either of us was able to utter; it was as if I had rung the bell to start a boxing round with multiple participants and no referee. The first to respond was immediately interrupted, and from then on no fewer than three people were speaking at once, with insults and threats freely traded. 'Mr X, how *dare* you accuse me of treachery, when *your* people ...'. 'Mr Y, just you repeat that outside and you'll go home with two black eyes ...'. Much of the initial conflict sprang from an assertion that under British law a Roman Catholic could never become Chancellor, later amended to Lord Chancellor, but after that it was impossible to make sense of anything. At one stage I feared that blows would be exchanged. After about fifteen minutes of this, the chairman at last made himself heard, saying it was time to resume their session, thanking us for our presence, and hoping we had learned something from the discussion! It was as if the bell had rung to signal the end of the round, and all the councillors filed meekly back into the council chamber to resume their discussion of how to entice more tourists to Enniskillen.

I cannot speak for Chris Murphy, but I certainly learned something from that visit. It was that when you give men and women power and responsibility to decide matters of vital importance to themselves, their families and their community, they will work together to achieve the improvements they want. But withdraw all other powers of democratic decision over their daily lives from them, as has been the case in Northern Ireland for at least twenty-eight years, then you produce a situation in which sectarian prejudice will flourish.

I had long been fascinated by Northern Ireland. When I was a political correspondent it was the habit of the Unionist Government in Stormont to invite a group of lobby correspondents and gallery reporters to Belfast during a parliamentary recess, and I took up this invitation every couple of years. After showing us over the Stormont Building and introducing us to some of its politicians, they took us to some of the modern industries they had succeeded in bringing to the Province. I was a Unionist myself and still am, but though our hosts kept us away from meeting leaders of the Orange Order, there was no mistaking the strong Protestant basis of our hosts' judgement and culture. On one such visit in the late 1960s I and Maureen Tomison, a close lobby friend, used a free afternoon to make contact with Gerry Fitt, recently elected Republican Labour MP for Belfast West; a local election was under way, and Fitt went to great trouble showing us how the Republican machine operated. News of our enterprise was received frostily by our Unionist hosts, who took it as an abuse of their hospitality. On a later visit, when the Civil Rights protest movement was under way, I remember meeting a very senior officer of the Royal Ulster Constabulary, a tall man of distinguished bearing whose name alas I cannot recall, who foretold with chilling accuracy how the Civil Rights movement would be taken over by men of violence who would use bullets and bombs to coerce Ulster into joining the Republic in the south. Some of my colleagues scoffed, calling him a paranoid Orangeman – yet the subsequent Ulster tragedy fulfilled every word of his grim prophesy.

Heath's decision to scrap the Stormont Government and impose 'direct rule' from Westminster was probably the worst political decision he ever made. Of course it made sense to direct security operations from Whitehall, but the trouble was that with direct rule came all the responsibility which Stormont exercised for local government matters like housing, health, planning, drainage and the like, which from then on had to be decided by legislative order brought before the House of Commons late at night. As a consequence, from 1971 Northern Ireland became nothing short of a democratic slum. The IRA case, as pressed in the USA and elsewhere, was that Britain was the 'occupying power' in Northern Ireland, ruling it as if it were a colony. Our Government protested that this was not so, that our interest was to protect the rights of the majority and the minority alike – yet the prevailing culture in Whitehall, including the Northern Ireland Office, was that Ulster *was* best governed like an old colony, incapable of accepting responsibility for running its own local affairs. The result was that a whole tier of local government, which elsewhere in the British Isles gave stability to politics and valuable training for many politicians, was woefully absent in Northern Ireland.

A succession of Secretaries of State accepted this prevailing culture and had little instinctive understanding of the nature of this part of our kingdom. When Humphrey Atkins became Thatcher's first Ulster Secretary, the following story is told of his first briefing. His officials showed him a map of the Province, marked out by counties. Atkins listened attentively, then placed his finger on an area of blue on the map. 'What's this?' he asked. 'That, Secretary of State, is Lough Neagh.' This interior lake covers no less than 153 square miles of Ulster, yet a senior British minister had never even heard of it!

But Ulster need not have remained a democratic slum for so long. When Thatcher became Tory leader she entrusted Airey Neave with shadow cabinet responsibility for Northern Ireland, which he undertook with great diligence. He concluded quite early on that any notion of forcing the majority and minority to share power in a new devolved legislative assembly was futile, and that responsibility for running their own local affairs should be restored to the people of Ulster. Majority and minority politicians would be represented together on local council committees (the council having been elected under the Irish system of proportional representation), while an ombudsman, such as the Stormont Government had proposed before it was abolished, would adjudicate on any complaints of infringement of civil rights. Northern Ireland would have more MPs at Westminster as indeed its population merited; in fact, this had already been enshrined in legislation in the

dying days of the Callaghan administration, to come into effect following the next revision of parliamentary boundaries. Accordingly the
Conservative manifesto in May 1979 promised: 'In the absence of
devolved government, we will seek to establish one or more elected
regional councils with a wide range of powers over local services.' It was
an open secret that Neave preferred 'more' rather than 'one', but mention of the possibility of only one was included to placate those
Unionists who still hankered after Stormont rule.

This was the Neave policy, and when he was blown up as he left the
House of Commons car park at the start of the 1979 election his policy was blown up with him. It was never tried. Instead, the new Ulster
Secretary, like all his successors, reverted to the Whitehall orthodoxy of
'neo-colonial' government. Jim Prior, in his memoirs, pours great scorn
on what he calls the 'policy of integration' proposed by Neave and supported Sir John Biggs-Davison, himself a Roman Catholic, Thatcher's
PPS, Ian Gow, Julian Amery and many other Tories including myself –
not to mention Ulster Unionists like Enoch Powell. Yet proper representation of Ulster in the House of Commons had already been conceded under Callaghan; all that remained was to give Ulster citizens the
same democratic control over their local affairs as was enjoyed by their
fellow citizens in England, Scotland and Wales.

Would the Neave policy have worked? Who can answer this with any
certainty? Of course no-one in his right mind ever pretended that this
policy would persuade the IRA to call off its campaign of terror and
intimidation; that would have continued regardless. But giving Ulster a
local government structure would have made for better governance
than Whitehall could ever provide; it would have offered political scope
for leaders in the majority *and* the minority communities, and might
have avoided the sheer frustration that led some Unionists to support
their own terrorist organisation; certainly it would have offered proof to
the world that the British Government was not ruling Ulster like an old
colonial power. No, the lesson I learned at Enniskillen still holds good:
give a divided community responsibility for improving its lot, and its
citizens will rise to meet that challenge; deny it that democratic right,
and you give positive encouragement to extremism.

All this explains how, after co-ordinating back-bench opposition to
Prior's timid plans for trade union law reform, I found myself opposing
his proposals as Ulster Secretary for 'rolling devolution' of legislative
authority to a new Ulster assembly in which minority Republicans
would slowly gain equal power with majority Unionists. I believed he
was putting the cart before the horse. If only local government could
be returned to Ulster, why then would it be necessary to devolve leg-

islative power at all? Prior's proposals seemed an exercise in futility. Yet he was obsessed by the need, as Whitehall and the Ulster Office saw it, to share legislative power with a minority whose allegiance lay with the Republic of Ireland. Of course much can be gained by co-operation between north and south across the shared border, but today we see the Prior policy enshrined in the Good Friday Agreement, under which Dublin is given a share of executive power over part of the United Kingdom. Will this work, and put an end to the threat of terrorism for good? We can hope, but again, who can tell?

So, with Prior's Northern Ireland Assembly Bill, the rebels of the right were back in business, though in smaller numbers. As a constitutional measure the bill's committee stage had to be taken on the floor of the House, so with Jim Molyneaux, Powell and other Unionists we organised an effective filibuster. When it comes to expanding a natural nine-minute speech to last for ninety, no Irish MP needs to take any lessons from the English! After all, the filibuster was developed to perfection by Irish MPs in the nineteenth century. As usual, we spoke until a closure was moved, which we then voted against to take up still more time. It was a battle involving only Conservatives and Unionists; the Labour Opposition took no interest, its benches often deserted save for their shadow spokesman and a whip. In the end the Government's patience ran out, and a guillotine motion was pressed. I believe I am right in stating this was the first time a Government has ever used a guillotine to silence a determined section of its own benches rather than the Opposition.

We knew we were caught in a very different ball game from our attempts to strengthen Prior's Employment Bill. Then, we knew we were reflecting a sentiment in the party, that we were putting down foundations for the future; now, with the Falklands War under way, both the party at large and the mainland press took no interest whatsoever. Then, we knew we had the tacit support of some cabinet ministers; now, though Thatcher and Howe had their doubts about the efficacy of Prior's proposals, we received no encouragement from them.

I began by co-ordinating the efforts of those Tory MPs – Amery, Biggs-Davison and the rest – with strong Unionist feelings, but I came to rely more and more on Chris Murphy to do the donkey-work. In the early months of 1982 I knew I was a sick man; my soaring temperature was controlled only by courses of penicillin, at night I found my sheets soaked with perspiration and I was suffering bad cramps. My doctor thought some relaxation in the sun might help, so I asked John Cope, then pairing whip, if I could be excused for a few days after the Whit recess to convalesce in Crete with Helen. His face lit up: 'Of course,

George, of course. Take as much time as you like – until this Irish Bill
is through!' But in Crete, when my tablets ran out, my temperature
soared again. A local doctor prescribed a different course of penicillin,
and all was more or less well. On coming home I suffered bouts of fever
alternating with courses of penicillin for a further month; I continued
to vote to obstruct Prior's bill whenever possible, but I left co-ordination of the revolt to others.

Prior got his Bill through as expected, and a Northern Ireland
assembly was tentatively established in the impressive Stormont
Building. I later visited it and talked to its Speaker, Jim Kilfedder, also
MP at Westminster for North Down, as kind and gentle a Unionist
politician as you could ever meet. But before long the assembly col-
lapsed under its own contradictions, boycotted by the very Republicans
whom Prior had set out to help.

I have never witnessed a more dejected and fractious House of
Commons as that which met in emergency session on Saturday 3 April,
the day after the Argentinean junta had invaded the Falkland Islands –
British territory beyond dispute and recognised as such under international law. I had cancelled my constituency surgery to attend, and most
other MPs had done the same. Labour was naturally critical that the
warning signs had never got through to Whitehall, and on the Tory
benches we felt shame that we had allowed British territory to be invaded under our Government. It was a considerable feat of Thatcher's to
raise our spirits from the depths, announcing that a Task Force of naval
destroyers, aircraft carriers and troops would be dispatched to the
South Atlantic to free our subjects, but still there was a desire to find
scapegoats. Foreign Secretary Lord Carrington and Defence Secretary
John Nott were given a very rough time that evening at a special meeting of the 1922 Committee, Carrington – who as a hereditary peer had
no experience of Commons politics himself – faring particularly badly.
By Monday he had resigned, to be succeeded by Francis Pym. The next
day a subsidiary War Cabinet was set up; led by the Prime Minister, it
comprised Pym, Whitelaw and Cecil Parkinson.

The effect on the public was much the same as when Winston
Churchill called the nation to arms in 1939 and 1940, with only a left-
wing/pacifist fringe objecting. In the Tory Party the old conflict
between Wets and Dries appeared suspended, though before long it re-
emerged in different form, with some Wets arguing that even when our
forces reached the Falklands they should never invade to regain British

territory so long as there was the remotest chance of agreeing a compromise (i.e. a sell-out) with the Galtieri regime. A leading Wet,
Michael Mates, argued in the smoking room that public opinion would
change 'once the body-bags are flown back home', and, predictably,
Heath used Commons debates to argue that the exercise was futile and
would gravely damage Britain's trading interests throughout South
America. Given his strong feelings against the Fascist General Franco
of Spain when a student at Balliol, Heath's trust of dictators in the
post-war world is indeed remarkable.

In such a situation, the role of back-bench groupings like the 92 is
pretty minimal. However, we did play a role at one critical stage,
though whether it influenced the course of events I have no means of
knowing. In the early stages of the war the United States played a highly equivocal role, with politicians like Jeane Kirkpatrick, US
Ambassador to the UN, arguing that Britain had no proper role in the
South Atlantic anyway. The Falklands War dominated the leader page
of the *Sunday Express* for weeks on end; once I wrote a challenging article under the headline: 'What are friends for, Mr President?' The inim-
itable Cummings captured the feeling well with an accompanying car-
toon of Reagan and Thatcher walking through a rainstorm, Reagan
with a big umbrella over his head, Thatcher dripping wet. The caption
had Reagan saying: 'When it stops raining I'll lend you my umbrella –
I'm a pal!' The American Secretary of State, Al Haig, came to London
with ideas of what he thought might be a compromise solution;
Thatcher pointed out all the flaws, and insisted that General Galtieri
could not be allowed to profit from his aggression, but the Cabinet
reserved judgement until Haig's proposals were put to the
Argentineans. Predictably Galtieri rejected them out of hand; he was in
possession, and even sharing sovereignty with the UK would for him be
a backward step. But Haig continued his attempts to broker a deal,
while all on the right viewed him with great suspicion.

Our suspicions that there might be a weak link in the War Cabinet
came after a Commons statement by Pym on 20 May, in which he
implied that our Task Force would not make any landings until the full
potential of negotiations had been exhausted. If this was the case, then
Galtieri would have every incentive to continue procrastinating until
the severe South Atlantic winter weather made any landings impossible. Later that evening Pym was ordered back to the Commons to insist
that this was not what he meant at all – but by then our suspicions were
aroused. I could recall Pym's reluctance, when he was shadow
spokesman against the Callaghan Government's devolution plans for
Scotland and Wales, to go for the jugular by calling for a referendum

provision to be inserted. Any wobbling by Pym when it came to retaking the Falklands was very serious – especially as he was flying to Washington the following day to continue the dialogue with Haig! Patrick Wall strongly smelt a rat, and we agreed to summon an emergency meeting of the 92 to consider the situation. This revealed that many of us would feel obliged to resign the Tory Whip if the merest fraction of sovereignty over the Falklands were to be ceded to the Argentine aggressor. But how best to make this threat known? We decided to bypass the usual whips' channels and go straight to the top, to the member of the War Cabinet who was also Party Chairman: Parkinson. He readily agreed to receive a deputation from us later in the evening, when we warned him of twenty to thirty resignations unless the retaking of the Falklands was seen through to its conclusion. Parkinson promised to convey our warning to the Prime Minister and other members of the War Cabinet, and I have no doubt he did.

How accurate our fears turned out to be is confirmed in Thatcher's own account of the war in *The Downing Street Years*, for, while in Washington, Pym swallowed hook, line and sinker the latest Haig proposals, under which all forces in the area would withdraw within seven days and disperse altogether in fifteen, all sanctions against Argentina would be lifted straight away, while, worst of all, Argentinean representatives would make up part of a 'Special Interim Authority', under whose rule the Argentines would be free to send their own settlers to the islands and acquire property rights. It is hardly surprising that Thatcher describes this as 'conditional surrender'. Pym even embodied these proposals in his own recommendations to the War Cabinet on 24 April, but mercifully these were rejected by all the other members. I have no doubt that Thatcher would have stuck to her guns in any event, but it is quite possible that our warning served to strengthen the mettle of other ministers.

Later, as our troops were closing in on Port Stanley, I wrote in the *Sunday Express* on 30 May of the effect the war had had on us as a nation.

> First, we have rediscovered our National Unity ... Second, we have rediscovered National Leadership ... Third, we have rediscovered National Pride – the pride that comes from fighting alone for an undisputably just cause ... Finally, we have rediscovered National Confidence. For a quarter of a century the British people have lived under the shadow of the Suez fiasco in 1956, when we tried to act boldly in defence of our interests and failed. That single disaster cast a terrible blight on our view of ourselves and what we were capable of doing. Perhaps the greatest thing the Falklands invasion has done has been to lay that ghost of Suez. We

have fought for our interests, and indeed for those of all free peoples, 8,000 miles across the world, and we are succeeding. We *are* masters of our own fate, once we fix on our objective, and pursue it with ruthless determination. Our years of psychological retreat are at an end.

The final surrender came on 14 June. The Prime Minister announced it to the Commons that evening, and opposition leader Michael Foot was generous in his congratulations. All acknowledged her sheer determination and fortitude, but only those close to her knew the emotional strain she suffered with every report of casualties. This was the only occasion in the Commons when I have had to fight back tears.

It does not fall to many backbenchers to speak to an enthusiastic audience of more than 5,000 in London's Royal Albert Hall. The experience was mine thanks to the Sikh community in Britain. I made a number of Sikh friends when I was preparing to fight Coventry South in 1970, and I have always found them very loyal in their friendships. I kept in touch with several of them, in particular with Dr 'Paul' Bedi. By 1982 he had moved with his family to Southall in west London, and it was his brainchild to organise a World Sikh Festival over the second weekend of July. A model of the holy Golden Temple was carried with great reverence at the head of a long procession down Park Lane on the Saturday, followed by a mass rally in the Albert Hall. On Sunday a gathering was organised for Sikh families in Hyde Park, where the atmosphere was that of a giant picnic. Here I encountered Bernard ('Jack') Weatherill, then Deputy Speaker of the Commons, and Lord Avebury, both long-standing friends of the Sikh community. A few days before, I took a deputation of senior Sikhs to meet the Prime Minister in Downing Street; she showed great interest in their culture and the moral values entwined with it, and later gave me a message to read at the Albert Hall rally.

The audience at the rally was made up entirely of Sikh men and their older sons. As well as speaking myself, to enhance the prestige of the occasion I had arranged for two junior ministers to speak as well: Timothy Raison from the Home Office, where he was in charge of immigration matters, and Sir George Young, whose responsibilities at the Department of Environment included inner-city renewal. Raison was the first of the guests to speak, Young the second. Wisely, both stuck meticulously to their civil service texts, but as they spoke I became aware for the first time of the unique way in which a Sikh audience registers its appreciation. It does not simply clap those passages of which it particularly approves; instead, a respected elder rises to his feet and shouts an exhortation meaning 'blessed is he who speaks', to which the entire audience responds: 'God is the ultimate truth'. When this happens, a wise speaker waits for the exhortation to be completed, but neither Raison nor Young had a clue what was happening, perhaps thinking the respected elder was just a heckler, and plodded on. As a result, parts of their speeches were not heard by the audience at all, and I learned from their experience when my turn came. I began by reading Margaret Thatcher's message of greetings and goodwill, then I launched into my theme, which was that whatever discrimination or taunts Sikhs suffered from the ignorant, their resilience lay in pride in the Sikh traditions and values they upheld. My speech was interrupted by many shouted acclamations. I was followed by Lord Avebury, who recalled the wisdom of the Sikh gurus.

At the start of the following week my bottle of penicillin tablets was again exhausted, and immediately the familiar symptoms returned. I finally made an appointment to see a consultant at Westminster Hospital in Horseferry Road, where I was admitted straight away, and remained for another ten weeks. The same blood poisoning that struck me down in 1975 had returned, due to a malfunctioning heart valve. My first visitors were six leaders of the Sikh community, concerned to hear through Bedi of my plight. Two, wearing 'Ali Baba' slippers with curled-up toes, made a great hit with the nurses on duty. Another early visitor was my friend Ian Gow, PPS to the Prime Minister.

My spell in hospital taught me the concern that Margaret Thatcher always had for her friends. Each summer Conservative Prime Ministers held three receptions, usually timed to coincide with the Queen's garden parties at Buckingham Palace, to which were invited ministers and back-bench MPs, together with their spouses. Helen and I were due to attend one two days after I entered hospital. Gow rang Helen at her office to convey the message that the Prime Minister wished her to come early to Downing Street in order to receive a personal letter of good wishes addressed to me. I was amazed that with all her burdens of office she could attend to such detail – but that was Margaret. Over succeeding weeks Gow visited me regularly; he was a great believer in the restorative effects of alcohol and on one occasion, with a broad beam on his face, he produced bottles of gin and dry Martini from a carrier bag. Unfortunately he did so within view of the staff nurse in charge. 'You can't bring those in here!' she told him sternly. Gow protested, eliciting from me a promise to consume only a little at once, but to no avail. It was the only argument I witnessed in

'A youngster with ears standing out from back-and-sides cropped hair': myself at the age of twelve.

'A total suspension of rational judgement': in uniform as a national serviceman.

'All human life is here': as a trainee journalist.

Norman Tebbit inspiring a Conservative Way Forward fringe meeting at the 1991 party conference in Blackpool. On his right is Cecil Parkinson, and on his immediate left John Bercow and Nick Gibb, both now MPs.

Opposite

Constituency duties 1: Conservative party workers keep Reigate free of litter.

Constituency duties 2: Kenneth Baker (Mole Valley), myself and Humfrey Malins (Croydon North West) promoting a Young Farmers' Cowpie Rally.

Smile please: photocall with John Major.

Opposite, from top

With Chief Mangosutho Buthelezi, an old friend from South Africa, at Ulundi.

At the Children's Trust, introducing Joan Collins to a patient being rehabilitated following brain surgery. On the left is unit manager Dr Stephane Duckett.

Opening ceremony at the East Surrey Hospital. Left to right: Geoffrey Howe (Surrey East), Norman Fowler (Health Secretary), myself, Margaret Thatcher, Kenneth Baker (Mole Valley) and Ken Gulati (Mayor of Reigate).

Celebration party hosted by Joan Spiers (centre) for the campaign team following my reselection in June 1996.

We must not let Kenneth Clarke speak for Britain

BY SIR GEORGE GARDINER MP

LAST Tuesday will surely be recorded as Black Tuesday in the annals of the Conservative Party. It was the day when our Leader and Prime Minister stood at the Commons' Dispatch Box and announced to the world his abject surrender to Chancellor Kenneth Clarke and Deputy Premier Michael Heseltine over European policy.

It was the day when, in obeyance to Clarke's orders, he threw away his party's strongest card in the coming election — a pledge that under a re-elected Conservative government, Britain would keep out of a European Single Currency, the inevitable precursor to a United States of Europe, and that sterling would be safe.

It was the day when Clarke effectively became Prime Minister, ensuring that the key to 10 Downing Street was passed to Tony Blair by the outgoing tenant. Small wonder that Labour MPs were cock-a-hoop and there was gloom on countless Tory faces across our benches.

For it has long been common knowledge that a majority of Cabinet Ministers, Tory backbenchers, our constituency workers and indeed the electorate at large, believe we have gone far enough in integrating with the European Community or Union, and that the time has come to call a halt.

Equally, it is common knowledge that among Cabinet members, Clarke, Heseltine and John Gummer thought differently — and that Clar[...]

people before or during the election. So in the campaign he and Malcolm Rifkind — and Michael Howard, Peter Lilley, Michael Portillo and Brian Mawhinney too for that matter — will have to stand on platforms saying: "So sorry we can't say whether we're going to abolish the pound or not. You see the negotiations won't finish until June. Come back and ask us then."

The voters will fall about laughing and rightly so.

Yet the reality is that in the next election the majority of Tory candidates will give their personal pledge against joining a single currency.

This was established in a survey of all adopted prospective candidates that John Townend MP, chairman of the backbench finance committee, and I conducted last September.

There is no way that a Conservative Cabinet would ever be allowed by the party to recommend joining the Euro — so why not come clean and say so?

WHAT makes my blood boil is not just the way the Cabinet has been hijacked but that Conservative Party workers across the country have been hijacked too.

Central Office knows the score — how umpteen regional conferences and scores upon scores of constituency executive committees have called for a pledge to shun the Euro.

These are the people who do the party's work, yet they are being treated like dirt. Conser[...]tive principles have bee[...] my bones sinc[...] one [...]

'John Major stood at the Dispatch Box playing the role of ventriloquist's dummy'

Several respe[...] [...]ical corre[...] in my bloo[...] [...]nts were [...] [...]he Pr[...] [...]eenage

My article in the Sunday Express *on 8 December, 1996, together with the illustration, which gave my Reigate opponents the chance for which they had been waiting - to reopen the proceedings to force my deselection.*

My calling card for the 1997 general election, with snuggly friend.

My adoption as Referendum Party candidate for Reigate on the steps of Reigate's Old Town Hall. On my left is Bill Westnedge, and on my right Douglas Simpson.

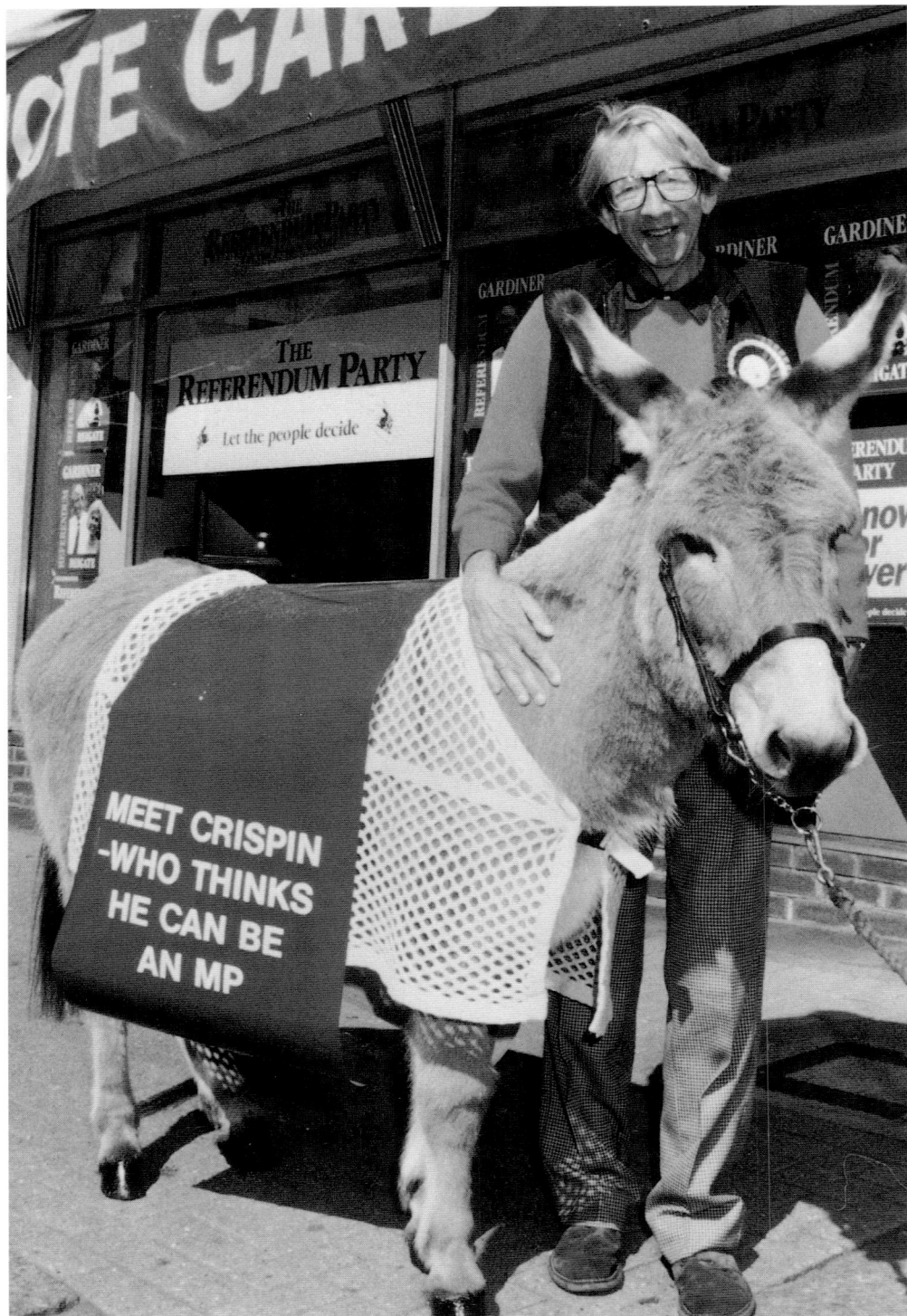

Gloves-off campaigning. My Tory opponent, Crispin Blunt, had told his party workers: 'You could put up a donkey as the Conservative in Reigate, and it would win.'

which Gow was roundly defeated, and he had to take his bottles with him when he left.

After some days on a penicillin drip my fever subsided, and the drip was replaced by regular injections through a canula. I was put on my own in a side ward, where I was able to see my secretary every day and handle constituency correspondence. I was also able to use my portable typewriter, which meant I could resume writing articles for the *Sunday Express*, dictating them to a copytaker from a patients' phone in the corridor. Since May there had been a strike over pay by ancillary workers organised by the health service unions, and pickets were posted at the entrances to hospitals, certainly in London. At Westminster few of the staff seemed to take much notice; cleaners and porters still turned up regularly. I often asked the views of the nurses, who said they regarded the pickets as a stupid irritation. However, on 26 July there were two IRA bombings, one aimed at the Household Cavalry in Hyde Park and the other two hours later at the band of the Royal Greenjackets in Regents Park. Eight soldiers were killed, and fifty-three injured. Those injured in Hyde Park were rushed to Westminster Hospital, and as soon as the union chiefs heard what had happened they wisely called off their picket. After that the pickets never had the gall to return. During that health service dispute I wrote a predictable denunciation for the *Sunday Express*; John Junor, the editor, said he liked it, but when after two weeks it still did not appear I rang to inquire if anything was wrong. Junor's answer astounded me. The print unions in Fleet Street were the staunchest allies of the health unions, and had often threatened not to print strong opinions against them. 'Look, George, I just can't take the risk of losing a whole Saturday print run,' explained Junor. So much for fearless journalism.

My consultants decided that once the poison had been eliminated from my blood system I should have an artificial mitral valve fitted, which of course meant heart bypass surgery. It was explained to me that there was a risk, though it was minimal. Bypass surgery was common enough, and I had absolute faith in my surgeons. Margaret Thatcher wrote a note telling me to do whatever my doctors thought best. In thanking her I suggested she might take some of her own medicine; she had a medical problem at the time – I think with one of her eyes – and she had the reputation of not being an easy patient. My operation was scheduled for a Wednesday, and two days beforehand I sent an article to the *Sunday Express* for possible use while I was recovering. Despite the unusual circumstances of its writing, I remain proud of that article to this day.

It argued that the time had come for Tories to raise their eyes from present challenges, and consider what should be the big themes of our manifesto, ready for the next Parliament. My first suggestion was obvious enough: that the root causes of unemployment should be tackled by ever tighter curbs on inflation.

> Jobs are created not by governments but by customers. We can win these from the world if we keep our costs down – and if we leave more money in the pockets of our own people to spend as they choose. This means cutting income tax, and the State spending less. *The people's* priorities must decide where the new job opportunities blossom – not some bureaucrat distributing the fruits of their labours from Whitehall.

This had to go hand in hand with continuing trade union law reform and breaking the monopoly power of state industries wherever possible. But there was a bigger theme even that this: 'bold action to give the people a real chance to own a share of the resources of our nation. Years ago Anthony Eden pressed the ideal of a "property-owning democracy". It has assumed reality in housing, but nowhere much else.' Whenever part or the whole of a state industry is sold off it should be to their workers and to the public at large. 'Let us work for the day when not only do most families own their home, but Mum and Dad have their own private pension schemes and a bundle of stocks and shares stuffed in a desk drawer too.'

With the benefit of hindsight all this might seem pretty obvious now, but in August 1982 it was pretty radical thinking. Upon taking office the Thatcher Government had begun selling off some state-owned industries – National Freight, Cable and Wireless, British Rail Hotels, Britoil, Associated British Ports and British Aerospace – and in many cases the workers involved were given the opportunity to buy shares. But the full potential of privatisation in spreading share ownership to families who had never before even seen a share certificate had yet to be understood. The word 'privatisation' did not appear anywhere in the 1979 manifesto.

I awoke from my anaesthetic with tubes coming out of my chest and a bruised rib cage that was sheer agony. But I had the satisfaction of reading my article in that Sunday's paper. By Tuesday another note came from Downing Street, congratulating me on my (non-existent) courage in writing such an article while preparing for surgery, and saying how closely my enthusiasm for a *genuine* property-owning democracy mirrored Margaret's own. The scene was set for the next stage of the Thatcher Revolution. I felt well pleased.

CHAPTER SEVEN

The Enemy Within

'At one end of the spectrum are the terrorist groups within our borders, and the terrorist states which finance and arm them. At the other are the hard left operating inside our system, conspiring to use union power and the apparatus of local government to break, defy and subvert our laws.'

Margaret Thatcher, the Carlton lecture (1984)

JUNE 7, 1983. This was the election meeting I shall never forget. Until then the day had been unremarkable; in my Redhill HQ in the morning I attended to administrative matters and put the finishing touches to my speech, then at 2 o'clock sharp set off on my usual afternoon 'flying canvass' in the streets, avenues and closes of my mainly suburban, part-rural constituency. This was not a canvass in the strict sense of the term, no checking of voting intentions against the electoral register, but simply an exercise in meeting the people, or 'glad-handing'. My secretary slowly drove my car, with large 'Vote Gardiner' placards and a public-address system mounted on the roof, down the road, announcing my presence and inviting those wanting to meet me to alert a member of the team calling at their doors, while I walked along the pavement to respond to beckoning waves. We knew only a small number of householders would be at home, which was what we wanted, for it meant we could cover far more streets in the time while leaflets were stuffed into every door. So long as I met at least some voters in each road, who later in the day would spread the word that I had been round, the exercise was fully justified. Meanwhile, between announcements the loudspeaker played pop music or well-known choruses from opera; there was an element of razzmatazz to my campaigning.

I opened every campaign with a meeting in the south of the con-

stituency, and two days before polling had one in the north. Normally
they were conducted by the association chairman, but on this occasion
we thought it would be nice to ask the president of the local branch to
officiate, an opportunity he seized eagerly. So there I was, in leafy and
wealthy Walton-on-the-Hill, making my final rallying call. My speech
extolling Tory policies and deriding the Liberal–Social Democrat
Alliance (my only real rivals) went down well; alas, no heckling of the
kind that made election meetings of old fun, but well-thought-out
questions. When the last of these were answered I expected the chairman to wind up with a call for everyone to turn out to vote for me when
Thursday came – but not a bit. I knew that this chairman was besotted
with badgers and the need to preserve them, yet was aghast when he
launched into a speech rallying the audience to support not me, but
them. He then put a succession of questions to me: would I press for
an end to gassing, would I sponsor a Private Member's Bill? When I
had finished answering he went on to invite more questions on badgers, but by then the audience had dwindled from some fifty to nearer
five. So at last he wound up: 'The best of luck on Thursday, George –
and when you're returned, don't forget our badgers!' You bet I
wouldn't; nor would I forget the experience of an election meeting
chaired by someone who was taking a single issue to this extreme.

There was never the slightest chance that Margaret Thatcher would
not win the 1983 election. The electorate felt little love for her, but it is
a weak Prime Minister who seeks affection anyway. However, the determined lead she gave the country during the Falklands War earned for
her admiration and respect, while Labour leader Michael Foot was
known mainly for his carping criticism of that campaign and for his fervent support of unilateral nuclear disarmament despite the threat
posed to British and European security by the Soviet Union. But public opinion had begun to turn in the Government's favour before the
Falklands campaign even began. As more than a million council-house
tenants were either seizing their new freedom to become home owners
or indicating their interest in doing so, the public began to understand
more clearly what Thatcherism was all about. The same purpose was
served by the new freedom opened up by the Government in telecommunications, driven by Kenneth Baker, then Minister for Information
Technology. The days when an exporting company in my constituency
had been told by the GPO, at that time still in charge of telephone
installation, that it would have to wait six months before having a telex
point installed were long gone. The proposition that 51 per cent of
shares in a privatised BT should be sold to voters in the first truly 'public' flotation conveyed the same Thatcherite message. The first

Telecommunications Bill fell casualty to the early election and had to be reintroduced in the new session. The driving force behind both was Baker, who had an intuitive understanding of the tremendous potential offered by competition in telephones, multifibre cables, mobile phones and the like; today's homes and businesses little realise how much they owe to Baker's driving enthusiasm. All these factors gave Margaret Thatcher her first landslide majority.

The Government's post-election honeymoon was not to last long; indeed, for the first twenty months of the new Parliament almost nothing seemed to go right. It had been argued that Parliament had been able to flex its muscles from 1974 to 1979 only because the Labour Government had a majority of just three, soon to be eroded, yet after 1983 Parliament became just as assertive with a Tory majority of 144. Rebellions were frequent, often led either by Ted Heath or Francis Pym, predictably sacked as Foreign Secretary after the election; the old Wets were back in business with a vengeance. The 1983 October party conference, which should have been a victory celebration, was totally overshadowed by news that Parkinson had made his secretary pregnant, and eclipsed by his eventual resignation (see Chapter Nine). A back-bench rebellion (in which I joined) defeated the Government's recommendation on MPs' pay. There was a succession of rebellions on local government legislation; Heath led a revolt against rate-capping high-spending local councils, while Pym led a revolt on the rate support grant settlement, which had disappointed many Tories in the shires; Heath, Pym and Ian Gilmour led opposition to scrapping the Greater London Council, while the Lords threw out the 'paving bill' to cancel the 1985 GLC elections. The Wets rebelled over cuts in overseas aid, while Keith Joseph, now at Education, antagonised even the right by proposing increased parental contributions towards student maintenance costs, thus hitting directly at middle-class families, and was forced at a stormy 1922 Committee meeting to backtrack. Geoffrey Howe got the Government into more hot water by announcing in January 1984 that trade unions were to be banned from GCHQ Cheltenham, the radio station that received all our overseas intelligence information, for which he was now responsible as Foreign Secretary. He was quite justified in doing so, since a strike in 1981 by civil servants employed there had gravely endangered national security, though many of us thought that the subsequent trouble was far greater than the principle was worth. Meanwhile, the Labour Party was rising like a phoenix from the flames under its newly elected Leader, Neil Kinnock, and the Tories were suffering disastrous by-election results.

By late 1985 the outlook could hardly have been more gloomy.

Thatcherites like myself who spent most weekends defending the Government at political suppers across the country found our activists surprisingly less disturbed than many at Westminster, and I used my regular *Sunday Express* articles to spread an encouraging gospel. But in fact what kept our party workers enthused was undoubtedly the renewed challenge to democratic authority mounted by Arthur Scargill from his power base in the National Union of Mineworkers, and the increasingly vociferous challenge to defence policy from the Campaign for Nuclear Disarmament.

The miners' strike began in March 1984 and lasted for nearly a year. The miners were dragged into it through an overtime ban, technically in protest against a pay offer. The NUM's rules required that a *national* strike had to be supported by 55 per cent voting for it in a *national* ballot, and it was highly unlikely that Scargill could get his 55 per cent. So instead the NUM executive got round their rule by staging a *regional* ballot in the militant Yorkshire coalfield over the closure of one pit, then inviting other regions to strike in sympathy. The Midlands coalfields of Nottinghamshire and Derbyshire did hold a ballot – and voted 73 per cent against strike action; this turned out to be Scargill's Achilles heel. We had been given plenty of warning of what was coming, so in the previous Parliament, Energy Secretary Nigel Lawson had built up heavy stockpiles at the power stations and coal depots; this, together with production from the Midlands, stepped up output from the oil-fired and nuclear power stations and coal imports meant that the Government, with determination – and it required every ounce of that – could see the strike through. Yet other unions gave Scargill the strength he needed: the National Union of Railwaymen by blacking all movements of coal by rail, and the Transport and General Workers by fighting physically against movement by trucks and organising sympathy strikes of dockers over coal imports. Scargill was also helped by Kinnock's waffle in the Commons, which led many Labour supporters into believing this was no more than a strike to improve workers' rights.

The violence employed by those supporting Scargill was truly terrifying. Even in Yorkshire some brave men continued working, and the threats against them from the picket lines extended to their wives and children. In order to gather material for my *Sunday Express* articles I made two visits to Yorkshire, standing safely behind the police lines as rebel miners were driven in coaches at daybreak to the pithead. Afterwards I visited some of these men in their homes; I found they were tough as nails, with a burning conviction that they were not going to be bullied around by men like Scargill. I saw the lead shot that had been fired through the kitchen window of one while he ate, and heard from the wife of another who had been spat upon while doing her shopping, and whose children had received threats at school and were afraid to walk the short distance home without an adult to protect them. The truck drivers who kept the coal moving to the power stations suffered gross intimidation too, and in South Wales a taxi driver carrying a miner to work was killed when a three-foot concrete post was dropped from a motorway bridge onto his taxi.

Meanwhile Scargill made no attempt to conceal that the motive for the strike was not economic at all, but political. His impossible demand that *every* pit be kept open, however uneconomic and at whatever cost in subsidy, until the very last ton of coal had been extracted, and the violent means adopted to achieve it, were intended to defeat democratic government itself. This was finally underlined by his contempt for the courts of the land. This was a strike that was totally Marxist-inspired.

Not surprisingly, the Scargill challenge brought Wets and Dries together in the parliamentary party, not least because one of the heroes of the Wets, Peter Walker, was proving highly effective as Energy Secretary in communicating the Government's case to the press. Occasionally the right was regretful that greater use was not being made of judicial processes to bring Scargill down, but rarely did that reach the surface. On one occasion I was approached in the lobby by Leon Brittan, then Home Secretary, who was having to take the strain of the heavy burdens placed on our police forces in the course of the strike; he was worried that Walker was dragging his feet and not allowing Coal Board chairman Ian MacGregor to pursue action through the courts as he wished. I suppose Brittan thought that either through my articles or through the 92 Group I could bring public pressure to bear on Walker, but I could not see that this would achieve any constructive purpose. I thought Walker was doing a good job.

Perhaps oddly, the memory of Britain's victory in the Falklands War also helped to reinforce public and party morale. We had triumphed over a foreign aggressor, it was argued, so why should we not triumph over an equally ruthless enemy here at home? Thatcher captured this sentiment when she spoke to the assembled 1922 Committee on the eve of the summer recess of 'the enemy within'. Some left-wing commentators saw this as an attack on miners generally, whom most of us held in respect, but in fact she was referring to the hard left and to terrorists as well. Later she used a speech to the Carlton Club in November to make this clear, and some of her words head this chapter. Remember too that earlier that year we had seen WPC Yvonne Fletcher shot by officials within the Libyan Embassy (representing the same regime that later helped to fund the strike), and the month before the IRA had bombed the Grand Hotel in Brighton with Thatcher as a target.

There was also another 'enemy within': the Campaign for Nuclear Disarmament, which then had the official support of the Labour Party. Though most of their demonstrations were peaceful, they succeeded for a while in harnessing a great deal of support from the young and cost the Ministry of Defence heavily in protecting our defensive installations against attack. One particularly ludicrous example of this was the 'Peace Camp' outside the Cruise missile base at Greenham Common, where a motley collection of half-crazed women lived in the hope of achieving martyrdom by throwing themselves under the wheels of the vast trucks bringing the missiles in. But CND's efforts also helped to unite the Tory Party and the general public, and nothing that Heseltine did subsequently as President of the Board of Trade (or even as Deputy Prime Minister) equalled his brilliance as Defence Secretary in ridiculing CND's propaganda. Here again we had a Wet minister acting with the wholehearted support of the right. The eventual collapse of CND, its balloon appealing to the ideals of youth punctured, owed no small part to Michael Heseltine's efforts.

So it was that by routing Scargill, who exemplified all the thuggish elements of post-war trade unionism, and by making the pacifist CND irrelevant, Thatcher added to the laurels won in the Falklands War. Yet these triumphs were won at a cost, and it can be argued that it was during these battles that the seeds of her own eventual downfall were sown. For although these conflicts were all-engrossing, this was the period in the Tory Government's history when the crying need was for intellectual investigation into the radical plans needed to bring efficiency to the National Health Service, to raise educational standards, to give more power to parents, and to install effective restraints on the ever-burgeoning demands for social security. It is true that good progress was being made with privatisation, sustained by very broad discussions within the party, and early in 1985 Baker, William Waldegrave and Lord Rothschild presented to cabinet ministers their scheme to replace local government rates with the community charge, yet the eventual decision to switch was made without any proper intellectual inquiry throughout the party. The result was that none of these radical reforms were begun till after the 1987 election, so that all the anxieties associated with them, though very few of the benefits, had become apparent when Thatcher's leadership faced its crucial challenge in the autumn of 1990. If these reforms had had their gestation after the 1983 victory, then the outcome of that challenge might have been very different. But the Scargill strike and the threat from CND were all absorbing, and vital thinking time was lost.

----- ❦ -----

From the late 1980s onwards the 92 Group was without doubt the strongest engine of back-bench pressure on government policies other than over Europe, on which the group was divided. Early in 1984 Patrick Wall decided that as he had no intention of fighting the next election he would stand down as chairman; he therefore invited its members to elect a successor and, since the 92 was growing all the time, to make a new departure by electing a secretary and supporting steering group of five to share the administration. Hitherto Wall had done everything, with my help in organising our slate for back-bench committee elections. He accordingly sent a letter to all members recalling how the group had grown in size and influence under his chairmanship, but unfortunately included the boast that our activities were never reported in the press. This was tempting fate too far; inevitably some MP's less-than-loyal secretary sold the story, with the result that political correspondents and gossip columnists had a field day gloating over how much they knew (in reality, very little). Before one of our subsequent dinners Anthony Bevins, political editor of the *Independent*, crouched in a car opposite our venue in St Stephen's Club to record our membership for his readers; alas he left too early to record the late, arrivals, and included in his list other MPs attending a totally different function.

Most members expected me to stand for chairman, though Peter Hordern, who had been in the group from its beginning, put his name forward too, with the support of some older members. There was nothing personal in his bid, and when I won by a sizeable margin he congratulated me generously. John Townend was elected unopposed as secretary, and on the steering group were Bob Dunn, Ralph Howell, Jill Knight, James Pawsey and Ivor Stanbrook. From then on we met fortnightly in my office, and were usually sustained by a glass of sherry. Access to the full list of members was restricted to Townend and myself, and I always refused access to others who might require it for their own purposes.

There was a demand from our members for more regular discussions than our four dinners a year allowed, so we instituted a policy committee, open to all our members except ministers and whips. It was felt that people might speak more freely if whips were not present, but invariably it was agreed that I would report the gist of the discussion to the Chief Whip after each meeting. We convened on an ad hoc basis in a room on the less busy upper committee corridor to discuss specific issues, with the discussion led either by a back-bench member or more usually by an invited minister. I made a point of inviting ministers who were not necessarily drawn from our membership; Michael Heseltine, Douglas Hurd, Kenneth Clarke, Kenneth Baker, John Moore and Ministers of State were invited, as well as, more predictably, Norman Tebbit, Michael Portillo, Peter Lilley and John Redwood. Some ministers used the policy committee to test responses to a policy before it was made public, as Schools Minister Angela Rumbold did before the initiative for grant-maintained schools was finalised.

One such policy group meeting in February 1986 turned out to be eerily prophetic. Morale in the party was at a low ebb; the previous month Defence Secretary Heseltine had resigned over the future of Westland Helicopters, soon to be followed by the departure of Trade Secretary Leon Brittan over authorising the leaking of a confidential letter critical of Heseltine; the Prime Minister's standing was badly dented, and our constituency supporters were asking what was going on. The opinion polls looked ominous, we fully expected to lose the pending Fulham by-election, and the Wets were briefing political correspondents that perhaps Thatcher should go before the next election. All this was enough to convince the steering committee to convene a policy group meeting to discuss simply 'The State of the Party'.

The fifty plus who attended the meeting were not in good spirits, but thankfully Party Chairman Norman Tebbit was there to listen and sum up. Anger was expressed over the appointment ten days earlier of Gerry Malone, a noted Wet, as Scottish whip in preference to the more obviously qualified Michael Forsyth; this led on to accusations that the whips office was not being as loyal as one would expect. Several Members then claimed that Tristan Garel-Jones, a senior whip and committed Wet, had over recent days had been moving round the Members' tea and smoking rooms asking colleagues whether they thought the Westland saga had been handled properly (without actually specifying by whom), whether they thought the Prime Minister was in touch with people, giving just a hint that perhaps she might soon choose to stand down. The effect was to put into many colleagues' minds thoughts that were never there before. It was the same tactic Garel-Jones used with devastating effect when Thatcher was genuinely under threat in November 1990. The almost unanimous view of the group was that I should straight away see Chief Whip David Waddington (no Wet he) and report to him that we took a very poor view of Garel-Jones's 'loyalty', which I did.

Naturally Waddington passed on our concerns, and the next day a very shaken Garel-Jones cornered me in the lobby to protest his total innocence. I replied that even if it had not been his intention to destabilise, that was certainly the impression he had been giving. He went off muttering that the 92 could not be more wrong. That, so far as I was concerned, was the end of the matter, but alas one of our members leaked the story to the political editor of the *Mail on Sunday*, Peter Simmonds, who reported what he called the 'civil war' under the headline 'Sack the Wet Whip, says Tory Right'. In fact we never called for his sacking; all we wanted was to fire a shot across Garel-Jones's bows, and our members reported to me that he was indeed far more circumspect in his tea-room conversation for many weeks afterwards.

The hard test of the 92's influence was always the elections at the start of each session to the 1922 Committee executive, followed by all the back-bench subject committees. These elections were held on different days and at different times, and the key to success was turn-out. If the party was on a one-line whip, meaning that an MP could be away even without pairing with a Labour Member, then turn-out was low. Of crucial importance to the organiser of a slate was to enthuse all those who were sent it. As chairman of the 92 I continued to organise what we called the 'Sound Slate'; it took the form of small slips of paper that could easily be inserted in a breast pocket, so that before filling in their ballot papers our members could double-check the recommended names. All the slips were left on the Members' message board before lunch on the day in question. I sent the slate not only to all 92 members but also to many others (including those lined up for membership) who asked to see it. I also easily obtained a copy of the 'Wet Whip' circulated at the same time (though not usually as efficiently) by the Lollards grouping. I always attended the ballots, and made a mental note of any of our members who were missing in order to give them a quiet reminder the next day.

The 92 decided its slate at a dinner without a guest speaker, in the 'spill-over' period after the summer recess but before the new session opened. To determine who should be on our slate for the 1922 executive we had our own internal secret ballot, conducted at the same dinner. Obviously we could never determine how our members actually used their votes, but it was a rule that no member would put himself forward against the 92's official nomination; some occasionally broke this rule, but they were lucky to escape being dropped by the group. We never went through a formal expulsion procedure; it was simply agreed by consensus not to send an offending member invitations to future dinners or meetings of the policy group. We received one or two resignations from people who had moved leftwards in the party, but none of any consequence.

The most difficult back-bench elections were always those at the start of a new Parliament; familiar faces had gone, replaced by new ones who knew very little of where many of their senior colleagues stood on the crucial policy issues. The steering committee therefore agreed a new system for recruiting newly elected members: prospective candidates in the safest seats were vetted beforehand and soon after arrival invited to a drinks party, either in my office or in a room off Westminster Hall. At the party our steering committee would get to know the new Members and offer them any advice they sought on finding their way around; immediately afterwards we agreed to make a number of them full members of the 92 without even the formality of election at a dinner, after which they became our agents in recommending the 'Sound Slate' to others in their intake. They could also propose other new members at their first dinner. Thus in the first elections of a new Parliament the 92 Group began with a head start, and many of our strongest members were recruited in this way. I also used to enlist one of the 'new boys' whose political leanings were not yet known to the Lollards to get himself invited to its preparatory meeting and then to brief me on its priorities and tactics in the coming elections.

To win back-bench elections and to bring pressure to bear on ministers meant we needed *numbers* – and an early decision by the steering committee was to increase membership steadily from the forty or fifty it then was to around a hundred. When I stood down as chairman in 1996 it had reached 107, including three who had since been made peers. But of course increased size brought its own problems in establishing a common line; though there was always general agreement on economic priorities and encouraging individual responsibility against the dependency culture, it was harder to get agreement on European policy and impossible to obtain on 'conscience issues' such as capital punishment and abortion.

From 1983 onwards there was no doubting the success of our strategy, and it was not long before we had established as chairmen of all the important back-bench committees either our own members or others whom we backed as 'sound men'. There was a period, indeed, when *every* back-bench chairman came from our ranks. Occasionally we came to an understanding with those organising the 'Wet Whip' to share joint vice-chairmanships; it was important that the Wets should have some representation, albeit small. Why was dominance of these committees so important, you might ask? First, because their officers shaped the discussion at committee meetings, which were always watched and analysed by whips; second, because they had instant access to ministers; and third, because their chairmen were frequently invited onto radio and TV programmes in the absence of a minister to ward off Wet attacks on Government policies. If they were called in to ward off Labour attacks, then so much the better.

The 1983 election produced a notable group of Tory radicals, most of whom quickly joined the 92. However, our periodic policy group meetings did not satisfy their need; they wanted a group of their own to work up detailed proposals for future policy and therefore formed a supper club to work on their first booklet *No Turning Back*, published in November 1985, and in consequence gave themselves that name. Its members were Chris Chope, Michael Fallon, Michael Forsyth, Eric Forth, Neil Hamilton, Gerald Howarth, Rob Jones, Peter Lilley, Francis Maude (son of Angus) and Ian Twinn; many had been friends when the Federation of Conservative Students was the advance guard of Thatcherism in the universities. They were joined by Michael Brown (elected in 1979) and Angela Rumbold (from a by-election in 1982). *No Turning Back* made policy proposals covering four areas: education, employment, health and housing – and certainly foreshadowed the subsequent reforms in education and health. Subsequently Michael Portillo joined the group after his by-election win at Enfield Southgate in 1984, and then John Redwood, former head of the Prime Minister's policy unit, after the 1987 election. Until the Major years, when many of its original members had become ministers, the group had a significant impact on government policy.

Whenever a cabinet reshuffle was in the offing, the 92's steering committee made recommendations on promotion to the chief whip, whose job it was to take such soundings, and often directly to Thatcher herself. We pressed successfully for Cecil Parkinson, Norman Tebbit and Kenneth Baker in turn to be appointed Party Chairman.

I also pursued the radical agenda through Conservative bodies outside Parliament. I was a vice-president of the Selsdon Group, a discussion forum drawing on London and the Home Counties, set up to promote free-market policies. I belonged to the Bow Group, Thatcherite through most of these years, and wrote a research pamphlet for them on further reforms that were required in trade union law. But most illuminating of all was my experience of the Monday Club, to whose executive I was elected.

The Monday Club had an interesting history. It was founded in the late 1950s to give a voice to 'true blues' (as the terminology went then) to counter the recently founded Bow Group, allegedly run by 'pinkos'.

An early member – surprisingly in view of his subsequent history – was Richard Needham. The club was strong in London and in certain regions, notably Hampshire and the West Country, and was organised by Cedric Gunnery, a large and genial bachelor who appeared to operate most of the time from his London club, and was the essence of the old English gentleman. By the time I became involved the club certainly had its head-bangers, but in control were serious and principled right-wingers like Gunnery and David Storey, a Home Counties solicitor, as chairman. Through the 1960s and 1970s it was above all else 'Old Imperialist' – adamantly opposed to dismantling the British Empire and fanatically supportive of Ian Smith after he had unilaterally declared white Rhodesia independent. When power was eventually handed over to President Mugabe in the new Zimbabwe, the Monday Club was left hopelessly adrift, needing fresh objectives to fill the vacuum.

A few Tory MPs were prominent members, but all because they saw the club as a vehicle for pushing their personal agendas. Julian Amery was there because of his old imperial interest; Teddy Taylor wanted to disseminate anti-Common Market propaganda (a natural follow-through from the club's imperial agenda); Harvey Proctor used the club to urge repatriation of Commonwealth immigrants; and some Ulster politicians came anxious to bolster the union. The club also urged restoration of the death penalty, a policy which united all the MP members except for Amery. In joining, I too brought my own agenda: to make the club a right-wing advocate of Thatcherite, free-market economic policies; I saw the need for a nationwide body to counter pressure from the Tory Reform Group. The Monday Club provided further weekend platforms for me across the country and at party conference fringe meetings, where I spoke either on the need for further privatisation or to bring back capital punishment.

Late in 1985 the club published my research paper on privatisation, in which I attacked the retention of the gas industry as a monopoly (for which I received a rebuke from Energy Secretary Peter Walker), and urging full privatisation of British Coal and British Rail, which few Tories then thought remotely possible.

I also had some success in stripping the Monday Club of its 'racist' inheritance. When the executive concluded its tortuous task of redefining its aims, I got the anti-immigrant commitment watered down to purely *voluntary* repatriation, which was something of a defeat for Proctor, who also sat on the executive. Harvey Proctor was a complicated man, for whom I developed a respect that survived the rumours of his peculiar sexual proclivities. One of the executive's tasks was to vet proposed new members in order to prevent any infiltration by those with a National Front background; in such discussions, Proctor always insisted that even the vaguest suggestion of such involvement should be a rigid bar. In October 1985 he, T.E. Utley, the distinguished commentator on the *Daily Telegraph*, and I were invited to Durham University Union to oppose a motion of no confidence in Her Majesty's Government; when the local leaders of the National Union of Students learned of Proctor's involvement they declared the debate 'black' and mounted a noisy picket line outside the Union building to dissuade students from attending. Even worse, the Labour MPs who were to speak for the motion pulled out at the last moment, saying they would not cross a union picket line. The organisers of the debate were distraught. Proctor said that if it helped he would pull out too, but Utley and I would not hear of this; vital principles of freedom of speech were at stake. So the students provided their own speakers for the proposition, and we decided among ourselves to be gentle with them. Of course we won the debate – it was not our eloquence, but rather the screaming minority outside that made sure of that! And Proctor did not mention immigration once.

A weakness of the Monday Club was that all its officers could be thrown out and its policies reversed simply by packing an AGM; there was no protective council in ultimate charge as in other groups. The first sign of impending trouble came at an AGM in I think 1988, when someone seriously proposed that the club should seek a cross-Channel alliance with Le Pen's *Front Nationale*. We fought that one off, but soon there were special meetings to force Storey and Gunnery to stand down, while the air was tainted with a nasty smell of anti-Semitism and with the somewhat contradictory suggestion of a national campaign to hound out Moslems. I decided to sever all connections with the Monday Club immediately, and when I told Amery what was happening he resigned too. Right-wing advocacy is welcome, but when tainted with racial hatred it becomes totally repugnant.

Once the revolutionary challenge posed by Scargill had been routed, the next big blow for freedom was administered not by Thatcher or her ministers, but by press mogul Rupert Murdoch. Neither I nor any other backbencher played any part in this episode; I relate it here because I believe it delivered the knockout blow to the thuggish, hard-left enemy within our political life.

I have already alluded to the dire state of Fleet Street in the 1970s and 1980s, the demarcation disputes between print unions and black-mail of press management to sustain a regime of corrupt employment practices, and the total refusal by the unions to permit any use of the new print technology without ludicrous manning levels. There were even disputes over which print union should have sole charge of pho-tocopiers! David English, saviour of the *Mail* titles, once told me how his management had trawled the world to find one second-hand lino-type machine, used to set the lines of lead type that Fleet Street was still forced to use, while John Junor told me of new printing presses at Express Newspapers worth some £2 million that had been 'moth-balled' for years because of the print unions' intransigence. Not until I travelled to Trondheim, Norway, to meet an editor friend did I see what modern full-colour printing technology could do for a daily newspaper. But worse still was the ominous censorship in Fleet Street; even as fear-less an editor as Junor was afraid to print an attack on the health serv-ice unions lest printers sympathetic to those unions took reprisals on a Saturday night (see Chapter Six).

By late 1985 Murdoch despaired of any sensible deal with the print unions, and had established a brand-new works at Wapping equipped with the latest print technology. He made the bold decision to shift publication, initially of the *Sunday Times,* from Grays Inn Road to Wapping without the agreement or knowledge of the print unions; this required surreptitious planning, so much so that only a few of the edi-torial staff knew what was happening until the very last minute. Of course a printers' strike was inevitable, and pickets were mounted at Wapping; the journalists were reluctant to move, and some never did. So we had a situation in which an organ of the free press was being printed behind fortifications topped with barbed wire, while the vicious mob assembled every Saturday night, attempting to stop publication, became increasingly violent. Wapping became the mecca for every mil-itant trade unionist in the country, including those who had earned their dubious spurs on the picket lines at the pitheads. The intimidation mirrored that of the Scargill strike, with the new print staff and their families put at risk. Margaret Thatcher assured Murdoch early on that there would always be a sufficiently strong police presence to ensure safe entry and exit at the site for the staff involved, and for the trucks bearing the editions to the trains and wholesale depots. The Labour Party tried to 'black' all Murdoch titles – a pretty fruitless undertaking – while Kinnock ordered all shadow ministers not even to talk to Murdoch journalists. Altogether it took more than a year to quash the militants and see the last pickets withdrawn. Many harsh things have been said about Murdoch, but it is thanks largely to his steely determination – and that of his editor, Andrew Neil – that the British national press in the late 1980s became truly free.

After the 1983 election I decided to seek an even better contract with the *Sunday Express*; when I called on Junor for my usual Wednesday-morning consultation on my next topic, I proposed that I end my freelance status and join his staff. He was somewhat taken aback, but agreed immediately, offering the appropriate salary. I in turn was surprised when an office was found for me straight away on the editorial floor together with a desk, phone and an ancient upright typewriter which I found far too clumsy to use. In fact I continued to work from my office in the Commons, while my Fleet Street office was used by senior staff every lunchtime for a bridge school. On weeks when I was not engaged on writing an article I would submit leader ideas, which were often used; editors always like to have a choice on the day. As before, I saw Junor most Wednesday mornings, undertook any research necessary on Thursdays, and wrote from 7 a.m. to midday on Fridays before dictating my article or leaders to a copytaker. For this weekly commitment of roughly one and a half days I received from Express Newspapers far more than my parliamentary salary.

Junor was a bully of an editor, yet unlike many, I found him totally endearing. On the rare occasions when he did not like the article I had written, he would shout abuse down the phone; how could I write such drivel? Yet within hours he was back again, apologising for his rudeness and saying there had obviously been a misunderstanding between us over the line I was taking. When pleased with my work his praise was fulsome. I shared most of his right-wing prejudices over trade union power, law and order, anti-CND, tight government spending, the Wets, South Africa, and indeed much else. His home was not far from mine in Dorking, and during parliamentary recesses I often ran into him shopping at the local branch of Waitrose; he boasted he was the only Fleet Street editor who did his own weekly shopping, and so was unique in his knowledge of how prices on the shelves affected housewives or pensioners. Though at times he was eccentric (he once complained in his 'Current Affairs' column that the cheap Christmas crackers he bought did not contain gifts up to his expectations), his feet were always firmly on the same ground that his readers trod.

Only once did I have a serious spat with him, and that was when I voted to increase parliamentary salaries in line with the review body's recommendation, but by far more than the Government wished. Even though my political activities were in effect being subsidised by Express Newspapers, I knew all too many of my colleagues could barely fulfil their constituency commitments on their parliamentary salaries. Many of the new intake had like me been forced to cash in whatever pension policies they could to make good the deficit on their previous incomes. Proposals had often been made to bring MPs' pay closer to that of overseas legislators, but never had it been convenient for the government of the day to accept the full recommended amount. I was therefore determined to join in forcing the necessary increase, and thereafter have our pay fixed according to a formula outside our hands; I found it totally invidious to be required to vote regularly on my own salary.

Junor, however, had an obsession that MPs should get less than the average Fleet Street journalist, and wrote the previous week in his column that any Member who voted to exceed the Government's recommendation would be hounded by the *Sunday Express* for ever after, and certainly would never again be allowed the use of its columns. It was therefore especially disconcerting for him to find that one of his own feature writers had done just that. I was expecting a stormy meeting with him the following Wednesday, but not a bit; he had obviously thought the situation through very carefully. He wanted to keep me as a feature writer, but knew he would lose face if he printed my articles. He also knew that to sack me for exercising my own judgement as an MP would almost certainly be counted as unfair dismissal, and bring bad publicity. So instead he was emollient; had he been in my position, he said, he would have voted exactly as I had. Yet my action, coming so soon after his threat, made it impossible for him to feature my name for a while; let's just wait and see, he said. So I continued to write leaders, but nothing else. Time went by, and the absence of my name on the leader page became obvious. When I spoke at political suppers I discovered this had become apparent to readers too; indeed, some said they had written to the editor asking why I was no longer writing. It was some six weeks before Junor felt it safe to feature me on the leader page again.

Express Newspapers was acquired by United Newspapers in 1984, and Junor did well out of his share options. He soon made no secret that he wished to retire as editor; he had, after all, been in charge of his paper for far longer than any other editor in Fleet Street. There was a good deal of dithering over his replacement, but in 1985 the editor's chair passed to Robin Esser from the *Daily Express* – a very different kind of journalist, but one with whom I also got on very well. Junor, meanwhile, kept up his popular comment column. Later the paper moved from its distinctive premises in Fleet Street to new ones by Blackfriars Bridge, where it took advantage of the new print technology made possible by Murdoch's stand. However, as we got into 1989 I found my articles being used less frequently; when I tackled Esser about the reason for this he hedged for a while, then came clean: 'Your enemy, George, is no-one in this office – it's the proprietor.' He was referring to Lord Stevens, chairman of United Newspapers, whom I had never met. It was not long after that Esser was paid off, and I found I had little in common with his successor. Stevens then decided to get rid of all the 'old guard' – me, Junor, and others too. My direct association with the *Sunday Express* was at an end – eleven years that were my most enjoyable in journalism. Though I was occasionally asked to write for the paper under later editors, I spread my freelance net to include the *Daily Express*, *Daily Mail*, *Mail on Sunday* and *The Times*.

CHAPTER EIGHT

The People's Voice: At Home and Abroad

'In all disputes between [the people] and their rulers, the presumption is at least upon a par in favour of the people.'
    Edmund Burke, *Thoughts on the Cause of Present Discontents*
                                                                (1770)

'Boom! Boom! Boom!
That is the sound of a cowhide drum –
the Voice of Mother Africa.'
    Oswald Mtshali, *Sound of a Cowhide Drum* (1971)

THE MOST CONSISTENT pressure applied from the back benches on successive governments concerned the restoration of capital punishment for those found guilty of murder; it lasted more than twenty years, and while I was an MP I was part of every effort to reinstate the death penalty. A strong majority of the public, as measured by numerous and repeated opinion polls, strongly supported us, yet this was never reflected in the way the Commons voted. Each time the issue came up Labour and Liberal MPs were unofficially whipped against restoration regardless of the feelings of their constituents, whereas such votes always found the Tories split asunder. Among the Tories it was never a deciding factor whether you inclined to the left or the right; several Wets including Michael Mates were advocates of restoration, while out-and-out Dries like Ian Gow and John Biffen lined up against. Thatcher could always be counted to vote for restoration.

Parliament first voted to abolish hanging for an experimental period in 1965, influenced very much by the fact that an illiterate, Timothy Evans, had been executed for murders which it was later established had been committed by the much cleverer John Christie. There was also revulsion that the last woman to be executed, Ruth Ellis, was punished for a crime of passion against a treacherous lover. The experiment was confirmed by a Commons vote in 1968, though during those three years and after, as the annual figures for crimes of violence involving guns, knives and terrorist bombs shot up remorselessly, the majority of the public called for added protection. The call for an ultimate threat to deter murders of police or prison officers, soldiers, and women following sexual assault became particularly strident. There was also a general assumption among many Tory supporters in 1979 that the return of a Conservative Government would lead to the return of hanging for the most heinous murders; alas, they were to be sadly disappointed.

Those of us campaigning for restoration were often accused of being motivated by blood lust and a morbid desire for retribution; all the moral arguments, it was suggested, pointed the other way. This argument I always strongly refuted. In a *Sunday Express* article just before our vote on the issue in July 1979, under the headline 'If it is wrong to take lives, is it also wrong to save them?', I put a case for our defence:

> I fully accept that those advancing this argument do so sincerely. What I do dispute, and deeply, is the oft-stated assumption that they have a monopoly of morality on their side. The strongest argument for restoring capital punishment is an essentially moral one. I am not talking about retribution, of an eye for an eye and a tooth. I am as concerned as the Council of Churches to save life, not to take it. But surely my obligation does not stop at the lives of convicted killers. Have I not a stronger moral duty to do everything I can to save potential victims? Are their lives not God's gift too?
>
> Just look at killings in furtherance of theft, where the evidence that capital punishment was and would be an effective deterrent is overwhelming. Before abolition it was rare for burglars or bank robbers to go out armed. Now it is normal. Over the past ten years crimes involving firearms have jumped from some 1,700 to more than 8,000 each year.
>
> Nor are we talking just of gunmen. There has been a vast increase in victims battered or stabbed, often for quite small sums of money. In those ten years more than 500 men, women and children have been killed by those bent on theft in England and Wales alone. How can anyone pretend that there is not a strong chance that many of them would be alive today if a few exemplary executions had put the fear of death into every potential killer's heart?

I went on to cite the most recent example reported in the press:

> Only a few days ago two men got twelve years for killing a woman of
> eighty-four. They tied her to her bed, put tape over her eyes and mouth
> – and left her like that after taking the £400 she had saved to pay for her
> funeral. Perhaps they never intended to kill her; what is horrifying is their
> total indifference to whether she died or not. The existence of capital
> punishment would at least have prompted them to spare a thought.
> Where, I ask, is the moral virtue in those who denied that old lady that
> last shred of protection that the death penalty could have given her?'

The vote was on a motion put by Eldon Griffiths, who was parliamentary adviser to the Police Federation. Its purpose was to establish
the point of principle before any legislation was drafted. It stated simply: 'That this House demands that the sentence of capital punishment
should again be available to the courts.' It was defeated by 362 votes to
243, with many Tories joining the abolitionists.

The strongest argument against us then, as since, concerned miscarriages of justice: what if after a man was hung, fresh evidence was
uncovered suggesting that he was innocent after all? Much was still
made of the Evans-Christie case. Those who took this criticism head-
on argued that even the rare mistake should be weighed against those
potential victims whose lives had been saved by the existence of this
ultimate deterrent – but it was a difficult case to put.

Three years later, when Home Secretary William Whitelaw was taking a Criminal Justice Bill through the House, it was decided to raise
the issue again in a different context. Many had argued that the
Griffiths motion had been too general, and not attached to specific legislation; instead it would be better to offer amendments to this Bill covering specific categories of murder, so that MPs could choose which
should lead to capital punishment. Accordingly, Vivian Bendall drew up
four amendments covering terrorist acts that led to loss of human life,
murder by firearms or explosives, murder of police or prison officers,
and murder in the course of robbery or burglary, adding one catch-all
amendment: 'A person convicted of murder shall be liable to capital
punishment.' The strongest votes were recorded for the terrorism and
police/prison officers proposals, but again all were defeated heavily.

In October 1982 I decided to try to mobilise the Tory party conference in Brighton, and encouraged my constituency association to table
an amendment to the usual anodyne home affairs motion urging the
Government to give serious consideration to restoring capital punishment. I was named as the mover of the amendment, and indirectly
word was conveyed to me the night before from the National Union

executive, in whose hands the conference arrangements lay, that my amendment would be called. Other delegates were quite excited too. The same information was conveyed to Whitelaw, who was to reply from the platform; displaying his usual open generosity, he drew me aside and told me he would urge the delegates to reject my amendment – which of course was what I expected. He even included his reason for rejecting it in the advance copy of his speech circulated to the press, and so was as surprised as I was when the conference chairman got cold feet and announced at the start of the debate that he would not be calling my amendment. I suppose it was naïve of me to expect otherwise; any suggestion of allowing argument over deeply held principles at a party conference was more than enough to sending any National Union dignitary reaching for his smelling salts. Afterwards Whitelaw was apologetic, thinking that perhaps I blamed him for misleading me; but I knew the National Union mentality as well as he did, and later we joked about it over a drink.

After the 1983 general election, with a Tory majority of 144 and many new faces in the Commons, the stage was set for a further attempt at restoration. Leon Brittan was by then Home Secretary. Sir Edward Gardner, QC, crown court recorder and senior backbencher, proposed the motion: 'This House favours the restoration of the death penalty,' but first a series of amendments were put specifying categories. Albert McQuarrie wished to add 'resulting from acts of terrorism', Eldon Griffiths and Peter Blaker wished to specify murders of police officers, Vivian Bendall 'by shooting or causing an explosion', while I wished to specify 'in furtherance of theft'. All were rejected, after which Gardner's unamended motion was defeated by 223–368, with large numbers of Tories in the 368.

The next effort was in the run-up to the 1987 election, when it was felt that some anti-hanging Tories might bow to the obvious wishes of their constituents. Geoffrey Dickens used the ten-minute rule (in which ministers and the payroll vote usually abstain) to move: 'That leave be given to introduce a Bill to make it a capital offence to commit the murder of a child.' Again, defeat by 110–175. Four months later Sir Ian Percival, a former Solicitor-General making a final fling before his retirement, moved a new clause to Douglas Hurd's Criminal Justice Bill that: 'A person convicted by the unanimous verdict of a jury of the premeditated killing of another person or of knowingly and intentionally killing another person in a manner, or for a reason, or in circumstances which a reasonable person would consider to be evil, shall suffer death.' You could hardly get more legalistic than that – but still he was defeated by 230–342.

After the general election, with a Tory majority of 101 and again new faces in the Chamber, Roger Gale tried again, proposing that: 'The maximum sentence available to the courts upon a conviction for murder shall be death in the manner authorised by law. The jury shall have the power upon reaching the verdict of guilt of murder to recommend that such a sentence be passed.' This admitted the possibility of capital punishment by means other than hanging, and empowered a jury to bring pressure. Defeat again, by 218–341.

Despite all these defeats, public pressure remained strong, intensifying whenever a 'life' sentence was passed after a particularly atrocious murder. 'Let a life sentence *be* for life' was a persistent cry in the search for a meaningful deterrent, yet it would never be possible to limit judges' or indeed Home Secretaries' discretion in this way. There were repeated calls, too, for a national referendum on the matter, though I argued that this would tell us only what we knew from the opinion polls already, that around 70 per cent wanted the punishment for particularly atrocious murders to be death; even after such a verdict there would still be the need for legislation, which would bring us back to the same insurmountable hurdle. Only towards the end did I concede that such a result might induce MPs to change their minds, even though the chance of this was remote.

In December 1990, with Kenneth Baker as Home Secretary, new clauses were proposed to a Criminal Justice Bill again – that 'a person aged eighteen years or above who is convicted of the murder of a police officer acting in the execution of his duty shall on conviction be sentenced to death' (from John Greenway, a former policeman); that 'the penalty for murder shall be death' (Ivan Lawrence); or for 'murder by means of firearms, explosives or offensive weapon, or for the murder of a police or prison officer' (Teddy Taylor). All failed again.

The final attempt was in 1994, during the Criminal Justice and Public Order Bill introduced by Home Secretary Michael Howard. Elizabeth Peacock sought to add: 'The penalty for murder shall be death', while Greenway wanted the death sentence for 'the murder of a police officer in the execution of his duty'. Peacock's effort fell by 159–403. Greenway's by 186–383. Of those voting against Greenway, a hundred were Conservative MPs.

Thus the long onslaught to persuade Parliament to reverse its decision of 1965 and restore the death penalty came to naught. It was doomed to be so, since always the parliamentary pressure to restore it even to a limited extent came from within the Tory ranks; I have known Labour MPs who felt the same way as their working-class supporters that capital punishment had much to commend it, yet who never felt strongly enough to vote against their party's unofficial whip. Through those twenty years polls of public opinion registered between 64 and 82 per cent in favour of restoration, yet it made no difference; MPs exercised their own judgement regardless, and under our constitutional practice were entirely right so to do. Yet the voice of the people was ignored.

I still have no regrets over the stance I took. If that ultimate deterrent had been put in place there might have been occasional miscarriages of justice, but I remain convinced that those who turn to crime would not take the casual attitude to human life that they do now, and that many innocents who have died by knife or gun or other violent means would be alive today. But there is little certainty to history, and none whatsoever in what might have been.

Autumn 1991. I am sitting on the platform listening to Edward du Cann, 1922 Committee chairman, speaking to the annual conference of my constituency women's advisory committee, and my eye wanders across the mainly elderly audience, some accompanied by retired husbands. Suddenly it lights on an arresting pair standing alone at the back, one a middle-aged lady in a smart suit, the other a younger woman in full nurse's uniform – starched front and collar, full mid-length skirt and belt with badge clipped tightly round a slim waist. They could hardly have been members. As I sit nodding at du Cann's points, my rakish eye keeps straying back to that pair; if only we could have that kind of glamour more often at our women's meetings, I think to myself.

As I leave the platform for the lunch break, a message is passed to me that they are there because they want to see me urgently, so I make my way to them. They are from Tadworth Court, the country wing in my constituency of the famous children's hospital at Great Ormond Street in London. Eileen Childs is the unit administrator at Tadworth and Mo Atkins a senior staff nurse, and they have heard on the internal grapevine of administrators and consultants that the facilities for sick children at Tadworth Court are likely to be severely curtailed or even shut down completely. Was I prepared as their MP to join the battle to save it?

I know that all MPs have in their own constituency a hospital, home or hospice which they believe is something special, but I have always regarded Tadworth Court as something *extra* special. Since 1927 it had been part of Great Ormond Street (GOS), and was built around a splendid but decaying Queen Anne mansion. By 1981 all the patients had been moved from the mansion to a collection of buildings, some prefabricated, in the grounds at the back, and all stood at the edge of 62 acres of parkland, of which 25 acres were let out for grazing horses. It contained a home for nurses, though most of the staff were drawn from the adjacent village of Tadworth.

But the extra special thing about Tadworth Court was its patients. Before and during the war GOS used Tadworth as a sanatorium for children suffering from tuberculosis, their beds being wheeled out on to the mansion's veranda on dry nights so they could benefit from the fresh air. With the scourge of TB almost eliminated, GOS now used it for several categories of child patients: first, those with cystic fibrosis, a degenerative disease of the chest that could be held at bay by regular intravenous injections and therapy such as swimming; second, those suffering from severe and usually degenerative neurological conditions, such as Batten's Disease; third, a school for children with severe forms of spasticity; and fourth, a small number of orthopaedic cases. Ivan Lawrence, whose daughter had suffered from cystic fibrosis, explained the hospital accurately in the first adjournment debate on Tadworth Court in the Commons:

> The uniqueness of this hospital is that it is what some hospitals claim to be but few really are – a *home*. It is a place of happiness, providing care and hope for children who are terribly sick, and for some who have little hope of life. To those children, Tadworth is a second home to which they are happy to return time and again. It is a home where the parents can go to live for short periods with their sick children and be sustained themselves, where they can gain some respite from the despair of coping at home with the most handicapped of children. It is a place where parents who are cracking up under the strain can receive friendship, advice and help.
>
> Tadworth is no large multi-purpose hospital, where the nursing staff come and go, but a home where the same nurses meet the same children returning time and again for help and loving care, and the children actually run to greet them. It is a place where bureaucracy and strict timetables are secondary, and the needs of the individual child for physiotherapy, intravenous injections or a hot meal at any time of the night are paramount.'

In the months that followed my meeting with Eileen Childs and Mo Atkins I learned that every word Lawrence later uttered was true. I got to know the hospital and many of the parents of children drawn there from all over the country, and awaited with them the dreaded decision from the board of governors of GOS. That decision, to close Tadworth Court completely and transfer all its services to Queen Mary's Hospital

for Children at Carshalton, six miles away by road, was made at a governors' meeting at Tadworth Court on 17 November, 1982. Queen
Mary's had offered a thirty-bed ward for those with cystic fibrosis, multiple handicap or those needing respite care. Queen Mary's was not a
bad hospital, but certainly a bigger and very different one. As the decision was reached, there was no angry demonstration by staff and parents in the courtyard outside; all who were not on the wards simply
stood in total silence as the governors went in, and as they emerged.
And everyone – staff, parents and the GOS consultants – vowed that,
by hook or by crook, they would reverse that decision. The battle to
save Tadworth Court was on.

I include this episode briefly in my narrative for one simple reason:
that it shows how a backbencher with a flair for organisation can use it
for the benefit of his constituents and others further afield. From
November 1982 a substantial part of my time and efforts were devoted to this campaign, covering it from every angle and presenting ministers with an option that they could not refuse.

Ministers were especially important here because Great Ormond
Street, the Queen Elizabeth Hospital at Hackney and Tadworth Court
made up a special health authority, not part of the NHS regional structure but directly answerable to the Secretary of State. The GOS governors therefore had to submit their proposal direct to the Secretary of
State; this was Norman Fowler, and his Health Minister was Kenneth
Clarke. The authority was in financial difficulties, and Fowler had been
pumping extra funds into GOS so that it could cope with increasing
demands for intensive care and the latest advances in paediatric medicine, but this was a temporary expedient. The GOS governors argued
that Tadworth Court's running costs were £1.4 billion a year, and half
its beds were empty; selling the site for housing development would
yield some £3 million, easily covering the £400,000 a year they were
proposing to pay to Queen Mary's.

The closure proposal brought instant criticism from Fleet Street.
'Must the Caring Stop?' asked the *Sunday Times*. *The Daily Express*
headlined: 'Heartbreak of Happiness Hospital', the *Sun*: 'Fury as Dying
Kids' Hospital Faces the Axe', while the *Daily Mail* vowed: 'We must
fight to save this haven of hope'. The staff, led by Eileen Childs and Mo
Atkins, were no slouches in getting publicity; a group wearing their
nurse's uniforms went down Fleet Street calling at each newspaper asking to see the news editor.

With such publicity, gifts of money started to arrive at Tadworth
Court, much of it in the form of small postal orders from schoolchildren and retirement pensioners. As things stood these would have to be

sent on to the GOS authorities, yet this would defeat the gifts' purpose, since it was the governors who were trying to close the hospital down. So at the end of November I set up the Tadworth Children's Hospital Appeal Fund to receive all these donations, initially to fund our campaign, but I also inquired about registering it as a charity. It was at this point that the *Sun* newspaper weighed in behind us with its own 'The *Sun* Says Save Tadworth' campaign which it featured day after day, offering free car stickers and badges to its readers. This was real help when we most needed it, and explains why I have had a soft spot for the *Sun* ever since.

At the Commons, Lawrence was a great ally. Together we tabled two early day motions approaching the issue from different directions; they were cross-party in appeal, and attracted 160 signatures; I was particularly grateful to Ted Graham, who gave valuable support from the Labour side. Lawrence and I organised a lobby to put the case for Tadworth to Clarke; represented on it were staff, consultants, parents, The Spastics Society (since renamed) and the Cystic Fibrosis Trust. I also invited an American passing through London, John Harwood, who rang me to ask what was happening; he represented the Genesis Foundation, a wealthy trust based in Rhode Island, which came to play a crucial role in our fund-raising. Meanwhile, Lawrence and I were applying to the Speaker for adjournment debates; he was the first to come up in the ballot, and got the adjournment the day after our meeting with Clarke. I have quoted from his speech above, but he sat down before his fifteen minutes were up to make way for me. Clarke replied from the front bench; he could easily have left it to a junior minister, yet he handled the Tadworth Court issue himself throughout. In his speech he simply promised the fullest investigation into the governors' proposals.

By now we knew we were on our way. Harwood went to see Tadworth Court for himself the next day, then went to look at Queen Mary's. The comparison left him in no doubt, and soon afterwards he confirmed that the Genesis Foundation would make a matching grant to our appeal fund, meeting pound for pound all donations over a three-month period to a ceiling of £120,000 – provided that the Government guaranteed Tadworth Court a three-year life. Meanwhile I had meetings with Tim Yeo, later to become an MP and minister, but then working as director of The Spastics Society, as a result of which the society made a submission to Clarke showing how Tadworth Court could be saved by selling that part of the site not required by the hospital for housing development. By the end of December I had made my own submission to Clarke, not differing from that of The Spastics

Society, but setting out plans to raise an endowment fund to help with the continued running of the hospital. I received much help from Andrew Leslie, a reinsurance broker in the City of London, who had no doubt that with proper organisation and charitable status we could raise £500,000 – a sum beyond my wildest dreams.

Meanwhile I had to be on the alert at Westminster. Because of the number of Tory MPs writing to Clarke on Tadworth's behalf, the Conservative Research Department decided to issue a 'balanced' briefing, available to all in the Government whips office, and relying entirely on information supplied by the GOS Governors. I was furious and stormed in to see the chief whip, Michael Jopling, pointing out how biased a document it was. To his credit he withdrew it from the whips office and told the Research Department to prepare something more balanced. This they did, this time incorporating the case put by Lawrence, myself and The Spastics Society. In leading a campaign like this you have to keep your eye on different balls in the air all the time.

On 5 January, 1983, Kenneth Clarke made a full visit to Tadworth Court to meet parents, children and staff, and there is no doubt he was moved by what he saw. But still no announcement came from Fowler; it appeared that Clarke was recommending reprieve, but the matter was stuck on Fowler's desk, as still more details were required. The special projects executive from The Spastics Society, Barry Hassell, supplied them, and at the end of January Yeo wrote to Clarke pointing out the urgency; delay was having a detrimental effect on staff morale. On 7 February I secured another adjournment debate, not reached till 9 a.m., in which I summarised our rescue plan and the potential financial support from private sources. On the subject of the alternative proposals I said:

> First, Tadworth Court would be taken out of the Great Ormond Street Group and administered as a separate unit. This could take the form of a Special Health Authority or a newly formed Charitable Trust.
>
> Second, savings would be made in the running of the hospital and from removal of the obligation to maintain unwanted properties. [Tadworth Court had been left several cottages nearby, now mostly unoccupied.]
>
> Third, the respite care facility at the hospital would be opened out to take children referred directly to it by local authorities. The Spastics Society's experience here would be particularly valuable. Five neighbouring local authorities have already indicated interest in placing cases at Tadworth Court.
>
> Fourth, The Spastics Society itself will make an input to the management team.

I then covered the sale of land, and the real prospect of raising £500,000 from private sources.

> However, I must stress that all these donations will have to be returned, and all these firm pledges will go up in smoke, if the minister denies Tadworth Court the future that everyone wants.

Clarke again replied, regretting that no decision had yet been reached. Supporters from Tadworth Court, who had spent the whole night waiting in the Public Gallery, were deeply disappointed.

It was not till 13 March that I was tipped off to table a written question asking if Fowler had reached his decision, and the reprieve was announced the next day in a lengthy answer, which accepted in principle our rescue plan, though with variations. Tadworth Court would be run by a charitable trust outside the NHS, with public authorities meeting the costs of caring for the children they referred there. The surplus land would be sold, the bulk of the proceeds going to GOS. The small orthopaedic unit would be transferred to GOS as well. The hospital site would be leased to the new trust at a peppercorn rent, the endowment fund I had promised would be expected to contribute £70,000 a year, and the remaining costs would be underwritten by the Government for a three-year period. In short: victory! The voices of concerned parents had triumphed.

The second stage of the battle then began, to raise the £500,000 endowment fund I had promised. Immense help came here from Legal and General Assurance, whose main offices were in Kingswood, not far away from Tadworth. Legal and General promised to meet all my promotional costs. The first requirement was an appealing symbol or logo, for which I wanted a cuddly teddy bear with a bandaged arm. The significance of this was that children receiving treatment for cystic fibrosis received their intravenous injections through a canula on their forearm, protected by swathes of bandages. Legal and General's design department got to work, and before long christened their product 'Taddy Bear'. Taddy Bear was launched on 21 June, but planning for the three-month appeal covered by the Genesis Foundation offer had to be postponed because of the June general election. Meanwhile the first meeting of the trustees of my fund took place at the offices of Tuck and Mann and Geffen, solicitors, at 210 Strand; Bill Geffen, who lived in Surrey, agreed to be a trustee and our secretary, and saw through the application for charitable status free of charge.

The Children's Trust, newly formed to manage Tadworth Court, took over on 1 April, 1984, and its first director was Barry Hassell from The Spastics Society. Meanwhile my team were still working hard at fund-raising. At this time I had split up from Juliet, and in August took my younger son on holiday to Gloucestershire, staying in a glorified boarding house. While there I received a message to ring Kelvin Mackenzie, editor of the *Sun*, who came straight to the point: could I use another £50,000 for Tadworth Court? 'You bet!' I replied. His paper had run an appeal, called typically 'Give a Tiddler for a Toddler', asking readers who had saved all the old halfpenny pieces in jars or bottles to donate them to save an advanced bone-marrow unit for children that was threatened with closure. The response was so generous that once the bone-marrow unit had been rescued, the *Sun* still had £100,000 left, which they wanted to split between two children's charities. Thank God they remembered their campaign to save Tadworth Court two years before. The magnified cheque was ceremonially presented later that year by Brian Stevens, editor-in-chief of Associated Newspapers, who had been a friend years before when he edited TRN's *Newcastle Journal*. Meanwhile, our fund-raising had concentrated on some of the big charitable trusts, with the result that in the end we raised not the £500,000 I had promised, but £750,000.

Since then Tadworth Court and The Children's Trust have gone from strength to strength. Now they not only treat children suffering from cystic fibrosis, who with modern drugs stand a far better chance of a longer life that when I first became involved, and the sad victims of degenerative neurological conditions, but also run a good outreach service, have expanded St Margaret's to become a first-rate boarding school for cases of severe spasticity, and developed a rehabilitation unit for brain-damaged children that achieves marvellous results. Once you set aside all the Thatcherite causes for which I have fought at Westminster, the achievement I treasure most is my contribution to the continued care of very needy and special children at Tadworth Court.

———————❦———————

It was during the autumn of 1983 that the keener members of the British–South Africa Parliamentary Group assembled in a small committee room off Westminster Hall for our AGM. A hard core of around a dozen attended our meetings, though we had a larger membership than that; all took a keen interest in the troubled land of South Africa, and with the help of its embassy we met key politicians and businessmen, white and black, as they were passing through London. All our members were Tories, with the occasional cross-bench peer; Labour MPs stayed away, believing instead that the embassy should be boycotted and that our relations should be with the rebel African National

Congress (ANC). At that AGM I thought we had the officers for that session tied up nicely: John Carlisle (the 'Hon. Member for Pretoria South') would continue as chairman, while Nick Winterton and I would be the joint deputies. As we were about to begin we heard a clamour from the narrow corridor outside, and around twenty Labour MPs burst in. One pound coins were slapped on the table – the cost of annual membership. We were being ambushed!

We eyed each other angrily. Carlisle reported briefly on the past year's activities, and the treasurer reported a healthy balance. Carlisle then handed the chair to Winterton, his senior deputy, to conduct the vote for chairman, and the Labour posse proposed Donald Anderson, by far the most likeable Member among them, as chairman instead. But Carlisle, temporarily relieved of the chair, was delving among his papers, and produced with a flourish the rules of the group, one of which stipulated that those eligible to vote at an AGM had to have been paid-up members for, as I recollect, three months before. A furious argument then ensued, but rules could not be ignored, so the Labour contingent scooped their coins off the table and stalked out in high dudgeon. Soon after that a rival body was formed, the British–South*ern* Africa Group, for ANC sympathisers; the divide among MPs over South Africa thus became as deep and bitter as the divide in that country itself.

I assert categorically that those in our group were never supporters of apartheid; we looked forward to reform as keenly as any, but we knew this could not be achieved through the ANC's 'armed struggle' or by trade sanctions which only fostered in the whites a '*laager* mentality'. We mirrored very much the view of Margaret Thatcher herself – that of course apartheid was morally and politically unacceptable, but that Britain, as an old friend with strong historical and family connections with South Africa, should help and encourage all its politicians to make a peaceful transition into a modern democracy.

I fell in love with South Africa and its peoples on my first visit early in 1979, when Parliament was adjourned for the Scottish and Welsh referenda on devolution. Though I played such an active role in opposing the Labour Government's legislation (see Chapter Five), there was absolutely nothing an English MP could do to help in the referendum campaigns so I seized the chance to fly to Johannesburg. I had to pay for my flight there, but as soon as I stepped off the plane I was taken under the wing of the South Africa Foundation, financed largely by the country's big business corporations. It was supported by the National Government, but presented its guests with an unbiased view of the country and its problems. In Johannesburg and Pretoria I had my own guide who took me to meetings with politicians, business and religious leaders, including strong opponents of the Government. I remember most clearly my guide in Cape Town – a coloured (mixed-race) young woman; the coloureds' natural tongue was Afrikaans and they shared much of the culture of the Boers, yet they were then denied any role in national government. They were very distinct from the blacks, who had their own languages and cultures, and were very critical of blacks taking city jobs they believed were theirs by right. My guide was attractive, well-educated and of liberal persuasion; she lived with her family at Mitchell's Plain, a middle-class coloured township on Cape Flats. As she drove the car or stopped for a refresher she gave me sound lessons in the structure of South African society; she was convinced that apartheid would crumble, yet was totally opposed to the violence of the ANC; she said the system of Bantu education was a disgrace – which it certainly was – and that until it was reformed, blacks would never be able to pull themselves up by their bootstraps. She drove me to Stellenbosch, centre of the wine industry, and to Kyalisha, the vast squatter camp outside Cape Town with its tightly packed shacks of corrugated iron and plastic sheeting. On a subsequent visit I was shown the Government's attempts to replace Kyalisha with low-cost social housing, yet this was a race it could never win; every time I returned the squatter shacks had multiplied, spreading as far as you could see either side of the main highway.

I was not to return to South Africa till 1985, but in 1983 I was part of a Commonwealth Parliamentary Association delegation to Zambia. We were received with great charm by President Kenneth Kaunda, who gave us dinner where we drank South African wine – so much for those at home who lectured us for buying South African oranges. But charming though he was, it seemed to me he was trying to run a command economy, largely through his henchmen. When the world price of copper, the country's staple export, was high he allowed Zambian agriculture to decay; Zambia should have been the bread basket of Southern Africa, but wherever we went we saw tractors, no doubt provided through overseas aid, rusting in the fields. After a while, the price of copper slumped. Our High Commissioner told me of a rural school that had been provided with a new toilet block, but it was kept padlocked, while the children ran off into the bush to defecate as they had always done. Why was the toilet block locked? Because the school was still waiting for a minister to come to declare it open, the joyous event to be filmed and relayed to an admiring public by state-controlled television; such was the nature of Kaunda's regime. In Luangwa National Park I saw miles of tree stumps torn to their roots by unculled elephants; in later years ivory poachers did what the Lusaka Government should have done, in the process pushing the cull too far the other way.

In February 1985 I was back in South Africa, this time with my wife Helen, on a three-week tour organised for us by the Government's Information Section. Obviously they wished us to form a good impression of the country and its ministers, and many of the briefings, this time covering the security aspect as well, were of a propagandist nature. Their aim was not to sell the apartheid system to us, but rather to show how it was being reformed, proof of their desire to reach a political accommodation with the black majority. Unfettered access was provided to the Government's strongest critics, some of them dangerously close to the ANC, while editors and political commentators also contributed a caustic view. One vivid memory I have is of learning for the first time of the role played by the fundamentalist black churches in voicing the desire of many thousands of their members for peaceful change. The country's free-market system worked well, giving many enterprising black businessmen the means of advancement, though its overweight bureaucracy appeared to be a vast employment expansion scheme for whites only. Certainly there were elements in the ruling National Party who had doubts about the reformist views expressed by their ministers, but in general the approach taken by the Information Section was as liberal as could be expected in such a deeply divided country. A number of British MPs were given similar hospitality, which largely explains why the complexities of reforming apartheid were better understood at Westminster than in most western legislatures, though some did give support to the ANC on returning.

After this I made regular visits to South Africa, sometimes twice a year, including three to Namibia, under South African rule until 1994. Sometimes I was invited by the Information Section, often by the International Freedom Foundation (of which more below), and once by the coal mining industry in its battle against international sanctions. My final visit, shortly before the eventual multi-racial election, was at my own expense. Often my companions were the same Tory MPs who had consistently taken an interest in the boiling cauldron that was South Africa – the 'Africa hands', as we came to be called.

Pleading tolerance for the National Party's slow but steady reform of apartheid, already under way before my visit in 1979, and total opposition to trade sanctions, which hurt only the South African peoples, not its rulers, provided much meat for my parliamentary campaigning and for my regular articles in the *Sunday Express*. In May 1984 I wrote defending Thatcher's invitation to President Botha to visit Chequers on his tour of European capitals. 'An insult to Britain's black community' Liberal leader David Steel called it; 'like inviting Hitler' said Labour's Peter Hain; but I knew the Prime Minister was thinking long term, to how with firm but friendly understanding Britain could hasten the 'wind of change'. In 1987 I covered for the *Sunday Express* the by-election at Helderberg, where Dr Denis Worrall – lately ambassador to London for four years, architect of South Africa's latest constitution sharing parliamentary power with coloureds and Asians, and an old personal friend – was standing as an Independent. In 1984, my last article on South Africa was an exclusive interview with the new President, F.W. de Klerk – to the best of my knowledge the first he gave to a popular UK paper. As he told me:

> We must create a new South Africa, free of domination by anyone. White domination must go, there must be a genuine sharing of power by all races. We will soon take the initiative and put forward proposals for discussion.

All our hopes for South Africa were at last in sight of being fulfilled. The voice of *all* its peoples would then be heard.

However, by far the biggest spur to my invective was the need to counter mounting pressure from the liberal intelligentsia, from overseas governments and, inevitably, from the Foreign Office, to tighten trade sanctions. My opposition to seeking to effect political change though sanctions was deep, and continues to this day. It is not simply that sanctions are expensive to enforce and easy to avoid – both old Rhodesia and South Africa itself discovered that. My real objection is that sanctions never hit the rulers, only the ruled, and that even if sanctions *are* effective they obstruct rather than encourage political change within a society. I knew that if imports of South African wine or fruit were barred from Britain, the immediate result would be vast numbers of blacks in the Cape losing their jobs and being thrown into poverty before moving in despair to squatter camps like Kyalisha. I remembered the manager of a factory making leather goods in a black township outside Johannesburg, an enterprise supported by international charities, telling me that he was laying off workers because his overseas markets were being shut off. Whenever I met Chief Mangosuthu Buthelezi of KwaZulu in Ulundi, he made the same forceful point. I also remain convinced that the arguments against sanctions to achieve political ends in South Africa in the 1980s apply with equal force in the very different circumstances of Iraq today.

The pressure from the Conservative ranks on Thatcher not to yield to international, European Community and foreign office pressure to

tighten sanctions was strong and sustained; we knew her objectives
were the same as ours, but it was necessary for us to demonstrate constantly that the party at Westminster and beyond were totally behind
her. In June 1986, when she being bullied by heads of several
Commonwealth Governments (often with a considerable degree of
hypocrisy), Julian Amery and I organised a high-powered deputation to
her in Downing Street urging her to stick to her guns. Thank goodness
for the people of South Africa that was exactly what she did.

Several of my trips to South Africa were sponsored by the
International Freedom Foundation (IFF), an organisation based in the
USA and reportedly funded largely by international commodity bro-
kers. I believe it also received funds and certainly co-operation from
South Africa's Security Service, though it never sought to defend
apartheid. Remember this was the time of the Cold War, when the
Soviets were training insurrectionists and providing them with money
and arms across the world, not least in South Africa and over its borders. IFF's declared aim was to foster democracy throughout the
world, which it did in South Africa too. At a time when many in the
National Party still hoped for reform with institutional representation
along racial lines, the IFF executive director in South Africa, Russel
Crystal, insisted there could be no alternative to one man one vote for
open legislatures, ideally within a federal structure. IFF was definitely
not, as its critics claimed, a pro-apartheid front. At Westminster I
organised about ten of the Africa hands into a group called Friends of
the Freedom Foundation; we met monthly for lunch at L'Amicos in
Horseferry Road with IFF's London officers. In 1989 the IFF organised a monitoring group of international parliamentarians, which I led,
to witness the first free elections under UN auspices in Namibia. Later,
after the Berlin Wall was torn down, it opened offices in the Baltic
States and then in Moscow itself. I attended a Westerners' seminar it
organised in Budapest on fostering communication in countries throwing off the yoke of communism. But alas, IFF over-reached itself; after
President Bush was defeated its funding was severely curtailed, and it
retreated to become a Washington research institute.

Many of the 'Africa hands' were fascinated during this period by the
experience of Bophuthatswana, generally called simply Bop, one of four
independent self-governing territories established under the apartheid
doctrine of tribal separation. For this reason their independence was
never recognised internationally. Six other tribal territories, including
KwaZulu, which I also visited frequently, chose to remain constitu-
tionally within the Republic of South Africa. Bop, homeland of the
Tswana tribes, was divided into seven separate territories, later merged

into six, with a total population of some 2.5 million, and was governed
from its capital, Mmabatho. It was best known internationally for Sun
City, a big sporting, leisure and gambling complex built out of the
bush. The full tribal area became part of South Africa only as a result
of British betrayal in the nineteenth century. While the territory of
northern Batswana was made a British protectorate, later becoming the
Commonwealth country of Botswana, the territory of southern
Batswana was made a Crown colony with the promise it would never
be annexed to Cape Colony. The colonial administration tore up this
pledge in 1895, freeing the Boers and British settlers to seize the old
tribal lands. You can understand why in the 1970s the Tswanas welcomed even circumscribed independence, with the chance to be free
from apartheid.

   If there was a leader of our group it was Andrew Hunter, a former
teacher at Harrow School, who formed a deep love of the Tswana peoples and of their culture, and was a respected adviser to Bop's
President, Lucas Mangope. I came to know Mangope well – a
Christian, caring, conservative leader of his people, a good example of
the breed often thrown up by the tribal system.

   We were fascinated by Bop because it showed how a state within the
borders of South Africa could be governed well without apartheid and
with a free market. The Tswanas voted in their own National Assembly
(dominated by one party as in so many tribal states); Mangope was a
benevolent President whose Cabinet was made up of blacks and whites,
many of the latter having come from Rhodesia when it passed into
black rule, bringing with them experience in finance and administration. Relations with the white farmers, particularly around Mafeking,
were good, as they were with the white managers of the platinum
mines, which yielded good revenue. Bop was interested in us, first
because it yearned for international recognition, and second because,
like all other southern African states, it was competing for international investment.

   I paid many visits to Bop. On one occasion I was enlisted to conduct
a seminar for National Assembly members on how Westminster's democratic system worked; they were enthusiastic and asked intelligent
questions, but I strayed onto dangerous ground when I made fun of the
hereditary principle in the Lords; what was wrong with that, these
products of the tribal system asked? Then, in 1991, Hunter and I were
asked by Mangope to suggest how Bop should react to the rapidly
changing situation in the South African Republic itself. We had a nine-
ty-minute discussion in Pretoria with South Africa's Foreign Minister,
Pik Botha, who was obviously wanting us to act as go-between to

encourage Mangope to engage constructively in the coming negotiations with the ANC on a new constitution, rather than wait to see
where they would lead. We met the Foreign Minister of Botswana and
others in Gabarone, which at least put paid to the romantic notion held
in Bop that they could somehow link up with their kinsmen to the
north; and we went to Ulundi in KwaZulu, still an integral part of
South Africa and so automatically part of the negotiations, to establish
what common interest there was between Buthelezi and Mangope.
Buthelezi's Inkatha movement was by then engaged in a bloody war
with ANC units across KwaZulu and Natal. I quote from our report:

> It must be in Bop's interest to become fully involved in the constitution-
> al negotiations after the multi-party conference expected later this year –
> at the same time keeping its options open on whether to be part of a final
> settlement. The Governments in Pretoria, Ulundi and Gabarone – who
> share a number of ideals with Bop – all agree on this.
>
> Once in such negotiations Bop would have natural allies in arguing for
> a federal structure with maximum devolution of power to the constituent
> parts. These potential allies also believe their case would be strengthened
> by Bop's participation.

Subsequently Mangope agreed that Bop should have full observer status in the talks, with freedom to join in when its interests were affected, but the dream of a fully federal constitution was alas lost, with the
ANC insisting on central control.

Sir Robert Renwick took up post as British ambassador to South
Africa in 1987, and he was a positive spur to the cause of reform. I met
him regularly, either in Pretoria or at his residence in Cape Town's
Bishopscourt, with its lush garden overlooking Table Mountain. Once
de Klerk was installed as President, he looked to Renwick for helpful
advice in times of difficulty, and was always given it. Renwick certainly
gave advice leading to the release of Nelson Mandela and the unban-
ning of ANC in 1990, and on how to handle various fraught situations
as they arose. This, of course, was exactly how Thatcher had planned
events would work out, with help and advice from Britain leading to the
destruction of apartheid, instead of the counter-productive antagonism
shown by many other heads of state. I still feel proud of how she won
through, and of my own small part in the ensuing transformation of
South Africa.

It has always been an inspiration to me how peoples far less educated
and sophisticated than we think ourselves to be have risen to the chal-

lenge of democracy. On my first visit to India, when I travelled from Calcutta, where all the problems of the subcontinent are writ large, to Luchnow and then New Delhi, I found myself viewing the Taj Mahal and then Fatehpur Sikri on the day of the country's general election, when Mrs Gandhi was seeking to regain power. We were the last allowed into the deserted red city before the gates closed; the sight of those confident structures, built by the Mogul Emperor Akbar then later deserted when the lake supplying the city's water became salinated was impressive enough, but on leaving I was greeted by a sight I shall never forget: when we entered, the steps had been crowded with beggars, but now they were all crouched around transistor radios listening to the early election results. All were rooting for Mrs Gandhi, and cheers went up as some piece of news pointed to her winning. Here were the outcasts of society – blind, leprous or suffering other deformities – yet they were following this contest as if its outcome would make the slightest difference to their miserable lives!

Years later when I was in Namibia observing its first-ever free election under UN auspices I saw families forming orderly queues across the sand throughout the night, bringing their children with them, so as to be the first to cast their vote after having their thumbs smudged with indelible ink to prevent them voting twice. The same enthusiasm was evident in South Africa during the first free multi-racial election there. In Israel I have marvelled how its citizens cling voraciously to their democratic system, despite all the threats from their neighbours to drive them into the sea; you would have thought in these circumstances they might turn to some dictator offering safety, but not a bit. In my own lifetime we have seen the Hungarians, the Czechs and the Poles all making heroic sacrifices to throw off the Soviet yoke.

How sad it is therefore to see how in our own country, which with the United States was the birthplace of parliamentary democracy, our citizens' control over their own destinies is being slowly but steadily whittled away, not by a Government that despises the House of Commons, but by an ever-growing European bureaucracy seeking to take ever more power unto itself.

CHAPTER NINE

Crown Princes and Betrayal

'There is no act of treachery or meanness of which a political party is not capable; for in politics there is no honour.'
Benjamin Disraeli, *Vivien Gray* (1824)

'He who wields the knife never wins the crown.'
Michael Heseltine, *New Society* (1986)

'Treachery with a smile on its face.'
Margaret Thatcher, *The Thatcher Years*, BBC (1993)

NOVEMBER 29, 1989. The steering committee of the 92 are assembled at 10 Downing Street for a consultation with the Prime Minister. To the best of my knowledge we were all present – Vivian Bendall, Bob Dunn, Jill Knight, James Pawsey, Marion Roe, John Townend and myself. We were but six days away from the leadership ballot triggered by the challenge from arch-Wet Sir Anthony Meyer, but that did not particularly concern us; we knew the 'dripping Wets' would vote for him, but few others. (We were to be proved right; he scored only thirty-three votes, though the twenty-four who deliberately spoiled their ballot papers represented an ominous sign.) We also knew the Prime Minister had a very small team actively identifying possible waverers and that this team included Tristan Garel-Jones, by this time a Minister of State at the Foreign Office – we had heard him boasting about it. Our purpose was to warn her that, though the ballot result was predictable, a number of our members felt she was in danger of losing touch with backbenchers.

Thatcher greeted us quite effusively, pressing full measures of whisky on us all, and the discussion began amiably enough, but we all knew that Dunn had something he was burning to say. I gave him a nod, and he launched in:

'Prime Minister, we feel we must warn you to beware of Tristan Garel-Jones. He may appear to you to be totally supportive, but he's not. He's just waiting for you to put a foot wrong.'

Thatcher looked aghast.

'But ... Tristan,' she almost spluttered, 'he's *one of us*.'

It was our turn to look horrified.

'Bob's right,' we joined in. 'Tristan's – he's so slippery. You'd be well advised to keep him at arm's length.' But it was evident she did not believe us. In *The Downing Street Years* she records her surprise when, just one year later, Garel-Jones declined her invitation to act as a lieutenant in her planned second-ballot fight-back against Heseltine. Of course he declined – he must have been waiting for that moment for years. Also, had she but known it, the pessimism over her chances she encountered on that fateful evening when she saw her Cabinet one by one, and which so demoralised her, was largely the product of Garel-Jones' spin-doctoring.

Poor Margaret; she never was good at distinguishing between those who supported her because they shared her convictions, and those who cosied up to her in order to further their personal political ends. In the end she did learn – but by then it was far too late.

It is not up to any leader to determine who should succeed him or her, but it is prudent to start grooming some other cabinet colleague for the role. *In The Downing Street Years* Thatcher records how after her third election victory in 1987 she thought of retiring 'perhaps halfway into the next Parliament', and her view that her successor should come, not from her own generation, but the next:

> In the next generation ... there was a variety of candidates who ought to be tested in high office: John Major, Douglas Hurd, Ken Baker, Ken Clarke, Chris Patten and perhaps Norman Lamont and Michael Howard. But I did have the obligation to see that there are several proven candidates from whom to choose.

This was a pretty big field. But long before this there had been other crown princes whom she was known to regard favourably, and whose names would have featured in any Tory backbencher's reply to the lobby correspondents' age-old question, 'Who would follow if the PM were to fall under a number 11 bus?' But, alas, tragedy of a different kind was to befall them all.

Let us start with the first of the crown princes to come a cropper: Cecil Edward Parkinson. Six years younger than Thatcher, he had certainly got on well with her during his time as an opposition whip from 1974 to 1976, if not earlier; on becoming Prime Minister she made him Minister for Trade, and their personal friendship prospers to this day. He is very much in her mould, a self-made man of respectable but modest background, a natural Conservative since his youth, and deeply patriotic. He came into his own during the Falklands War, when he was a key figure in Thatcher's War Cabinet; from there he moved to become Party Chairman, arguably the political peak of his career. He built up to a brilliant election campaign, and could justifiably claim to be the architect of Thatcher's 144 majority in 1983. After polling day the highest offices of state were within his grasp – but that was before the world heard of Sara Keays.

Sleaze has never been far removed from politics, but it is necessary to distinguish between the two varieties: financial sleaze and sexual sleaze. Only a select few have merited the title of 'Grand Master of the Honourable Order of Sleazebags' by being involved in both. But many politicians have seen their careers brought to an end by financial sleaze; one thinks of Tory ex-Chancellor Reginald Maudling, tainted by his connection with the corrupt T. Dan Smith who secured through bribery council building contracts in the north-east in the 1960s, Labour's John Stonehouse, jailed in the 1970s not for running off with his mistress and feigning death by drowning, but for defrauding insurance companies for the benefit of his wife, and the Tory Tim Smith, who resigned in 1992 after admitting he collected money in brown envelopes from Harrods chairman Mohammed Al-Fayed. There have been Tory MPs 'persuaded' not to seek re-election after their dealings with local property speculators became known. Financial sleaze in politics has almost always been punished.

However, in matters of sexual sleaze the public and the press used to be much more tolerant. The first minister I knew to fall from grace after a sleazy relationship was John Profumo, war minister under Harold Macmillan; he had to resign not for sleeping with Christine Keeler, nor for the security risks of sharing her favours unbeknown to him with a Russian diplomat, but because he lied about his relationship in a personal statement to the Commons. This was the equivalent of lying under oath in court; that was what made his resignation inevitable, not the sexual indiscretion itself.

Tolerance of and discretion over sexual peccadilloes was still observed when I became a Member in 1974. Humphrey Atkins was opposition Chief Whip from 1974 to 1979, and had as his secretary in the whips' office a very personable young woman called Lulu. After a while it became obvious that she was pregnant, and everyone at Westminster knew Atkins was the father; Thatcher knew, MPs and their secretaries knew, and so did most political correspondents – yet never did any hint of this appear in newspaper columns. Atkins's wife stood by him, while he did the gentlemanly thing and made sure that Lulu and her child were well cared for. Never was it suggested that she had expected to become his wife. I can well remember Lulu proudly bringing her child one lunchtime into the Members' Bar ('the Kremlin'), where Labour and Tory MPs, including myself, tickled the baby's feet and made cooing noises as people normally do on such occasions. Yet *still* nothing appeared in the press; Atkins subsequently became Secretary of State for Northern Ireland and then Lord Privy Seal, serving as Foreign Secretary Lord Carrington's voice in the Commons, before receiving his well-earned peerage.

But Parkinson was not so lucky. He broke the news that he had a mistress and that she was expecting his baby to Thatcher on the night of the 1983 election, thereby casting a shadow over her celebration of the excellent result; before long the news was out – and so were the knives. So why did Parkinson suffer so badly, while Atkins escaped unscathed? There were similarities between the two cases: both men stayed with their wives, nor was there ever any doubt that Parkinson, a fairly wealthy man, would make proper financial provision for his mistress and their child; the stark difference was that, unlike Lulu, Keays expected her lover to leave his wife for her, and when scorned she exacted bitter public retribution. Ironically, there might have been less furore if Parkinson had ditched Ann to marry Keays; those who chose to take what they saw as the high moral ground never have been able to counter that point. There was also the difference that no other Tories ever saw Atkins as a long-term threat to their own preferment, whereas Parkinson was clearly in the road to the top and thus a sitting target for their vilification.

The Prime Minister clearly believed Parkinson had done the right thing in staying with Ann, and appointed him Secretary for Trade and Industry in the hope that the fuss would die down. But the matter would not go away, and it was with some trepidation that his friends, including me, prepared for the Blackpool party conference that October. I went to Blackpool early as usual, at the same time as all the journalists, in the hope of helping to set the tone through media interviews, and was invited to appear on several radio and TV programmes. Most of all I remember a BBC studio interview, with Parkinson due to come on before the end of the programme; never have I seen a politician so defensive and nervous. By this time my own conference receptions – held when we were in Blackpool at a Greek restaurant near the Winter Gardens – were a regular event, attended by Reigate's constituency activists and various parliamentary friends; these receptions became a useful venue for right-wingers when trouble was brewing, and on this occasion those attending expressed strong support for Parkinson. However, it became clear to me that his standing had suffered among the party's strongest supporters, not so much for having had an affair with his secretary but for his earlier apparent indecision over whether he wanted to stay with Keays or with his wife; this was taken as evidence of confusion of judgement, boding ill for a future senior minister who would be called upon to make difficult choices the whole time. When Parkinson came to reply from the platform to the trade and industry debate his nervousness was painful to behold, but he had the sympathy of delegates, who gave him a standing ovation which meant 'stick at it and we'll stick with you'. However, a further onslaught followed from Keays that made his position untenable, and within a week he resigned from the Cabinet. Not until after the following election did Thatcher deem it safe to bring him back into the Cabinet, where he served well as Secretary for Energy, completing the privatisation of the electricity industry, and at Transport. After Nigel Lawson's resignation I hoped he might become Chancellor – a job he would have done well – but the younger John Major was Thatcher's choice. Parkinson then knew he could go no further, and after Thatcher's downfall he returned to the world of business. His old jaunty confidence returned, and in 1992 he became chairman of Conservative Way Forward, which I helped to found (see Chapter One); in that capacity I heard him deliver some brilliant, tightly argued speeches commending the Thatcherite vision. He later brought experience to William Hague's leadership as Party Chairman, seeing through a root-and-branch reform of the party's organisation, yet the Sara Keays scandal dogged him for the rest of his political life.

Another crown prince to come to an untimely end was Nigel Lawson. Seven years younger than Thatcher, from the moment he entered Parliament in the same February 1974 intake as myself, he stood out as a brilliant economist and persuasive politician. After our second election defeat that year he was among the first to give his opinion openly in the smoking room that Heath's leadership was highly vulnerable. Under Thatcher's leadership he became a junior opposition whip and then front-bench spokesman on treasury affairs; both she and shadow chancellor Geoffrey Howe came to rely greatly upon Lawson's research and advocacy in developing their alternative to a prices and incomes policy. When Thatcher formed her first Government, Lawson was a natural Financial Secretary to the Treasury, and in two years was in the Cabinet as Energy Secretary. After the tactical retreat before Arthur Scargill, ordered by Thatcher upon David Howell early in 1981, it fell to Lawson to build up coal stocks away from the pitheads ready for the next and final confrontation.

1983 saw Lawson appointed Chancellor of the Exchequer – a rise through Government Office far more meteoric than John Major's a few years later. He was very much an 'economist's Chancellor', sharing with Roy Jenkins the distinction of having gained a First at Oxford in PPE. But he was also a Thatcherite Chancellor too, responsible for many tax reforms including the introduction of tax-free Personal Equity Plans (PEPs) giving ordinary people the chance to become capitalists, so underpinning the property-owning democracy. I always saw a touch of Disraeli about him, taking at times considerable risks with total confidence. Though he never gave any hint that he had leadership ambitions, if in 1988 you had asked Tory MPs who might prove to be Thatcher's successor, quite a number would have plumped for Lawson.

When the break came with Thatcher it was bitter. The causes of it are well documented in his memoirs and in hers; his exchange rate policy became one of 'shadowing' the Deutschmark, unbeknown to her, and culminated with the ultimatum, delivered to her with Foreign Secretary Howe before the 1989 European Council in Madrid, that if she would not give a firm commitment that Britain would join the Exchange Rate Mechanism (ERM), they would both resign. She bowed to their pressure, against her own better judgement – but never forgave either of them for it. The immediate cause of Lawson's resignation in October 1989 was the Prime Minister's refusal to sack Sir Alan Walters, her economic policy guru, whose advice ran counter to his, but by then Lawson was fed up and left to put his economic knowledge to better personal use in the City. So another crown prince bit the dust. His resignation was the first real warning of the destructive potential lurking within the European issue for the Conservative Party.

――――――――・◁◯▷・――――――――

By the time Lawson resigned yet another crown prince had been and gone: Norman Beresford Tebbit, darling of the right and viewed with a shrewd respect by many others in the party. I have already described his devastating role in opposition, and his reforms of trade union law as Employment Secretary. In 1983 he became Secretary for Trade and Industry, where he was responsible for a far-reaching reform of financial services.

On 12 October, 1984, I woke early at my conference hotel on Brighton's sea front. I had heard the urgent sound of sirens during the night, but that was not why I tuned into the first news bulletins; the previous day I had written an article for the *Sunday Express*, and I wanted to check whether there had been any overnight developments that might require me to make changes to it. As soon as I heard that the IRA had bombed the Grand Hotel where the Prime Minister and half her Cabinet were staying, and that there could be dead or injured people beneath the rubble, I immediately phoned John Junor at home. Yes, of course a totally different article was needed, and he wisely told me to take my time over it. I then dressed and walked the short distance to the Grand through cordoned-off and strangely silent streets to see the wreckage and talk to friends who had been inside.

Twelve days later I drove to Brighton to see my old friend Tebbit in his hospital bed. Much of his flesh had been torn away by the bomb, and he was in evident pain; but far worse than that was the knowledge that his wife Margaret lay elsewhere in the same hospital with wounds bound to paralyse her for life. We talked about the medical prognoses for him and for her, and he showed me some of the cards he had received, painted and written by schoolchildren, which touched him profoundly. He obviously had been thinking deeply about his future – *their* future – and it was he who brought the subject up, not me, along the following lines:

> You know, George, after something like this you think a lot about what your life's about. I know I shall be on my feet again, but Margaret will need a lot of care and nursing. One way forward would be to quit politics, but I'm buggered if I'm going to give these IRA thugs what they want. I'm going to fight on.
>
> But there's something else I've decided too. I believe that in Margaret [Thatcher] we've got the best Prime Minister we've ever seen; she has all the strength we need. But I've also seen how some colleagues can barely tolerate her, and are just waiting for the chance to pull her down. If that should happen then I won't allow her cause to lapse; I shall stand for election as leader myself.

I was amazed by the man's courage. There he was, a human wreck lying on his hospital bed, contemplating the most physically arduous job of all in politics – that of Prime Minister. However, as we came to find out, neither Tebbit nor his wife were short on courage. That evening, by coincidence, there was a 92 dinner at which I reported to members on how I had found their colleague – but naturally I said nothing of the fact that another crown prince had declared himself to me.

One year later, when Tebbit had recovered (though he still suffered strain from his wounds), we pressed successfully for his appointment as Party Chairman in place of the limp John Gummer, who, it should in fairness be said, was doing the job part-time anyway. Tebbit was very popular among the rank and file, and it was he who built the party up for its 1987 triumph. At the time of his appointment Thatcher thought he might even in time become her successor, but she saddled him with an unfortunate deputy chairman in Jeffrey Archer, who, though a good speaker, caused many difficulties by blundering into policies of his own 'on the hoof'.

We on the right hoped Tebbit would take a grip on the apparatchiks of Central Office, but in this we were disappointed. Though he did well to make the astute Michael Dobbs his chief of staff, he never conducted the purge of Central Office time-servers that was required; indeed, he ended up taking too much of their advice. His worst mistake was closing down the independent-minded Federation of Conservative Students (FCS), who had become the cutting edge of Thatcherism in the universities. The pretext was a call by one of its officers, Harry Phibbs, for former Prime Minister Harold Macmillan to be put on trial as a war criminal for his part in sending Cossacks in exile in this country at the war's end back to Soviet Russia and certain death. It was of course a preposterous suggestion, but was seized on by CCO apparatchiks who had wanted to shut down the inconveniently free-thinking FCS for years. Ironically, two of those FCS stalwarts are now on the Tory benches – John Bercow and Nick Gibb, both men of whom Tebbit would approve.

Tebbit also made a mistake over the Greenwich by-election in February 1987 by sending in as 'support' what even in Central Office were known as the 'B team', whose blunders became a joke in the national press, and who allowed the SDP's Rosie Barnes a clear run against an unpopular Labour candidate. As president of the Greenwich Conservative Association I brought in a team of canvassers from the 92 in support of John Antcliffe, a sound candidate, but we might as well have not bothered. Though he had an unerring instinct for detecting and exploiting the weak points in the soft underbelly of the Labour Party, Tebbit was not the best of administrators.

Thatcher always felt great tenderness for Tebbit and his wife after the Brighton bomb. Once, at Sunday lunch at Chequers, I watched as she

squatted beside the other Margaret's wheelchair and spooned food up
to her mouth. She knew that the bomb had been intended for her, and
felt deeply that an old friend should have been so crippled as a consequence.

As the next election approached she became unsettled over the
direction of the party's propaganda, formulated as it was by the Saatchi
agency, and gave equal weight to alternative suggestions fed to her by
Tim Bell, a competitor of Saatchis, supported by his own firm's opinion poll findings that were much more pessimistic than those of
Saatchis. A subversive mood of creative tension was thus built into the
campaign – as Thatcher later remarked, often more tense than creative.
Tim Bell's alternative strategy came to be espoused by Lord Young,
drafted into Smith Square to help Tebbit, all of which culminated in
'wobbly Thursday' a week before polling, when Thatcher openly questioned Tebbit's judgement. Young was a sound enough politician, but
lacked the experience of ever having fought an election himself; nevertheless, this was a situation that should never have been allowed to
arise. It served to confirm a feeling that had been growing in Tebbit's
mind that if he was to provide properly for his crippled wife as they
both grew older, he could not do so on a minister's salary. He could
earn far more using his experience of trade and industry in private business and exploiting his gift for the telling phrase in journalism – which
is what he did. In the event, contrary to predictions by many in the
press and by the BBC, Thatcher was handed a majority of 101.

Tebbit did not go to the Lords quickly, but remained MP for
Chingford till the 1992 election. He was thus still in the Commons
when Thatcher was badly mauled by Heseltine in the first leadership
ballot in November 1990. When she resigned he came under pressure
from many friends to throw his hat into the ring; for the likes of me, he
would have been a far better choice than either Heseltine, Hurd or
Major. He thought about it, but wisely rejected the advice. The time for
such initiatives was past; Heseltine had put his time out of Cabinet to
good political use, while Tebbit had not, and many colleagues who
loved him dearly would have judged that his health made him a non-
runner. But for the IRA, things might have been very different.

---------••⟨∞⟩••---------

Next of the crown princes was John Edward Michael Moore. He began
his political life as students' union president at the London School of
Economics, then while working as a banker in the USA he served the
Democrats and met his American wife Sheila. Thatcher made him a

vice-chairman at Central Office in 1975 to cover youth issues; Moore gave more attention to his physical condition than most politicians, and still played soccer. The youthful image stayed with him; after he joined the Cabinet in 1986 he was put in charge of the election planning group working on policies for young people; Thatcher remarks in her memoirs that he was 'the nearest we had in Cabinet to a young person' – and by then he was all of forty-eight. By contrast, William Hague was thirty-four when he entered the Cabinet, and thirty-six when he became party leader.

Moore was gentle and soft-spoken; indeed, it was often difficult to hear his conversation at all. He drew his friends from both wings of the party. I once joined him at his Wimbledon home when he was also entertaining Nick Scott, Wetter than whom one could not get. Partly because Moore was thought to be 'a bit of a trendy', and partly because of his manner and LSE/Democrat Party background, he was seen initially among colleagues as being of Wet inclination. But this was not so at all; indeed, by the mid-1980s it would have been hard to find a more convinced Thatcherite.

His most telling experience came in 1981, when as junior energy minister he saw the first strike threat over pit closures from Arthur Scargill; Secretary of State David Howell was all for fighting, but Thatcher ordered a tactical retreat. Moore knew that the cost of producing Welsh coal was not covered by its selling price to the Central Electricity Generating Board; foreign coal was far cheaper, but any idea of importing this instead of using British coal found other ministers and civil servants raising their hands in horror. Why, Moore asked himself, should this be so?

When in 1983 he was drafted to the Treasury he found that there was no such thing as an overall government strategy for future privatisations, so he set about providing one. Several cabinet ministers whom he consulted thought he was mad, believing it was natural that many industries, especially the public utilities, should remain nationalised. In January 1984 he produced a paper for the Cabinet setting out a five-year rolling programme for future privatisations. Thatcher was ecstatic, saying 'This is absolutely marvellous, isn't it?' as her eye roved around the faces at the Cabinet table. Not one minister dared to express dissent, so Moore's rolling programme became government policy. Its bold radical thrust mirrored what Tebbit was achieving with trade union law, and the later 'Big Bang' he brought to Britain's financial institutions. It was Moore's report, more than anything else, which convinced Thatcher that maybe she had found her eventual successor.

From November 1983 through to July 1985, Moore worked up a

series of major speeches arguing the economic and social merits of extending privatisation to *all* state industries. He argued that experience thus far showed how privatised industries improved their performance to the benefit of employees and consumers alike, how instead of being a drain on the Exchequer as they had been under nationalisation, they actually contributed tax revenue to it. He showed how the Treasury's gains from flotations could be used to good effect elsewhere. He extolled the benefits of creating a 'people's capital market', making capitalists of workers and ordinary families as never before. Finally he showed how, in the case of 'natural monopolies', privatisation induced the State to exercise its proper regulatory function. Over the years other ministers in charge of individual privatisations did much to champion their cause, but Moore was the first to bring all the arguments together to form a coherent rationale. The disciplined logic of these speeches achieved wide recognition in the press, and when asked to justify his views in TV interviews he proved to be a good popular communicator as well. Thus did the mantle of Thatcher's approval settle on his shoulders.

This was much remarked upon in the press, which hardly helped Moore's popularity with rivals who saw themselves on other rungs of the ladder. In 1986 Thatcher brought him into the Cabinet as Transport Secretary, and after the 1987 election made him Secretary for Health and Social Services. The ball lay at his feet.

On one occasion when Helen and I had been invited to Chequers for Sunday lunch, we arrived to find the Prime Minister in a fury. She had just been looking through the Sunday tabloids and lighted on what I seem to recall was the *Sunday Mirror*; the paper had devoted its entire front page to a hatchet job on the iniquities that the Tory Government was inflicting on 'our poor nurses'. Thatcher knew just how much extra her Government was spending in real terms each year on the NHS, and how much better the working conditions of nurses were now than under the previous Labour Government, when they were forced to work ridiculous hours of overtime to make ends meet. 'When are they going to learn the truth?' she stormed. 'What's Norman [Fowler] doing to answer this? Get Norman on the phone.' She disappeared to take the call, and returned slightly mollified. 'He's going to issue a statement – but this can't go on.' While Denis took our wives on a tour of Chequers, the politicians settled down to a discussion of how to improve the Government's public image before going in for lunch. But however much money was tipped into the bottomless pit of the NHS, examples of hard-luck cases continued to be exploited by the press. Many district health authorities had little idea of effective budgeting; they were in the habit of overspending in the first half of the year then cutting expenditure by limiting operations and closing wards in the second, at the same time 'shroud-waving' to pressure the Government into providing them with still more taxpayers' money.

By the 1987 election it was clear to all that the NHS needed major surgery; the only question was just how drastic. This was the task Thatcher gave to her rising new star, and it did not take long for Moore to convince her that all the radical options available should be fully reviewed. The complexities of this review are well covered in her memoirs; she chaired the cabinet committee working on the NHS reforms, the other principle members being Moore and Chancellor Lawson. But near-tragedy struck early in Moore's career as Health Secretary when he became critically ill with pneumonia; he insisted on returning to his desk before he was fully recovered, and the toll on his habitual energy lasted too long a time. Worse, while he was still suffering he gave one or two poor performances at the despatch box; his voice was particularly weak, and he never fully regained his confidence. Nevertheless, Moore was the inspiration of most of the reforms to give local hospitals more independence and greater incentives to improve performance, and for money to follow the patient through an 'internal health market', thus making the best use of resources. Sadly, Thatcher did not keep him at Health long enough for him to see the reforms through to fruition.

Feeling that Moore no longer had the stamina to promote NHS reform to the electorate, Thatcher decided in 1988 to split his department into separate ones covering Health and Social Security, and moved him to the latter. But he did not shine particularly there, and in 1990, in a cabinet reconstruction that was the most reckless Thatcher ever undertook (of which more later), she dropped him altogether. Nick Ridley got it right when he wrote in his memoirs: 'It might have been right to give him an easier job with less exposure; but to sack one of her best supporters, and an able man at that, was a sad misjudgement.' However, such brusque treatment did not prevent Moore, like Tebbit, rallying to her support when she faced the fateful challenge from Heseltine one year later. That was the true test of loyalty.

With Moore's career on the slide, it is often suggested that the next crown prince to have Thatcher's mantle of approval settled on his shoulders was John Major himself, though my own view is that this is merely a projection backwards from her vociferous support for his cause once she had resigned. 'John's *one of us*,' she said famously on that occasion, but then Major did have the ability to appear at one with whomever he was talking to last. When she brought him into the Cabinet as Chief Secretary to the Treasury after the 1987 election, his promotion was well-earned, having done a credible job lower down the line. I have recorded above how after that election she included Major among six others of the 'next generation' from whom the party might choose a successor upon her own retirement 'perhaps halfway into the next Parliament'.

It is true that after his cabinet appointment, Major's rise was rapid, but each promotion was in response to a crisis situation. In July 1989 she was determined that Howe could not continue as Foreign Secretary, but her choice was limited over whom to appoint as his successor; Hurd already had one of the great departments of state as Home Secretary, while Baker, who had been included in her list of seven two years earlier, was blocked by having been made Party Chairman only two months before, charged with preparing the party for the next election. In her memoirs Thatcher firmly states that in July she had still not decided whether Major was her 'preferred successor'. Again, when Lawson resigned as Chancellor that October she had to appoint a substitute quickly, and again Major was just about the only suitable candidate to hand. He was also arguably better qualified to be Chancellor than Foreign Secretary; his biggest misjudgement at the Treasury was to push Thatcher into signing Britain up to the ERM, though in fairness it should be said that virtually every Establishment body and national newspaper were arguing fervently in support of the same cause.

But was there not another crown prince whom no-one ever noticed – one Richard Edward Geoffrey Howe? Even though he was three months older than the Prime Minister, would he not at least have been justified in so regarding himself? After all, alongside the PM and Keith Joseph he was a driving force behind the Thatcher Revolution; it was he who as Chancellor had made her vision achievable, it was he who sided with her against Jim Prior to make meaningful reform of trade union law possible. His leadership ambitions were revealed when he threw his hat into the ring for the second ballot after the overthrow of Heath. If at any time in the following decade the proverbial number 11 bus had dispatched the Prime Minister, Howe would have been entitled to expect that the Tory Party might turn to him as her natural successor, just as Anthony Eden was seen as the natural successor to Winston Churchill.

Howe had held the Reigate seat before me, but after boundary revisions he stayed with the eastern and more rural part that became East Surrey. Though in my early years as an MP we did differ over capital punishment – I think my statements calling for restoration might have put unwelcome pressure on him from his party workers – we got on well and joined forces on many local issues. When he was Foreign Secretary he had the exclusive use of Chevening, a delightful country mansion in many ways superior to Chequers, and not far from his constituency; one Sunday Helen and I were invited to lunch with Nigel Lawson and his wife – throughout the meal Lawson kept complaining that as Chancellor he had no facilities to match these. Chevening has an elaborate maze, and after lunch all the guests were let loose in it, with Howe watching our progress from a raised bank alongside; I remember his shouted advice: 'To the right, George; do what you always do, *keep right!*'

Occasionally on mornings during a recess, I would drive to Chevening to sort out how we were going to handle some local issue, and I got to know Elspeth Howe quite well. Once, after they had returned from a visit to Egypt, I found her sitting on the polished floor sorting out their tourist photos – 'Geoffrey on a camel', 'us by the Sphinx', and the rest. She clearly loved Chevening. She also presented quite a contrast to most cabinet wives; they invariably took a very intelligent interest in politics and conversed well about them, but Elspeth was different: she was at root a politician herself, and would have fitted easily into the House of Commons.

Thatcher's decline of confidence in her Foreign Secretary has been well documented, both by him and by her. She felt that in the Foreign Office environment he was 'going native', accepting that department's traditional preference for following the international pack rather than seeking to influence it, and in the process losing his former faculties of analytical judgement. She frequently berated him in public, even more so when he became Leader of the House and supposedly Deputy Prime Minister. I once witnessed such a dressing down round the lunch table at Chequers; I looked across at Elspeth, and her face was thunder.

I earlier described Thatcher's reconstruction of her Cabinet in July 1989 as reckless. She was bound to incur Howe's displeasure in moving him from the Foreign Office, but she also dropped Moore and Paul Channon, two of her strongest personal supporters – and this at a time when two others, Lord Young and George Younger, were leaving at their own request. True, she did bring Parkinson back in, but this was cancelled out by elevating Chris Patten, an archetypal Wet. The Thatcherite core of her Cabinet had gone, and when Nick Ridley was required to leave after his off-the-record opinions on German reunification were reported, she was left dangerously exposed. That October she made another disastrous mistake by making Tim Renton her Chief

Whip. He owed everything to Howe's patronage, and one would have expected his personal loyalty to his friend and patron to have been at least equal to that which he felt for his Prime Minster.

When Denis Healey described being attacked by Howe as like 'being savaged by a dead sheep' it was cruel, but had an element of truth; Howe had little taste for the cutting invective needed for good Commons performances. The sheer vitriol that permeated parts of his resignation speech in November 1990 therefore came as a great surprise to many. The Prime Minister's rhetoric over European integration, he said, undermined the efforts of both the Chancellor and the governor of the Bank of England:

> It is rather like sending your opening batsmen to the crease only for them to find, the moment the first balls are bowled, that their bats have been broken before the game by the team captain.

The real sting came in the tail:

> The conflict of loyalty to the Prime Minister ... and of loyalty to what I perceive to be the true interests of the nation has become all too great. I no longer believe it is possible to resolve that conflict from within the Government. That is why I have resigned. In doing so, I have done what I believe to be right for my party and my country. The time has come for others to consider their own response to the tragic conflict of loyalties with which I have myself wrestled for perhaps too long.

The immediate quip from the waspish Charles Irving was that 'it took Elspeth ten minutes to write that speech, and Geoffrey ten years to make it'. It was common knowledge that Elspeth had never warmed to Thatcher, and because these words were so uncharacteristic of Howe it was widely assumed that his wife had a hand in writing them; his statement was Elspeth's revenge. Howe denied this in his memoirs, as one would expect, but nevertheless the popular assumption to the contrary has the ring of truth. When in July 1989 Thatcher offered him the post of Home Secretary, he did not give an immediate answer, saying he must discuss it with Elspeth first; not many cabinet ministers would have responded that way. She was, as I have said, as much a politician as he. But whatever the truth of that, the invitation to Heseltine to challenge for the leadership could not have been thrown down more clearly.

Heseltine was never a crown prince, rather a pretender to the throne – and a not-so-young pretender at that. He was the only minister to have served in Thatcher's first Cabinet and in Major's last.

Until Howe's resignation speech, Heseltine's familiar line on whether he should challenge for the leadership remained as he stated in the *Daily Telegraph* on 7 November: 'I am not going to take part in that process. I think Mrs Thatcher will lead the Conservative Party into the next election, and that the Conservative Party will win it.' He was observing his maxim quoted at the start of this chapter. But he could not resist the opening that Howe created for him. The next day he reneged on his pledge and announced that he would challenge the Prime Minister after all.

After Thatcher announced her intention to resign I went to Heseltine's office to invite him to set out his stall to the 92 (see Chapter One). He accepted with alacrity, then said: 'Tell me, George, which way do you think your boys will go?' I replied that I thought most members would support whomever they saw as continuing the policies and embodying the philosophy of the outgoing Prime Minister. 'Marvellous,' he replied. 'In that case, I'm their man!' It was with great effort that I stopped myself breaking into laughter. Heseltine might have been many things, but the one thing he was not was a Thatcherite. Neither was he, like Heath, a corporatist; he was above all an interventionist, believing that ministers were best placed to control the strategies and investment decisions of private industry, in co-operation with other governments.

I have often wondered what precise motive led him to stalk out of the Cabinet in 1973 in opposition to the wish of the directors of Westland, a relatively small West Country company making helicopters, to link up with the American Sikorski to avoid bankruptcy. Heseltine said he wanted 'a European solution', though no such solution was on offer. Afterwards he claimed his objection was to Thatcher's 'dictatorial attitude' in Cabinet; in fact he was given ample opportunity to argue his case, but was unable to convince his cabinet colleagues. Another motive might have been that as Defence Secretary he objected to the involvement of the United States in Britain's defence industries; such prejudice, applied to industry generally, was only too evident when he became President of the Board of Trade under Major. But the real issue was whether Westland's directors and shareholders should be free to decide what was best for their company; Heseltine's belief was that the Government, and more especially he himself, was better qualified to make such judgements on their behalf – the very antithesis of Thatcherism.

I have already referred to Heseltine's reputation as an Oxford student (see Chapter Three). After leaving university he got some capital together by running a London drinking club, then embarked on a very successful career in publishing, thus becoming a very wealthy man before entering professional politics. His strength has never lain in mastering a complete brief, but rather in relentless pursuit of just one part of it. He was not particularly successful as Environment Secretary after 1979 – except in concentrating attention on the renewal of decaying inner-city areas, hence the nickname 'Minister for Merseyside'. As Defence Secretary after 1993 he did a moderately competent job, but his brilliance lay in his high-profile campaign to denigrate the Campaign for Nuclear Disarmament and its call for Britain to 'ban the bomb' unilaterally. At a time when many young people and the so-called intelligentsia were being taken in, he won the argument by using language that people understood, talking for example about 'one-sided' rather than 'unilateral' disarmament.

Before quitting the Cabinet over Westland he seemed rather an aloof figure to most Tory MPs; he did have some close friends, but he was rarely seen in the smoking or tea rooms, and never in the Members' Bar. Most Tories knew him from his barnstorming performances at party conferences, always cracking good jokes at the expense of Labour leaders, but in intellectual content totally threadbare. When I heard the early conference speeches my skin used to break into goose pimples in embarrassment, and I would deliberately schedule my champagne receptions for Reigate delegates and right-wing friends for the end of Wednesday morning, which was the National Union's favourite slot to bring him on. When someone once asked if a TV set could be turned on quietly at the back of my party I obliged, and even provided sick bags beside the set in case they were needed, but that guest turned out to be the only one to watch.

However, once liberated from office, Heseltine made himself far more approachable. Any invitation to a constituency dinner was eagerly accepted. In July 1990 he accepted my invitation to speak at a dinner in Reigate; perhaps I queered his pitch slightly in my introduction, when I congratulated him on undertaking not to challenge Thatcher for the leadership, to loud applause, but when he went on to talk about Britain's destiny in Europe I noticed eyes starting to glaze over. There was a limit to Heseltine's platform magic.

The final dispatch of Margaret Thatcher was brutal and quick, following a saga characterised by muddle, incredible incompetence, treachery and, above all else, sheer blind panic by many of her trusted ministers. Many of the participants have recorded the tragedy from their own viewpoints: Thatcher herself, Howe, Baker, Ridley, Alan Clark in his diaries, and others too, though by far the most comprehensive account was made by the journalist Alan Watkins in his book *A Conservative Coup*. I shall not add to this collective record, save to present my own observations as a backbencher who was fighting to save Thatcher's premiership.

At the conclusion of her rally speech at the Bournemouth party conference in October 1990, the chant rose from her audience: 'Ten more years!', yet within ten weeks she was gone. What could explain such a cataclysmic departure? Two fundamental causes have often been cited: cabinet divisions over Europe, characterised by resignations of such heavyweights as Lawson and Howe, and fears among many Tory MPs that clinging to the unpopular poll tax would lose them their seats in the coming election. The view of Cranley Onslow, 1922 Committee chairman at the time, was that Europe had nothing to do with it; fear of retribution for the poll tax was the real problem. This merits further investigation.

I was always a strong advocate of the community charge, as it was named in the White Paper of January 1986, following a review headed by Baker and William Waldegrave. It proposed a flat charge on all adults for services provided by local councils, with rebates for those receiving social security benefits, to replace the income from domestic rates. Overspending by councils had become endemic, and under the existing system it had proved impossible to control; the worst offenders were Labour-led, but many in the Tory shires were no slouches when it came to extravagant spending either. I knew from my own constituency just how unpopular domestic rates were; the argument was familiar: why should a widow living on her own have to pay the same rates as a family of four or more wage earners living in an identical property next door? I can vouch that when the community charge was introduced in our 1987 manifesto it was a vote winner. The argument that all adults should pay something towards the cost of the community services they enjoyed was then seen as being above all else fair. I pressed the case more than once in my *Sunday Express* articles: we all paid the same for a car or TV licence, or for that matter for a loaf of bread, so why should we not all pay the same for our street lighting, refuse collection and education services? If local citizens wanted a high-spending council that was fair enough, for they would then have to bear the cost.

As planning developed it became clear that the poll tax would cost far more than the optimistic predictions of the Department of the Environment. There were then calls, often supported from the right, to shift the entire cost of education straight to the Exchequer, but that would have meant a totally centralised system, with no responsibility or choice for local councils. Through 1986 and 1987 the hard core of old Wets rebelled against the legislation. Michael Mates, joint secretary of the 1922 Committee and a close supporter of Heseltine, tabled with his master's encouragement an amendment for the charge to be 'banded' according to the individual's income-tax status; this proved on examination to be far too complicated, and clearly Mates had not thought his proposal through. Many Tories who initially supported him felt they had been taken for a ride, and in the following elections for the 1922 Committee the 92 Group succeeded in ousting Mates in favour of Peter Horden.

But too many mistakes were made in seeing the poll tax through. The 1986 Green Paper suggested a transitional period of up to ten years, during which the rating system could wither on the vine. But Ridley, when he became Environment Secretary, reduced the 'dual-running' period to four years and then scrapped it altogether. He was put under great pressure to do this by the 1987 Tory conference, where delegates feared that having two local charges running side by side would cause confusion. But the decision to introduce the new charge in one fell swoop proved a fatal mistake, since it meant that many who had hitherto paid no rates at all suddenly had to bear the full burden of poll tax. Another big mistake was to make students, who usually had two homes and received little income anyway, liable to pay at least 20 per cent of the charge; Baker, now Education Secretary, suggested that everyone under twenty-one should be exempt, thus removing much of the problem, but this was turned down. Another blow to public acceptance was delivered by Chancellor Lawson; the Treasury hated the idea from the beginning, and Lawson resolutely opposed using any Exchequer money to ease the transition. As Baker observed in his memoirs, 'if the Treasury is not prepared to support [the introduction of] a new tax, then that tax is doomed'. When the poll tax was finally abolished it required 2.5 per cent to be added to VAT to sugar the pill of the new council tax, a return to the old domestic rates in different form.

My own belief is that the death blow to popular acceptance of the poll tax was the arcane and Byzantine complexities of the system for allocating government grants to local authorities. The allocation was worked out through a computer, into which were fed all kinds of details of populations, their relative age ranges, comparative wealth and disadvantage, numbers of first- and second-generation immigrants, citizens with special needs and much more besides, all superimposed by a redistribution factor whereby residents in the wealthier South were penalised to help ease the transition for those in the North. This process determined how the Government's grant was divided, and 'Standard Spending Assessments' (SSAs) were supposed to ensure that everyone across the country obtained the same standard of local services for their charge; local councils were penalised if they spent above it. There cannot have been many Tory MPs who did not join in deputations to local government ministers protesting that their counties or districts were being unfairly treated and pressing for adjustments to the data being fed into the system. But as the weighting accorded to the data was changed to remove one apparent anomaly, so yet another appeared. The black joke of the time was that only three civil servants had ever understood the system: one was dead, another committed suicide, while the third was in a lunatic asylum.

The result of all this was that a high poll tax was blamed not on the spending decisions or even incompetence of local councils, but on the Government for the blatant unfairness of the distribution of grants from the Exchequer. The connection we wished people to perceive between a local council's efficiency and its consequent poll tax had been severed. How much more acceptable the poll tax would have been, in retrospect, if local councils had been left to cover all their costs from the poll tax and from the uniform business rates, free of arcane environment department calculations of subsidy, SSAs and the rest. Of course that would have meant the poll tax would be higher, but if matched by significant cuts in income tax, made possible by the abolition of Exchequer grants, that would have been palatable; at least it would then be clear where the buck stopped. I suggest that the poll tax failed, not because it was too radical a change, but because it was not radical enough.

So to this extent, I would agree with Onslow's judgement; by 1990 Tory MPs' collective fear of the electoral impact of the unpopular poll tax was strewn around like dry tinder, requiring only the spark of a cabinet fall-out over European policy to send it up in flames.

My first apprehensions over Margaret Thatcher's chances began on learning that the closing date for nominations for the leadership was being brought forward to Thursday 15 November, with the first ballot the following Tuesday. This meant that during this crucial period she would be away from Westminster altogether, staying in Paris for the Security and Co-operation in Europe Summit. In her memoirs she admits this might have been a misjudgement, but explains it thus:

> It would have been absurd for a Prime Minister of eleven-and-a-half
> years' standing – leader of the party for over fifteen years – to behave as
> if she were entering the lists for the first time. Tory MPs knew me, my
> record and my beliefs. If they were not already persuaded, there was not
> much left for me to persuade them with.

One can see her point, but faced with such a challenge, any Prime
Minister must be seen to be out there fighting. Of course she could not
make offers of promotion to disappointed backbenchers, but then she
had never done that in 1975 when she was entering the lists for the first
time. Her explanation ignores entirely the role of flattery; MPs like to
feel that their leader values their personal backing. Thus the field was
handed entirely to Heseltine, who approached even those he must have
felt were unlikely to support him, devoting the entire weekend phoning
them at home; Vivian Bendall was called from the shower by an
'urgent' call from him. I do not believe that Heseltine made offers of
promotion to anyone, but he did drop hints like 'we need to promote
unused talent', and he certainly promised a better alternative to the poll
tax. When Major later shrewdly gave him the task of finding such an
alternative it quickly became apparent that Heseltine had not a clue
even where to start.

   The absence of the Prime Minister from the ring to defend her title
might not have mattered if her campaign team had been even remotely
efficient, but alas, they were not. Indeed, even to refer to a 'campaign'
at all was a misnomer, since to all appearances it did not even exist. It
was supposed to be led by George Younger, who left the Cabinet in
1979 to become chairman of the Royal Bank of Scotland, and for this
reason can fairly be described as an 'absentee leader'. Supposedly working under him were ex-minister Michael Jopling (Watkins describes him
accurately as 'the phantom campaigner'), Thatcher's PPS Peter
Morrison, ex-ministers John Moore and Norman Tebbit, and backbenchers Gerry Neale and Michael Neubert. Thanks to Younger's regular absences his role as leader effectively passed to Tebbit in the final
days. Much missed was Ian Gow, in her team to counter the earlier
Meyer challenge, but since then assassinated by the IRA. Tristan Garel-
Jones, also in that earlier team, complained afterwards that he had not
been included, and that he could have tipped the balance in her favour,
but she was better off without him; he might have netted a few Wet
votes, but his presence if known would have alienated more than it
gained; certainly his efforts for Hurd in the second ballot did nothing to
increase the Foreign Secretary's vote above a paltry fifty-six.

   Worse than useless was the blindly optimistic Morrison; Clark
records in his diaries how on eve-of-poll afternoon, the most critical

point in the campaign, he called at Morrison's office to convey his anxieties; he found him 'asleep, snoring slightly in the leather armchair,
with his feet resting on the desk'. Clark woke him sharply, only to be
told: 'Quite all right, old boy, relax.' What did the arithmetic look like?
'Tightish, but OK.' My experience of Morrison's sheer incompetence
was much the same; after nominations closed the previous Thursday I
cornered Morrison behind the Speaker's Chair. 'What can the 92 do to
help?' I asked. 'No need to worry, old chap. Everything's under control.' Nevertheless I pressed him to give me his contact phone number
for the weekend, which he gave me from memory; when I tried to ring
it on Saturday I found the number did not even exist. By Monday
Tebbit had effectively taken over the running of Thatcher's campaign;
as experience was to prove, this was far too late.

The evening before the first ballot I called a meeting of the 92 to
rally support, and found our members bitterly critical over the absence
of any proper Thatcher campaign. Several complained they had not
even been asked by a member of her team for their support. I could
have told them that Neubert was sitting among them, noting in his
mind those speaking strongly in her favour, but I was urged by Neubert
not to do so; 'discreet canvassing' was the order of the day. He took his
intelligence back to base, but to my knowledge he never thanked those
who had voiced such support, nor asked their opinions on known
waverers. Such canvassing was not 'discreet' but downright ineffectual;
even a doorstep canvasser asking a child of eight how all the adults in
her household were intending to vote would get a better perspective
than this. We agreed to meet again on Thursday to assess the result, but
by this time I, like Clark, was deeply despondent.

To win outright under our rules Thatcher needed not just a simple
majority, but 50 plus a further 15 per cent of all those entitled to vote,
which of course gave a value even to abstentions. The result, declared
soon after 6.30 p.m., not directly to the full 1922 Committee waiting
in committee room 14, but via the press outside, was:

Margaret Thatcher	204
Michael Heseltine	152
Abstentions	16

Thus, though she won a simple majority, she failed to clear the 15 per
cent hurdle by just four votes. So near – and yet so far. There would
have to be a second ballot, in which only a simple majority was needed
to win, but which fresh candidates could enter. The grim news was conveyed to the Prime Minister in Paris, and as arranged she came out
fighting: 'It is my intention to let my name go forward for the second

ballot.' It is hard to convey my own depression; I knew that supported by a proper campaign, efficiently managed and involving her, she could have swept the board.

The next twenty-four hours were ones of indescribable confusion, with normally level-headed ministers in blind panic over how to 'stop Heseltine'. Never have I seen such collective loss of nerve. When the 1922 executive met the following morning we were, not surprisingly, divided; most thought Thatcher was best placed to beat Heseltine this time round, but there was a minority calling for the field to be 'opened up', meaning that Hurd and possibly Major should be freed of their obligation to her and allowed to stand as candidates. But meanwhile, other dark deeds were afoot, so let us look more closely at the efforts of three *dramatis personae*: John Wakeham, another victim of the Brighton bomb, a former chief whip, now Energy Secretary, and with the reputation of being a 'good fixer'; the current chief whip, Tim Renton; and the ever ubiquitous Tristan Garel-Jones.

It should be stressed that many leading Wets were emphatically *not* supporters of Heseltine; indeed, they saw him as little more than a populist orator with only a tenuous intellectual grasp of political issues. Ken Clarke detested him, Chris Patten distrusted him, while Garel-Jones feared the consequences for the party if it were led by him. Wakeham, though not as Wet as they, agreed, as did John Gummer.

On returning to London, Thatcher asked Wakeham to take charge of her second ballot campaign, asking him to recruit some younger blood to her team and suggesting he ask Garel-Jones and Richard Ryder to be his 'chief lieutenants'. She was greatly taken aback when both men refused; the warning about Garel-Jones given to her by the 92 steering committee a year before was becoming hideous reality. In fact, throughout this period, Wakeham, normally the smooth fixer, was in a confused dither, unable to distinguish his arse from his elbow. The day *before* the first ballot a secret meeting between Clarke, Gummer and Wakeham was held in Wakeham's room, when they agreed that if Thatcher failed to achieve an outright win the next day she should be allowed to return from Paris with dignity, before being persuaded by cabinet colleagues like themselves to withdraw so that Hurd, or possibly Major, could see Heseltine off. Yet on the day *after* she failed to clear the 15 per cent hurdle, there was Wakeham accepting the job as her campaign manager and assuring her that she could win. Then he arranged that on the same evening she should see her cabinet colleagues one by one – this planted the kiss of death. No doubt throughout he had the best of intentions, yet there was no evidence of any effort to rally support.

Renton was a most unfortunate choice as Chief Whip. Most good

Chief Whips rose through the whips' office, but not he. Politically he was a lightweight, owing everything to the patronage of Howe. He was appointed PPS to Foreign Secretary Howe in 1983, the following year became a junior minister and for two years after that was Minister of State at the Foreign Office – all under Howe. He was as much a Europhile as his master, and would hardly have welcomed Thatcher's famous Bruges speech in 1988 in which she made a hard pitch in favour of a Europe of nation states. When Renton was moved to the Home Office he and Howe remained close, and when Howe knew he was to be moved from the Foreign Office he urged Thatcher to make his old friend Chief Whip, which she did largely to appease him. With Howe as Leader of the Commons and Renton as Chief Whip, they made a cosy pair.

But Howe's man was not a success. His tastes were too artistic for this often brutal job, his manner at times foppish. He doted on two King Charles spaniels, and I once watched in horror as he allowed them to defecate all over the lawn in front of Chequers. Rather surprisingly for a whip, he once reprimanded John Townend, a wine merchant by trade, for cutting across some friend in a business deal involving Chilean wine, calling Townend 'a shit', whereupon Townend said he would take no notice of the weekly whip unless Renton apologised.

When the chips were down, Renton decreed that the whips' office should preserve neutrality, which was only right and proper; Humphrey Atkins did the same when Thatcher challenged Heath. But after the first ballot result, Renton's advice played a crucial role in undermining Thatcher's confidence.

Thatcher arrived back from Paris on Wednesday morning, still insisting: 'I shall fight on.' But by noon, ugly rumours were spreading through the corridors and offices of the Commons: the whips' office had undertaken a trawl of back-bench opinion, it was said; they had found that support for her was falling away fast, and she was likely to quit after all. The reports seemed odd to me, since I had been in my office all morning and taken many calls from colleagues, but none from any whip asking my opinion; furthermore, not one of her supporters who spoke to me that morning had been approached by a whip either; the so-called 'trawl' thus sounded a very one-sided affair. Renton subsequently pleaded that time was too short to allow his 'soundings' to be wide-ranging; according to Watkins, what the whips did 'was to allow – to encourage – people to come to them'. It seemed the whips had fallen for the oldest trick in the book: a small string of backbenchers knocking on their door, just to say that although they had supported Thatcher in the ballot the day before, they thought it would be in her best interests and those of the party if she stood down – whereas it was most unlikely they had ever been among the 204 voting for her anyway. The whips would hardly know, since they had no access to canvassing returns. Confirmed Thatcherites had little respect for Renton, knew that Sir George Young – inexplicably back as a whip – was a strong critic of Thatcher, so hardly thought it worth giving the whips' office their view. Soon after, the chief whip gave the Prime Minister his gloomy assessment.

By mid-afternoon Thatcher was still determined to stay in the race; leaving Downing Street to make her statement to the Commons on the Paris summit, she told the press: 'I fight on, I fight to win.' After the Commons statement Tebbit took her into the Members' tea room, where she soon learned backbenchers' opinion of how appalling her 'campaign' had been. After that she saw Parkinson, who told her she should stay in the fight and could still win. Then, almost by coincidence, Francis Maude, not in the Cabinet, came to her and began what became a familiar litany: that of course he would support her, but that she could not beat Heseltine.

Then, soon after 6 p.m. in her room at the Commons, the final denouement began; cabinet ministers from the Commons were invited in one by one to give their views. What happened then is well recounted in her memoirs: Peter Brooke said he would support her, and that she could win; David Waddington promised support, but could not guarantee victory; Tom King gave support too, suggesting she might win if she promised to retire soon after. Wakeham again reported that the outlook was bleak, while Baker said she should stick at it and could win with a vigorous campaign. But Peter Lilley, Michael Howard, William Waldegrave, John Gummer, Chris Patten, Norman Lamont, John MacGregor, Tony Newton and Alan Clark (not in the Cabinet, but he insisted on seeing her) all said they would support her if she decided to stay in the race, but there was no way she could win it. Malcolm Rifkind also said her chances were nil, and even demurred on whether he would give support. As Thatcher later remarked, they were all repeating the same tired formula; it was as if they had collectively worked out the 'line to take'.

In truth, none of these ministers were remotely qualified to give any assessment of the strength of sentiment on the back benches, for the very reason that they *were* ministers. How often have I heard their complaints that the heavy demands imposed on their time by departmental duties prevented them from obtaining a feel for the opinions of those working and socialising within the Commons. Clark voices this complaint frequently in his diaries – and he was not even in the Cabinet.

Ministers may pick up some clues from their PPSs, but even that depends on how astute their bag carriers are. So how was it that no fewer than ten ministers had become so convinced that support for Thatcher was ebbing away fast, and so gave her identical advice? Surely there was some co-ordination?

Of course there was – so call on stage [*entrance left*] our old friend, Tristan Garel-Jones. The night before, once the ballot result was known, he called a crisis meeting at his home in nearby Catherine Place. Present at this clandestine gathering were Chris Patten, Lamont, Rifkind, Newton, Waldegrave and Clark – all of whom gave Thatcher the standard line next evening that there was no way she could win. Four others were present who were not among those she consulted: John Patten, Douglas Hogg, Alan Howarth, Tim Yeo (PPS to Hurd) and Richard Ryder (who, like Garel-Jones, refused to serve on Thatcher's reconstituted campaign team the next day). Clarke and Gummer were not there, but remember that both had been at the meeting the day before in Wakeham's room when they agreed that if Thatcher failed to clear the 15 per cent hurdle she should be persuaded to resign. As for Lilley, he appears to have reached his own decision against her standing, though upon what basis we do not know.

This meeting was later named the 'Catherine Place Conspiracy', but such a description is frankly ludicrous; the participants were far too diffuse in their positions in the party spectrum to make it remotely credible that they could form a 'plot'. Garel-Jones has since stated that if there was a preference among them for an alternative candidate it was Hurd, but this was not pressed to a formal conclusion. Garel-Jones's long-term ambition was always to get his close friend Chris Patten into the leadership, which probably explains why he supported Hurd rather than Major; Hurd, then sixty, would present less of a blockage than Major, at forty-seven. Far from being a plot, the explanation of their behaviour is far more simple, and relates to human frailty: it is that a group of highly excited men, in a blue funk that Heseltine could be elected leader and without any knowledge themselves of the potential strength that Thatcher still possessed, just panicked.

But what did Garel-Jones intend should be the outcome of their discussion? Clark mentions in his diary that a full week before the vote, Garel-Jones told him on his car phone that 'he thinks he can fudge up a solution that will keep H. out', but did not say what that solution was. Could it have been the idea that Clark proposed later: that Kenneth Clarke should stand to split the Heseltine vote? Or was it that Thatcher should stand down so that Hurd or Major could see Heseltine off? Who will ever know? Few can begin to comprehend the Byzantine workings of the Garel-Jones mind.

When the 92 Group gathered at 6 p.m. on the Wednesday there were bitter recriminations from the sixty or seventy present over the sheer incompetence of the Thatcher team, and a conviction that with proper organisation and her own participation she could go on to improve on her simple majority against Heseltine. It would have helped if Tebbit had been there, but at that time he was on hand to give any help that Thatcher required in her interviews with cabinet ministers. Suddenly there was a commotion at the door; David Maclean, a junior minister, and I think one other, brought news that Thatcher was under tremendous pressure from cabinet members to withdraw, and that Renton was telling her that her supporters were deserting her. 'It's no use you sitting here talking,' he shouted, 'while downstairs the whole thing's falling apart.'

We immediately ended the meeting, while a group of us charged down to her room to demand to see her. This group was hastily assembled, and included not just steering committee members like Townend but also Maclean, Chris Chope, Edward Leigh and several others. Our arrival coincided with that of Portillo, who had just heard the same news. We were met by Morrison, looking sicker than I had ever seen him. 'You can't see her,' he said. 'She's busy with members of her Cabinet, then she's got to go back to Number Ten to write her speech for tomorrow.' (In the interval Kinnock had tabled a censure motion.) We dug in our heels: 'We're staying here till we see her.' It was subsequently reported that Portillo was so angry he grabbed Morrison by his lapels, pushing him to the ground, but this was not the case. We were simply determined, and Morrison promised he would see what he could do. Portillo, as a Minister of State, was shown in first, and to the best of my recollection stayed when we were finally ushered in. We found Tebbit standing behind her; he knew the battering she had received from ministers, and said to himself: 'Thank God the 92's arrived.'

I then knew nothing of this battering, and began by saying 'We've come to bully you, Margaret' – perhaps not the best opening in the circumstances. But she listened patiently while I put our case: 'The reason you fell just short of an outright win was that you had no campaign worth calling a campaign at all. You ceded to Heseltine all the advantages. But you have strong support, and with you out there and seen to be fighting you'll win more. For God's sake, Margaret, don't quit now.' She retained her dignity throughout, but I could see she was close to tears. Her eyes struck me as like a puppy's who had just been given a cruel beating. 'But what's all this I hear, George, about our supporters deserting in droves?' *Deserting in droves!* The words sounded to me like Renton's – so I went on to expose the myth of the 'whips' trawl'. 'I've yet to find a 92 member who's been asked his voting intentions by the whips since last night's result,' I declared. Others then came in, backing up my arguments, some citing the national interest involved too. The Prime Minister, obviously relieved to learn there was still a strong body of MPs still loyal to her, promised to sleep on it overnight – but I could see that her mind was made up.

I returned to my Dolphin Square flat heartbroken, and for the only time in my adult life cried myself to sleep. This woman had achieved more for her country than those assassins had ever done, or for that matter ever would. Of course she had her faults, but she never deserved such cruel treatment as this.

CHAPTER TEN

Pursuit and Principle

'*Shall I make it clear, boys, for all to apprehend,*
Those that will not hear, boys, waiting for the end,
Knowing it is near, boys, trying to pretend,
Sitting in cold fear, boys, waiting for the end?

Shall we make a tale, boys, that things are sure to mend,
Playing bluff and hale, boys, waiting for the end?'
                    William Empson, 'Just a Smack at Auden'

APRIL 6, 1994 – Ultimatum Day. I am sitting in the sumptuous drawing room of Tony Geddes, committee member of one of my Conservative association's wealthier branches at Walton-on-the-Hill. With him is the current chairman, Margaret Benson. They have welcomed me with smiles, and Geddes has put a gin and tonic in my hand. We talk about the immaculate garden spreading before the windows of his conservatory, then Geddes comes to the point. 'We've been thinking, George; we suggest it would be appropriate for you to retire as our MP at the next election. You've had quite a good innings, and many professional people are going for early retirement these days. It would be nice for you to go out with dignity.' All delivered with due Surrey decorum; you could almost see the service revolver alongside the gin bottle on the silver tray.

I have to say that his suggestion did not come as a great surprise to me. My relations with Geddes and the Walton-on-the-Hill Committee had been difficult ever since the build-up to the vote on the Maastricht Bill the previous summer, when he sent faxes pleading for me to support John Major and swallow my strong objections to the Bill. This is one paragraph from the fax sent on 19 July, 1993:

> We have all been very unhappy about the damage we perceive to have been done to Government by some of the tactics adopted by Conservative Members who have been trying to kill Maastricht. In our view this issue is now so fundamentally part of Government policy (both internally and internationally) that Conservative Members who oppose Government in this matter on Thursday will not only damage the standing of the party in the country, but damage also the standing of the country internationally. We believe that they should, rather than continue being a thorn in Government's side, resign their seats to make way for Conservative candidates able to provide the Prime Minister with more loyal support.

I replied pointing out the immense national issues at stake, and reminding them that when Maastricht was debated at a party meeting in Reigate (which no Walton-on-the-Hill committee member bothered to attend) the voting was 2–1 against ratifying the treaty (see Chapter One), but my arguments were a waste of effort. They were not interested in Maastricht; they believed that the leader of the party's judgement was invariably right, never to be questioned by his MPs. To this day I do not know whether Geddes even had an opinion on the Maastricht Treaty; for him, loyalty was the only issue. He really had missed his vocation; he was a natural for high office in the National Union.

I told them at that drawing-room meeting that I was fifty-nine, by no means old for a politician, and had every intention of fighting the next election. I had no desire to 'do a Ted Heath', but planned to retire soon after reaching the age of sixty-five. They had clearly expected this reply, and their response was rehearsed: 'In that case, George, we have to warn you that Walton will press for an open selection of our next candidate, so that you can be judged alongside others more loyal.' Menacing suggestion had changed to ultimatum. From that moment the hounds were unleashed; the pursuit of me had begun, and Geddes became the brains behind the campaign to deselect me.

Next in the chamber of horrors plotting my removal was one Angela Fraser, a borough councillor for Chipstead and a Surrey county councillor too, with wits as sharp as her tongue. She was the widow of former Tory MP Ian Fraser, a distinguished whip made lame during the war who became a champion of ex-servicemen's associations. My relations with her had always been prickly. She was queen bee of our branch at Chipstead, a small but quite wealthy community and consequently had influence in the Conservative association; with her stark black hair and pinched face, she was known by many in the association as the 'Black Witch'. Her principal ally in the Chipstead branch was one Chris Robinson, who had been conspicuously rude to me at one of the branch's social events.

In 1994 there were only two branches where my critics held the levers of power – Walton-on-the-Hill and Chipstead. Another wealthy branch was Kingswood, distinguished by big houses at the end of rhododendron drives; my towers of strength there were Joan Spiers and her fellow Kingswood councillors, though there were some critics. The remaining branches were all supportive, and produced some close friends. A smattering of Euro-enthusiasts could be found in Reigate, Kingswood and Horley, though in all cases we were on amicable terms at that time.

My strength in the Reigate association was my reputation as a hard worker for my constituents – in popular parlance, 'a good constituency member'. This was something that my critics never questioned; they knew they would be howled down if they did. When one critic did get to his feet at my June 1996 selection meeting to suggest that what an MP did for his constituency hardly mattered, he was greeted by a wave of laughter. A few MPs deride their constituency 'surgeries' as a tedious bore, but I have never agreed. Anyone with even a glimmering of interest in the human condition must find the wide variety and unpredictability of personal cases fascinating, quite apart from the challenge of helping people in difficulty. Wider issues too – pressing for road improvements, saving the remnants of our rural heritage from developers, reducing air and noise pollution and urging the provision of a better choice of schools – are equally absorbing. I have always reckoned that well over half my desk time at the Commons was spent on constituency casework.

The Reigate constituency as then defined was split by the North Downs escarpment. Above the hill were large tracts of green-belt heathland, dotted with quite wealthy commuter villages like Chipstead, Kingswood, Tadworth and Walton-on-the-Hill; below the hill were the larger and older towns of Reigate, which had sent its first member to Parliament in 1297 and was quite affluent, and Redhill, founded as a railway town on the London–Brighton line in the nineteenth century, where a number of light industries were based; further south lay more areas of green belt, the villages of Sidlow and Salfords, also with light industry, then at the southern tip of the constituency the town of Horley, principally serving Gatwick Airport. The Conservative association had branches in all these areas; Reigate and Redhill had several branches, the most powerful being Reigate North.

The line of the North Downs did not merely divide the constituency physically; those living 'above the hill' seemed to have totally different social attitudes to those below. Though for most of my time the borough council was dominated by Conservatives, there was constant friction within the Tory Group, and I worked hard to avoid getting caught up in their squabbles. I once incurred displeasure by suggesting to Tory councillors that they should make way for a Labour mayor from time to time, but it was a long time before they stopped hogging the mayoralty for themselves.

The president of Reigate Conservative Association has few formal duties, but the most important is to take the chair at the AGM when officers are elected. The president in 1994 was county councillor Douglas Simpson, whose political experience dated back to when he was a mines manager in the South Wales coalfield. It was at that AGM, the first after my Maastricht rebellion, that a Euro-enthusiast from Reigate – the same man who had suggested a Maastricht debate in the confident belief it would show overwhelming support for ratifying the treaty – first suggested that the selection procedure should be opened up ready for the next election. Simpson slapped him down in no time at all; that, after all, is what good chairmen and presidents are for. The Chipstead and Walton-on-the-Hill representatives stayed silent, biding their time.

The main responsibility for running an association lies with the chairman. In 1995, Mary Newstead, like her fellow officers anti-Maastricht, came to the end of her term, and we were looking around for a successor. In the end Daniel Kee, county councillor, past chairman and president, and a very loyal friend helped me to persuade one Michael Steele, a retired gunner, to take over the task. So here was the next of the *dramatis personae* in my tragedy – Major-General Michael Steele. He was a slight but nimble man, a peacetime professional soldier to the core, but unfortunately had no experience of politics; he was concerned above all to play everything according to the rule book, rather than give a determined lead and bang a few heads together. He seemed personally supportive but, as I was to discover, that support was not to extend very far. By this time the association had no agent; so many members had left in protest over either Major or his Government's performance that we could no longer afford one.

Following their drawing-room ultimatum, Geddes and his crew did not let up, despite my efforts at Westminster through the 92 Group to present a public face of unity and help Major to make a fresh start. Efforts by me and the Major-General to arrange for me to meet members of the Walton-on-the-Hill committee to talk things through met with rejection; I even booked a meeting hall in the village where I could hear in private the views of *all* branch members, but the meeting had to be called off when the local officers made clear they would boycott it. However, they found it hard to find another stick with which to beat me – until Major threw down the gauntlet, challenging his critics either to 'shut up, or put up'.

I have explained in Chapter Two how in the 1995 leadership election I remained publicly neutral till the eve of the ballot, when I declared for Redwood. Prior to that I consulted privately with a wide range of my local party officers, councillors and recently defeated councillors, asking whether they thought we stood a better chance of winning the next election under Major's continued leadership, or under a new leader. The result was that 55 per cent favoured sticking with Major, and 45 per cent were in favour of change – the latter including a couple of association officers. I was surprised by the narrowness of the majority for Major, and wondered whether I ought to make allowance for all those who had deserted the association over the past two years because they could no longer stand him. I therefore used my vote to try to secure a second ballot, so that the party could choose from a wider range of candidates. In asking for views I made it clear that the survey was purely consultative, and when Major eventually won I saw it as being my task to win over the 45 per cent to see some hope in the situation. But Geddes and his friends did not see it this way, and not surprisingly accused me of flying in the face of my local party's wishes. Interestingly, my support for Redwood figured far higher in the dissidents' propaganda against me than my rebellion over Maastricht ever did.

After this, it became obvious that I faced a serious fight to secure reselection. A big factor was the impending boundary revision; the Reigate constituency was to lose Horley, where I enjoyed very strong support, and gain the northern village of Banstead, which I had represented before 1983, but where the principal branch officers now had close links with Geddes, now chairman of the next-door branch. The choice of candidate would thus be made by a reconstituted association, excluding many of my closest supporters but including very identifiable critics. However, I remained confident, knowing that I had very strong supporters. 'Let battle commence!' was my view.

After winning his leadership ballot Major appointed Brian Mawhinney as party chairman. I rather liked Mawhinney; his demeanour was something like that of an undertaker, with a menacing look suggesting he would deliver a hard punch to anyone tampering with the coffin – appropriate, perhaps, since it fell to him to dust down the coffin of the once proud Tory Party – but he was usually a shrewd assessor of people and, despite his fiery temper, could often get the best out of them. On 12 July I arranged to meet him on the Terrace, at the quieter end reserved for Members and senior officers of the House. On arriving he removed his jacket and rolled up his shirtsleeves; it was indeed a balmy evening. I began by congratulating him on his appointment, and inviting him to be guest speaker at an early dinner of the 92, which he accepted with alacrity. I then told him of the challenge I was facing in Reigate, and of the decision I had reached after much careful consideration. 'I am confident I can win this one, Brian – but there is something I must tell you. If by any chance I were to fail and not be reselected, I would apply for the Chiltern Hundreds [the means by which an MP resigns his seat] at the earliest opportunity.' His eyebrows shot up; 'a difficult by-election' was written all over his face. As you might expect, he told me he thought such a reaction would be unwise; better, surely, to wait and judge my feelings if such a misfortune were to occur. But I was adamant, so he accepted my decision with regret, and promised to do whatever he could to help.

The same day I conveyed my decision to Alastair Goodlad, newly appointed chief whip; he too tried to dissuade me, but soon accepted the situation. He wished me luck, and offered to release me from the whip any evening if my presence was necessary in Reigate, unless the Government was in dire straits. That night I went to Portillo's office to tell him; he let out a low whistle and said, 'That's risky', then smiled: 'I didn't know, George, that you were a gambler.' Two days later I told the Major-General, who went as white as a sheet; he too tried to persuade me otherwise, but in the end gave up. By the following weekend my news was out.

Why did I reach this decision? Obviously the Government's slender majority – when the whipless nine were back, it was still in single figures – made my threat very relevant. But my reasoning went further than this: it was all too easy, I told myself, for persistent moaners in a constituency party to desert an MP who had served them well for twenty-one years, with no trace of scandal, making him a scapegoat for the unpopularity of the party; should they not be forced to take some responsibility for their actions too? Besides, what would be my position at Westminster if everyone knew my party workers had declared their lack of confidence in me? I would be nothing more than a lame-duck MP, and that was something I was not prepared to accept.

If I did have to resign it would still be open for me to fight an ensuing by-election as 'Conservative Candidate', rather than 'The Conservative Party Candidate'. There is no copyright on the word

'Conservative', which is why Central Office always insists that the latter description appears on the ballot paper. This would certainly split the Conservative vote, and it is doubtful if a credible candidate from the Central Office list would present himself in these circumstances. However, I and my friends would have to bear the cost of my campaign. I decided not to come to a conclusion on this till after the event, but I was not greatly attracted to this course of action.

An amusing interlude came in July when the arch-Wet Peter Bottomley, seeking a safe haven in place of his marginal seat at Eltham, told the BBC he was thinking of applying for Reigate. When I asked him what he thought he was up to, he pleaded limply that he had been given to understand the Reigate association was seeking an open selection. I wonder who could have told him that?

Mawhinney was as good as his word. On 27 October he came to an association lunch in Reigate; after the usual message extolling all the Government's works, he settled down to the real business – boosting my position. I still recall with affection his character reference: 'George is an experienced Member of the Commons – not always an easy colleague, but highly respected.' The contingent from Walton-on-the-Hill occupied one table, staying silent, asking no questions. Mawhinney's belief was that time was a great healer, and accordingly urged the association to postpone the candidate-selection process for up to a year. It would have suited me to clear the matter up sooner, but I acquiesced. I was in regular contact with David Simpson, Central Office's regional agent and a real professional, who could not understand why the Major-General did not knock some dissidents' heads together.

Viewed from one perspective, you might see my Reigate situation as having all the high drama of an attempted political assassination, without any regard for the party's public standing; on the other hand, you could see it as an exercise in Toytown politics, with individuals paying off old scores against each other that had little to do with me. Either way, the battle from the autumn of 1995 through to summer the following year became increasingly bitter. On one occasion my secretary, Sarah Farquharson, received an intemperate phone call from Chipstead telling her that 'everyone here knows he's dying from heart disease'! My heart bypass operation was in 1982, since when I have been perfectly healthy.

I was often asked what I thought motivated the dissidents, and it was hard to give an answer; there was no question of them thinking I was a lazy MP. Of course anyone who holds a seat for twenty years incurs some enemies. The majority of Tory county councillors were against me because in Environment Secretary Gummer's push for unitary local authorities I had sided with the borough councillors, most of whom wanted to link up with next-door Tandridge, to the exclusion of the county. A few councillors, I knew, had close links with the left-wing Tory Reform Group, and more – including the Black Witch – had always been carpingly critical of Thatcher and of my strong support for her. Some were straight Euro-enthusiasts, though not enough to matter. But overlaying these groups was what I later termed 'the Toffee-Nosed Tendency', who were not interested in political issues as such but felt I was not sufficiently 'county' or 'Establishment'.

It is a vital part of an MP's job to meet constituents, including party members, on a regular basis; how else is he to know what is happening in the real world? Party members equally expect to see their MP taking an interest in them. I always gave high priority to attending local party functions at weekends when I did not have invitations to speak in other constituencies. However, determined efforts were made by certain dissident officers to prevent me meeting party members at the branch events they arranged. One critic in Kingswood organised a smart evening reception, for which tickets were offered to branch members on a selective basis and to identifiable dissidents from outside; determined efforts were made to keep the gathering secret. Of course I knew about it, and the next day received full reports from my Kingswood supporters who had managed to slip under the net.

A more blatant example came from Chipstead branch, where Chris Robinson was chairman. On Saturday 30 March, the branch was to hold a Spring Lunch in the roomy home of his deputy; no advance notice was given in the association newsletter (organisers of such events usually welcome members from other branches), and forms applying to attend were circulated only in Chipstead. Some loyal friends in the branch, Steve and Val Pittman, obtained an extra form and sent it to me. Two days before the event, the deputy chairman received my form and accompanying cheque. Consternation reigned; Robinson was rung at work, and he hit the ceiling. On the Friday he rang not me but my Commons secretary Sarah Farquharson. 'There's no question of Gardiner coming to our Spring Lunch,' he stormed. 'He's not welcome. If he came half the people there would leave in disgust. He's hated in Chipstead.' Sarah is no shrinking violet, but he reduced her to tears; when she recovered she rang me, read her shorthand note, then said: 'You're not going to take any notice of this are you, George? You've *got* to go to that lunch now!'

How right she was. I went to the Pittmans' home on Saturday morning, and over a drink we worked out our tactics. We would walk to the deputy chairman's house just as most people were arriving; if I were

refused entry, Steve would engage whoever was on the door in argument while I slipped in with Val. If the deputy chairman asked me to
leave his home, then of course I would do so, but we thought that
unlikely. When we got to his drive we found ourselves walking behind
Councillor Fraser. 'Good afternoon, Angela,' I said. As she spun round
her jaw dropped and you could say her eyes were on stalks. More com-
posure was shown by the deputy chairman's wife at the door, who welcomed me in with a smile. For the next ninety minutes I had very ami-
able conversations with branch members present, apart from
Robinson, who studiously avoided me. I was waiting to warn him never
to speak to my secretary like that again, but I was not given the chance.
As the news spread that he had ordered me not to come, several people came up to say they were glad I had ignored him; they *expected* to
see their Member. Not one person walked out. Victory – but to fight
this game demanded the hide of a rhinoceros.

The dissidents had their own co-ordinating committee, called
GROG (Get Rid Of Gardiner). I put together my own campaign team
under the chairmanship of Michael Berry, a middle-aged business
executive, who was one of the first in the association to perceive the
essential weakness of Major. Originally our meetings were at his home
at Kingswood, then at Danny Kee's in Reigate North, and finally at the
home of Gillian Ryan, Chairman of Reigate South-Central Branch,
where parking was easier. Intelligence reaching the group from all
branches proved to be highly accurate, and we knew exactly where each
member of the local executive council stood.

With Central Office's David Simpson breathing down his neck, the
Major-General fixed the crucial executive council meeting for Friday
17 May. The resolution before the meeting was to approve the adoption
of me as prospective conservative candidate. Geddes tried to argue that
instead there should be a resolution inviting nominations for an open
selection, but Simpson insisted that Reigate adhere to the required
rules in seats where the sitting Member wished to continue. The executive was made up of five executive officers, two representatives from
each branch, one from the ladies' committee and another from the
Redhill Constitutional Club. Vice-presidents (usually former presidents), including two of my strongest supporters, Danny Kee and
Douglas Simpson, were allowed to speak, but not to vote. David
Simpson was in attendance.

If the executive passed the resolution it would be put formally to the
next association AGM the following March, or earlier if the general
election came sooner. If the resolution fell, I had the right to appeal
over their heads to a Special General Meeting of all paid-up members

of the association. I judged my position would be stronger there than on the executive.

I knew the executive result would be very tight. My campaign group had done their homework, and we knew exactly where my support lay and where it did not; the only thing we were not certain of was how the president and chairman would vote. One member of the executive had given notice he would be absent because he would not have time to get back from his work at Milton Keynes; he represented a minor branch whose committee was so small they could not even produce a substitute. But this in itself was an ominous sign; he had always been a strong personal supporter, and I thought he could have got to the meeting had he so wished. His wife, Mary Newstead, was now president; when chairman she had been firmly supportive of my position over Maastricht, and only that summer had actually urged me to vote for Redwood in the leadership contest. Her husband's absence tended to confirm rumours we had heard – that she had changed sides.

The meeting was attended by thirty voting members: a full house apart from the single absentee. I explained in ten minutes why I should be their candidate, and why I would resign the seat if I lost the association's confidence. There were few questions, and Geddes complained about being 'blackmailed'. The Major-General pleaded with me to withdraw my resignation suggestion; I replied that I could not, since in the event of deselection I would be a lame-duck MP with no clout in pressing constituents' cases. The executive then proceeded to vote by secret ballot.

One of our vice-chairmen was a young man called Henry Smith, a strong supporter of mine; three years before he had written commending my Maastricht stand, I had followed his letter up, recruited him as a member and now he ran our political supper club. Just as he was about to drop his paper into the ballot box, the president innocently intervened: 'You can't vote; you live outside the constituency.' Smith had certainly moved house to Crawley, but on checking before the meeting with Central Office he had been told that as an executive officer his vote was still valid. What he should have done was to appeal straight away to David Simpson before the ballot closed, but Smith was still somewhat inexperienced in politics and let the chance slip. Only later did he make a fuss, when it was again confirmed that his vote would have been perfectly valid – but by then it was too late.

With Smith not permitted to vote, the motion to reselect me was lost by 15–14. The arithmetic made it obvious that both the president and chairman had voted against me. However, if Smith had not been prevented from voting the result would have been a tie, from which an interesting situation would have arisen – the chairman would have to exercise his casting vote. My friends claimed he would have had no option but to follow the convention set by Speakers in the Commons and vote so as to retain the status quo – in other words, me. But I am not so sure; my guess is he would have cast it so as to leave the final decision to a Special General Meeting of all members, which even if I had won by a small majority I would have sought anyway. It also suited me for it to be known that I had lost by just one vote rather than because the chairman had voted to deselect me. I declared straight away that I would exercise my right to appeal to an SGM, where I sensed I would be on safer ground.

The Special General Meeting – or what I came to call the shoot-out – was fixed for 28 June in the main hall of Reigate Grammar School. The guns were drawn; high noon was fast approaching.

———·⟨∞⟩··———

Of all the campaigns I have ever fought, I found the one leading up to the June meeting by far the most stimulating and enjoyable. I had a first-class team in the constituency, led by Malcolm Berry and including six borough councillors, with grassroots intelligence supplied from every branch. In my Westminster office I had my secretary Sarah, who worked late into the evening printing off letters and address labels to all the association's paid-up members, and my research assistant Chris King, who had a genius for designing leaflets which I exploited fully. Together they spent hours stuffing, stamping and sealing thousands of envelopes, taking care never to use House of Commons stationery. I organised a tea for my supportive ladies at the Commons, though alas I did invite one who had assured me of her support two months earlier, but had since gone over to the enemy. I gave small receptions in supporters' homes to meet branch members with any doubts, and made many personal calls too.

When we began our fight, the incoming branch of Banstead Village was something of a mystery. We knew the branch officers were committed against me, but what about their members? We had the complete membership list, so one Monday morning I took a strong team to the village to canvass every member; we were surprised just how many were at home, though of course the proportion of retired people was high. There was a sense of adventure about the whole enterprise; my team felt they were crawling under the wire into enemy-held territory. In fact, we found that more than half the members we spoke to were supportive, and we made the necessary arrangements to give the elderly lifts to the grammar school and back on the big night. I knew that the Banstead and Walton-on-the-Hill committees were laying on coaches to ferry in my critics too.

The fact that if I lost and resigned, it would wipe out the Government's majority, already down to one, meant that national press and TV took a close interest. I gave many interviews and was the subject of several cartoons, all of which helped raise my local profile. *The Times* columnist William Rees-Mogg, whom I had known since the mid-1960s, wrote a supportive article under the headline 'Time to cultivate our Gardiners'. The *Daily Telegraph* had a first leader which concluded:

> None of Sir George's actions merits the drastic step of deselection. The final irony is that, if deselected, Sir George will stand down. The ensuing by-election might result in Mr Major being left with a minority in the Commons. Those attempting to remove Sir George would be the architects of the real betrayal, rendering even more vulnerable the Prime Minister they wish to support.

Former minister John Patten, himself hardly a right-winger, wrote a very helpful letter in the *Daily Telegraph*, saying: 'Over many years of dealing ministerially with his work on behalf of his constituents, I have always found Sir George the most tenacious and thorough of representatives, and full of integrity.'

On the Sunday before the meeting, the BBC programme *Around Westminster* filmed live a debate from a car park on the top of Reigate Hill. At two trestle tables sat four of the GROG campaigners and four of my own team, diplomatically spaced two yards apart; behind both stretched the stunning panorama of the Surrey and Sussex Weald. The interviewer was Jon Serpel. The GROG team was made up of Councillor Fraser, Patsy Robinson, a former county councillor, Sir Brian Hill, of construction industry fame, and a man few members had ever heard of called Victor Mannion. On my team were Douglas Simpson, distinguished by his familiar cloth cap, Councillor Richard Bennett, leader of the Tory Group, Councillor Joan Spiers in resplendent summer dress, and Victoria Bowles, an attractive young mother. There was no doubt which team won the glamour stakes – and later the BBC team thought mine won the argument too. Europe was never mentioned; it was purely a question of loyalty to the party leader on one side, and integrity on the other. Joan Spiers put my case well:

> With Sir George, what you see is what you get. He's a good hard-working constituency MP – articulate, intelligent ... I don't want a puppet. I want someone who speaks, says the truth, argues his corner. Sir George never ducks the issue.

But I did not do nearly so well with Reigate's local paper, the *Surrey Mirror*. Its political correspondent, one Steve Taylor, followed the same rule as I did as a young journalist: that the first duty of a journalist is to make trouble. I knew all the techniques he employed backwards, but now I was no longer either poacher or gamekeeper; this time I was the game, and Taylor used his gun with damaging effect. At one point someone suggested that if I fell, Sebastian Coe might be offered the seat in the consequent by-election; all it took was a phone call from Taylor to some idiot in Walton-on-the-Hill who said that sounded a good idea, and straight away the paper's front page proclaimed that Coe was being lined up to take my place. When the Press Association rang his agent in Falmouth to ask how his existing constituents felt about their MP deserting them all hell broke loose; Coe issued a strong denial that he had ever even contemplated such a move and that he hoped I would remain Reigate's MP.

However, we had great fun with a report which appeared in the *Observer* on 23 June – the Sunday before the shoot-out. The paper's reporter, David Harrison, began his survey of the Reigate battle with an interview with Angela Fraser. Under the headline 'Sir George fights Tory dragons', it was vintage journalism:

> The accent is cut glass, the words pure venom. 'One cannot help one's looks. but he hasn't helped himself. He has made no effort with his appearance over the years.'
>
> The target of this personal attack is Sir George Gardiner, Euro-sceptic Tory MP for Reigate, Surrey. Sir George is used to criticism but this is true-blue Reigate and the critic is Angela Fraser – pillar of the local Tory establishment, Surrey's deputy lord lieutenant, county and borough councillor since 1979, education committee member and school governor.
>
> In an elegant sitting room at the town hall, Mrs Fraser adjusts her floral dress and goes on, buttoned-up, polite and vicious. She describes Sir George as charmless at tea parties and other constituency gatherings. 'He doesn't even try to look as if he is enjoying himself. At surgeries he gets things done, but his heart never seems in it'.

The moment I read this I roared with laughter. 'Silly cow,' I muttered; had she not the sense to see that a paper like the *Observer* would use her to send up snobby Tories? I cut the report out lovingly, and next day put it into Chris's hands. Within an hour he produced the mock-up for an A4 leaflet, reproducing the start of the *Observer* report and alongside it my comment in bold type:

> I'm sorry about my physical appearance, Councillor Fraser – but I was just born ugly.

We ran the leaflets off fast, and included them in my last-minute appeal to all party members whom we had not written off as confirmed opponents.

On Tuesday I had lunch with Sarah Womack, a political reporter on the *Daily Express*, and showed her the leaflet, which she stowed in her handbag; she could see its potential. Next day she had a nice exclusive, headlined: 'Don't drop me just because I'm ugly, says MP Sir George', in which she repeated the old crack that I looked like 'Dracula left out in the rain'. Other papers followed up fast on the question of whether ugliness mattered in politics. The *Evening Standard* had a straw poll on 'The beauties and the beasts of the Commons', gallantly restricting it to men. The beauties were Jonathan Aitken, Seb Coe, Ian Lang, Bernard Jenkin and William Waldegrave; the beasts David Mellor, John Bowis, Rhodes Boyson, Douglas Hogg and Michael Fabricant. Michael Portillo managed to score as a beauty and a beast. After my reselection the *Sunday Telegraph* devoted a whole page to looking back on the controversy, with big photos comparing me again with David Mellor, but also with Robin Cook and John Prescott. After reporting how the knives had been out for me, Jenny McCartney wrote:

> The sharpening sound was audible. Suddenly Sir George bared his sinewy neck. His hang-dog eyes looked deep into the souls of his persecutors. 'I am sorry about my physical appearance, but I was just born ugly,' he wrote.
> Reprieve. Daggers were sheathed; hatchets quietly buried. Gardiner avoided deselection by the skin of his candour. Heck, you wouldn't kick a guy who knows he's ugly – would you?

It is not up to me to comment on the truth of this; I can only confirm that the Black Witch's brew did me no harm at all.

But back to the shoot-out. The doors were to be opened early; we guessed the hall would fill quickly, and that members would have to wait some time before proceedings began. Chris therefore designed a folded A4 leaflet reproducing helpful press articles to give them something to read; that morning Cecil Parkinson wrote an article in the *Daily Telegraph* urging Reigate members to back me, so we ran that off too and made sure everyone in the audience had a copy. Meanwhile in another room countless reporters were assembling, marshalled by one of my former Commons secretaries, Fiona Antcliffe, and my CWF ally Mark Allatt.

Before the meeting I was in buoyant mood; I expected to win. I had booked a room off Westminster Hall for the Monday morning to announce my application for the Chiltern Hundreds if I were to fail, but I sensed I would not need it. I acknowledged there would be ingrained hostility, but I knew my campaign had been far better than that of my opponents. The 'ugly MP' incident had injected some much-needed humour. All my workers had their tails up.

The shoot-out began with the Major-General announcing he had received a letter signed by 117 back-bench Conservatives, led by 1922 chairman Marcus Fox, saying it would be a great loss to the 'broad church' of the party if I were to be deselected. Signatures had been collected by John Townend, Jim Pawsey and other friends, and came from all sections of the party – Wets and Dries, Europhiles and Euro-sceptics. The only MP refusing to sign had been arch-Wet Nicholas Scott, so I watched his own subsequent deselection with mild amusement. The Major-General also read a message of support from chief whip Alastair Goodlad. Conspicuous by its absence was any supportive message from my MEP, Tom Spencer.

When I faced the throng of some 530, I knew I could succeed only by taking an aggressive line. Deselection of a sitting Conservative MP had happened before, I said, but only in one of two circumstances: the first was when he had been bone idle, rarely seen in his constituency; not even the 'malcontents in our midst' could claim that I fitted that description.

> The other reason for deselecting an MP has been his involvement in scandal, usually sexual. Now tell me: what scandal have I been involved in? I'm all ears. Who was the out-of-work actress I bedded, slipping down my Chelsea shorts before getting on with the job? Where is the love child I fathered at – of all places – a Conservative party conference? What backhanders have I taken to promote some Middle Eastern cause on the floor of the Commons? Where is the sleaze? Tell me – please.

I then dealt with the charge that I was being disloyal to Major – 'a monstrous charge, which I utterly refute'. It was Major who invited a leadership ballot, and he invited MPs to vote according to their judgement. There had never been any suggestion that my local survey was binding, but purely consultative.

> In the end two thirds of the party backed John Major, and that was the end of the matter. Immediately we all closed ranks – and I find it utterly amazing that the malcontents in this association want to reopen that argument all over again. I have since given him my full support.

I reminded them of Winston Churchill's words, quoted at the start of this book.

> I have always been loyal to the Conservative Party. Tory values are in my

bones and in my blood – and I've argued for them consistently at Westminster. Sometimes that has brought me into conflict with the Government of the day, but still I've argued them ... I'm a conviction politician, and I know I share those convictions with most of you.

It was because I put loyalty to my country and to the grassroots of my party first that I rebelled against ratifying the Maastricht Treaty, supported at the time by a majority of my local party workers, by a majority on the executive – and by all my executive officers, from the president downwards.

But that was not the point. In the end, on a matter of such supreme national importance, of whether we were to take a step towards a United States of Europe or not, I had to exercise *my own judgement*, and that I did.

The crucial point of principle to be settled at that meeting was the old Burkean one:

Is your Member of Parliament sent to Westminster as a mandated delegate or as a representative; is he sent purely as lobby-fodder for the whips, or is he expected to exercise his judgement on the most vital national interests of the day?

When my colleague Chris Gill had the Conservative whip unwisely withdrawn from him, a TV reporter asked his local party chairman what he thought. The chairman's reply went straight to the point: 'If we'd wanted to send a sheep to Westminster we'd have gone and bought one from Ludlow Market.' I have never been a sheep at Westminster, nor do I intend to become one ...

Blind obedience, unthinking devotion, the abandonment of judgement, voting like an automaton and refusing even to contemplate an alternative view – that is not democracy, but its denial ...

Let me make quite clear my position on Europe: I have always supported what used to be called 'the Common Market'. I campaigned for a Yes vote in the referendum ... But let me tell you why I will never vote to scrap the pound and join the euro, for to do that would be to give an unelected committee of central bankers total power over our currency, our interest rates and essentially our taxation too. Our Chancellor would not even be allowed to advise them. A nation that loses its currency loses its nationhood too. Parliament would become a provincial assembly, 10 Downing Street a glorified Mayor's Parlour.

The rights of Britons have been won over more than seven centuries – the power of the king being shared first with the barons, then with knights, then with yeomen, in the last century with property owners, and now with every citizen. This is the birthright of every Briton – and you will never find me selling it out for a mess of *potage au feu* and *bratwurst*.

Finally, I explained why I would resign straight away if the vote went against me, then added:

> The malcontents say they are prepared to risk a by-election in order to get rid of me. Well, they can vote for a by-election if they want one – be that on their heads.

The applause was deafening, the majority of the audience giving me a standing ovation while the rest simply sat in silence, many with arms folded. But I knew I had made a good speech – a politician usually does when his back is to the wall. The Major-General then called on Geddes to make a statement in opposition; he rambled over several quite diffuse points, and after five minutes there were calls of 'Come to the point!' and 'Sit down!' He may have been a good organiser, but he was no speaker. I then took questions from all sides – and I sensed I was winning. In the end the vote to adopt me as prospective candidate was passed by 311–206 – a convincing majority of 105. A further resolution pledging me 'wholehearted support to secure [my] return to Parliament at the next general election' was then put forward and carried without dissent.

My wife Helen, sitting in the front row, came up and threw her arms around me, tears in her eyes. I had been able to withstand the brickbats of the past fourteen months because I had the necessary hide of a rhinoceros, but for a wife in such a situation the stress is quite intolerable, as women she had thought were our friends rang with weasel words asking her to persuade me to stand down 'to avoid being hurt'. Then a big kiss from Sarah, who had been in the fight from the start.

Even allowing for my optimism, my victory was still one to savour – for I had won it on my own terms.

———⋘———

> On Tuesday afternoon [Major] stood at the Dispatch Box, playing the role of ventriloquist's dummy in response to probing by Blair. Yes, the 'wait-and-see' policy would stay. No hint or lead for the British people before or during the election. So in the campaign he ... will have to stand on platforms saying: 'So sorry, we can't tell you whether we're going to abolish the pound or not. You see the negotiations won't finish until June. Come back and ask us then.' The voters will fall about laughing, and rightly so.

That from my article in the *Sunday Express* on 8 December, 1996, above it the damning illustration of Major as a lantern-jawed ventriloquist's dummy sitting on the knee of a beaming Clarke. I have described this article and how it came to be written in Chapter Two, and it provided the opportunity to reopen the Reigate battle for which Geddes and his friends had dreamed. 'Oh dear, George,' one of my loyalist friends remarked, 'you've laid yourself open with that. If only you had kept your head below the parapet till after the election!' His comment was kindly meant, but there was more than a grain of truth in it.

Following my reselection in June I made efforts to build bridges with the leading dissidents, but my attempts were rebuffed. Joan Spiers held a party around her swimming pool to celebrate my victory, but she and my campaign manager Malcolm Berry warned me that the dissidents were only waiting for the chance to strike back. My article certainly gave them that chance – but evidence that my opponents were scheming to mount a fresh challenge at least ten weeks before I even wrote that article has since come to light. For on 3 February, 1997, after the sordid circumstances of my eventual deselection in January were reported in the press, one Len Lambert, who was membership secretary for Maldon Conservative Association and on the mailing list of the European Movement, sent a letter to party chairman Mawhinney, from which I quote:

> On Tuesday 24 September last year I was telephoned by a lady who said she was a political co-ordinator of the European Movement. She said she had been given my name as a 'Conservative activist and a supporter of the European Union', and asked me if I could assist her with contacts living in Surrey and in particular in the Reigate constituency.
>
> When I asked the purpose of her inquiry she was quite frank and said: 'We are on the offensive now and we are going after the anti-European maniac Sir George Gardiner.' She said they were trying to recruit people primarily of Conservative persuasion to join the Reigate Conservative Association but 'anyone who supports the European Union would be useful' ...
>
> When I replied that it was difficult enough trying to get existing members to pay their subscriptions and I doubted if there was much point, she became rather impatient and said *money was of little consideration* [my italics]. I was very busy at the time and asked her to ring me back later. On reflection I wanted to know more of this, but unfortunately when she rang later that afternoon I was out, and heard nothing more from her.
>
> At the time I placed little importance on this conversation ... it was not until I saw the news reports on 30 January concerning the deselection of Sir George Gardiner that I understood the relevance of the above conversation.

He then asked Mawhinney to inquire whether there was a conspiracy 'motivated from outside the Conservative Party to deselect Sir George', whether there was 'an organised campaign of long standing to circumvent the six-month voting rule on the deselection procedure', and whether those recruiting new members to the Reigate association over this period 'against existing recruitment trends' had any connections with outside bodies like the European Movement. As he wrote, 'there are implications here which could well affect other constituencies'. When Mawhinney replied on 10 February he sidestepped Mr Lambert's inquiry concerning the influence of outside bodies, stating simply that he understood the recommended model rules of the National Union had been followed.

I have never met Mr Lambert, though I have spoken to him by phone. His account certainly has the ring of truth, and there is no reason why he should invent such a story. However, I find it hard to believe that the European Movement would involve itself in such an exercise. Lambert certainly made a relevant point in asking whether this exercise was designed to circumvent the 'six-month rule' whereby a member's subscription had to be of six months' standing for him or her to have a vote in any selection or deselection procedure. For remember this: my victory on 28 June simply made me *prospective* Conservative candidate. The final decision to drop the word 'prospective' is always made at an association meeting open to paid-up members at the very start of the election campaign, though usually attended only by key workers. Was it the plan of Lambert's caller and like-minded friends in Reigate to spring an ambush and deselect me at the very last minute? It could have worked, and Central Office would have been only too willing to offer a choice of immediate replacements.

Before Christmas I knew the leaders of my opponents were organising a petition to secure another Special General Meeting, to discuss the situation following my article. Geddes had most of the names of my June critics on his database. There was nothing I could do about this over the Christmas holiday, and on 29 December I flew with Helen on a visit to Khartoum. On returning on 6 January, I made immediate contact with the Reigate association office, where Diane Pike, who ran the office and had received basic training to serve as my election agent, told me that 126 paid-up members had petitioned for a Special General Meeting to 'discuss a motion of no confidence in Sir George Gardiner as our MP'. I said I should send a letter straight away to all members, whereupon she told me that sixty-eight had been recruited over the last couple of weeks. I asked to see a list of these new members, which as MP I had every right to do, and she gave one to me.

I then made an amazing discovery, for of these newly recruited members, forty-six had each paid only £1 annual subscription, while four had responded slightly more generously with £2. Unlike the Labour and Lib-Dem parties, the Conservative Party then had no minimum membership subscription, though married couples would usually subscribe £10 upwards. A mere £1 would not even cover the annual cost of postage to them from the association office. This also might explain the remark made to Mr Lambert by his caller that 'money was of little consideration'. What we were seeing here was blatant 'entryism' of the kind last employed by the Trotskyite Militant Tendency in their efforts to deselect moderate Labour MPs in the 1980s; in fact it was even worse, since at least the Trotskyites paid the Labour Party's minimum subscription, which to the best of my knowledge was around £15. As Mr Lambert also said in his letter to Mawhinney: 'We would certainly not permit this kind of infiltration, for the express purpose of unseating an MP, in my constituency. It is reminiscent of the worst excesses of the Communist Party.' But even worse than that, twenty-two of these entryists were among the 126 members who had requisitioned the SGM, which was now fixed for 30 January.

When this highly dubious, though technically legal, tactic was drawn to the attention of Central Office they decided to turn a blind eye. The truth is that I no longer had the support of Mawhinney, not because of my declared support for Redwood, but because of the exercise Townend and I conducted the previous summer showing that a majority of prospective candidates did not agree with Major's 'wait-and-see' policy and were opposed outright to scrapping the pound. He felt I had betrayed him after he had supported me in my earlier selection battle; an old friend of mine close to him at Central Office told me he was describing me as his front runner for the title 'Shit of the Year'. Later, the Major-General received a letter signed by a substantial number of members requesting that, if the no confidence motion were passed, it should be followed immediately by a motion to deselect me.

On getting this list of new members with the amounts of their subscriptions, I made several photocopies and gave them to my old campaign team, hastily reconstituted. It was of course my intention that they should make it known throughout the association what was happening. Inevitably a copy reached the press, and on the night of Friday 10 January, I received a fax from Andrew Grice, political editor of the *Sunday Times*, of the document I had already seen. That Sunday a report appeared headlined 'Tory infiltrators target Gardiner', in which I was quoted as saying:

> This is entryism through the bargain basement. These people have been recruited with the sole purpose of fixing the vote against me on 30 January. The meeting will cost the local party about £1,200, so the wreckers are getting good value for their paltry £1.

The topsy-turvy, Toytown nature of what was happening became

almost laughable when the Major-General announced an inquiry into
the source of the leak, and even asked me whether I was the culprit –
as if the crime lay not in the blatant entryism but in making it public
knowledge!

I also scrutinised carefully the 126 names on the requisition for a
special meeting, mostly drawn from the 'difficult' northern branches,
and was surprised to see on the list Sir Bryan and Lady Nicholson.
Until 1996 Sir Bryan was chairman of the CBI, and I had always
enjoyed a friendly relationship with him. So what was he doing on that
list? I supposed it was because he was a well-known and fervent
Europhile.

On 14 January Geddes rang the Major-General to say he had in his
possession a letter signed by more than fifty paid-up members requesting that if the no confidence motion were carried it should immediately be followed by another motion to deselect me, so negating the vote
the previous June. The fact that me losing the first motion could trigger the second was doubly damaging.

The danger to me lay in the fact that under the twenty-eight-day
membership rule, all the entryists who joined the association before 2
January – and I suspect it was more than the sixty-eight on that first list
– were entitled to vote on the motion of no confidence, though not on
the deselection motion it could trigger, for which the six-month
membership rule still applied. The tone of the first debate would almost
certainly influence the outcome of the second.

I told the Major-General I had considerable doubts about the propriety of the proceedings he was proposing for the Special General
Meeting, on which he was guided by Central Office. For a start, the
motion of no confidence in me as Member of Parliament obviously had
to be confined to my existing constituents, thus excluding members
from Banstead, but it should also cover representatives of all branches
of my existing constituency, which included Horley. They, after all, had
as much right to judge my suitability as their MP as those in other
branches, and their inclusion would certainly have tipped the balance
in my favour. Then there was the legality of the deselection procedure
itself. The difficulty here was that, though there were clear party rules
governing the deselection of a *sitting* MP to ensure he was treated fairly, there were no rules governing the deselection of an MP who had
already been adopted. The only catch-all rule was one which stated
that, in the absence of other rules covering a situation, it should be for
the executive to decide their own rules and apply them. I contended
that the deselection procedures for a sitting MP who had already been
selected should be the mirror image of those governing a sitting MP

facing his first challenge. In other words, the executive should first consider a motion to deselect me, which if passed would give me twenty-eight days to appeal over its head to a Special General Meeting, untrammelled by any no confidence motion on which entryists could speak and vote. I accordingly gave notice to the Major-General: 'Whatever the result of the vote at that [30 January] meeting, I cannot recognise it could possibly invalidate the decision of the Special General Meeting of 28 June, when I was appointed prospective candidate in accordance with the rules of our party.' I also told him that I would seek legal advice.

But the Major-General did not put a straight deselection motion to the executive. With Central Office's encouragement he abrogated the executive's responsibility to the Special General Meeting, which would have before it no advice from the executive. He did call an executive meeting on 23 January simply to approve the arrangements he had already made for the Special General Meeting in five days' time – but he had a very close shave. By this time he had received an angry letter from the Horley Branch protesting at their exclusion from a vote of no confidence in their MP; he planned to send a letter refusing the request, but this was immediately challenged by Douglas Simpson. When approval of his proposed letter was put to the vote, the result was a tie, 11–11; the chairman then used his casting vote to approve. How often in politics are matters decided by the missing vote of an absentee, by someone turning up late or, as in the previous May, by one vote being accidentally barred; thus is history shaped. His arrangements for the Special General Meeting were then approved 12–11 – again, a very tight margin.

My short campaign leading to the 30 January meeting had little of the élan of that the previous summer. There was a much more sour feeling throughout the party, and morale was even lower. The previous June, the William Empson poem quoted at the start of this chapter summed up the mood quite well, but now there was a sullen acceptance of the inevitability of defeat; many old activists had given up, others were looking for scapegoats, of which I became one. After making allowance for the new entryists, the fact that the votes cast at the second selection meeting were well below the first showed how many of my real activists had become sick to death with the whole sordid exercise. I could see the meeting would be bitter, so I suggested to my wife that she stayed at home; she had been through enough of this already.

The debate on the no confidence motion was conducted partly along Oxford Union lines. The motion was moved and seconded by two who were good examples of what I subsequently called the Toffee-

Nosed Tendency: loyalty to whatever the party leader said and did was all that mattered. It was opposed on my behalf by Douglas Simpson and Councillor Phil Hitchins from Reigate North, both members of my campaign team; they put up a strong case for me as a hard-working 'constituency MP', a man of sound principle and independent judgement. Unlike the toffee-nosed pair they were experienced public speakers, yet I sensed they were fighting an uphill battle. There were short contributions from the floor, then it was my turn to speak. I began by recalling the vote in my favour at the 28 June meeting, 'properly conducted under our party's strict rules for candidate selection'.

> But even more important was the subsequent motion pledging 'wholehearted support' for me in the general election, which was carried unanimously. *Unanimously*. I don't recall Tony Geddes standing up to object. Yet he and his friends have been unable to accept that democratic decision, and are trying to reverse it tonight through the back door ...
>
> My critics allege in their circular letter to members that I have 'continued to undermine the Government'. What on earth are they talking about? What fantasy world are they in? Ever since Maastricht, and certainly since last June, I've *never* voted against the Government in *any* Commons division – unlike David Mellor and at least four other Tories. But they're not facing deselection battles in their constituencies.
>
> At that June meeting I also pledged to campaign against scrapping the pound and taking Britain into a European single currency – which would mean the end of a proud and independent nation. And I've done that too, knowing that the majority of the *Cabinet* agreed, that 90 per cent of *Tory MPs* agreed, that the vast majority of *grassroots Tories* agreed, and that according to the latest Gallup poll the *voters at large* agree by 2–1.

Nor could it be claimed that campaigning against a single currency was 'undermining the Government':

> The field was wide open to join in 'the great debate' for which John Major had called. So if Kenneth Clarke, Ted Heath, Hugh Dykes can do it from one side, why not Michael Howard, John Redwood and George Gardiner on the other?
>
> So what has changed since that motion carried unanimously on 28 June? Of course it's my article in the *Sunday Express* that has been the pretext for those who couldn't accept the June decision. I've accepted that my choice of words was over the top. With the wisdom of hindsight I would never make comparisons of that kind again. The cartoon was also offensive, though I had no control over that.
>
> If any of our members were offended – and I recognise that they have been – I've already apologised unreservedly. But please don't read into that article what wasn't there. It *wasn't* an attack on John Major. It was an attack on the two cabinet ministers who had thwarted him ...

I doubt whether many of those who signed the letter requisitioning this meeting realised the immense damage it would do to our party, nationally and locally. It was Andrew Howard, my Labour opponent, who remarked to one of our councillors last week: 'Your local party are the best election agents I've got.' If he meant *some* of our local party, he's dead right. When are we going to stop feeding our Labour and Lib-Dem opponents all the ammunition they could possibly need?

So let's use this vote to put all those damaging divisions behind us. [In the election] I intend to be out there fighting the Conservative cause, fighting for the values in which I've always believed, fighting to defeat Lib-Dem and Labour. Let's from tonight march forward together, to do just that.

But it was a vain appeal; the motion of no confidence was carried by 291–226 – a majority of sixty-five against me.

Next, the motion to deselect me, moved formally and falteringly by one of the Toffee-Nosed Tendency. My turn to speak again:

It will be no secret to you that I have grave misgivings over the constitutional propriety of this motion. I am not happy that it's been triggered by another motion in which our £1-a-head entryists were allowed to vote and speak. Nor do I believe it is natural justice to arraign a man on the same charge twice. I obviously reserve the right after this vote to take whatever legal action may be appropriate ...

I've always been honest with my grassroots workers, and I'll be honest now. I intend to fight as Conservative candidate in the general election that's almost upon us. I will fight for the same cause that I've always fought, for Conservative principles embodied in Conservative policies.

I then delivered what was essentially an election speech, concluding:

I'm a conviction politician, and I've always been so. And my convictions, I know, are shared by the vast majority in the Conservative Party – and outside too. I intend to stand for Reigate.

I answered questions, one from a woman who wanted me to promise never to write an article for the press again; just how Stalinist could you get? But the writing was there on the wall. I was deselected by 272–213 – a majority of fifty-nine. Triumph for the entryists. After making a brief and I think uncharacteristically bitter statement to the press and TV, I was whisked off to a wake at the home of Victoria Bowles, where Helen later joined us. A number there urged me to take my case to the courts, some pledging help towards the legal costs.

But in politics, as on the stage, the show must go on. The night after my deselection I was due to attend the AGM of the Salfords and Sidlow branch, always hard-working and loyal, part rural, part urban. I do not believe I have ever missed its AGM, and as usual I was invited to come to speak after they completed their formal agenda. When I arrived I found a bitterly critical motion of censure of their branch president, none other than Major-General Michael Steele, in full swing. I sat silently at the back of the hall while this was going on; after all, it would hardly be proper for me to contribute, though later Mrs Steele had the nerve to accuse me of not coming to her husband's defence. What on earth did she expect?

I had already engaged solicitors in London with experience in this field, and we had briefed counsel, who advised me to take my case to the Chancery Division of the High Court. Accordingly a claim was prepared, seeking the Court's declaration that the deselection resolution was 'void and of no effect' and an injunction restraining the Reigate association from taking any steps to select or adopt a new prospective candidate. We had to move fast as the selection process was already under way, and we succeeded in getting an early hearing.

Counsel's advice was against using the 'Horley argument' in justification of my case. Instead, the burden of our case was first that a Special General Meeting had limited executive power conferred on it under the association's rules, strictly confined to considering a sitting MP's request to override a deselection decision by the executive council, or to make the final decision between candidates recommended by the executive council; under the rules it had no power to deselect a prospective candidate already adopted, nor had the executive council the authority to confer such a power upon a Special General Meeting. The second part of our case was the 'mirror image argument', that the executive council should follow the same rules as applied to a sitting MP applying for reselection. Counsel for the association, briefed by Central Office, argued to the contrary.

Hearing the case was Vice-Chancellor Sir Richard Scott, head of the Chancery Division, best known to MPs for his report to the Government on the Arms-to-Iraq affair. Several of my supporters from Reigate attended court, and my family were with me too: Sebastian, who was studying law, sat with my legal team; Alexander, a political journalist for television, and Sophie-Maria, an independent film producer, sat in the row behind me, whispering their comments in my ear. Justice Scott often intervened to challenge my counsel, and I had the feeling he was not altogether satisfied with the answers. During the adjournment we crossed the Strand for lunch and a drink in the George. The judge would sum up and give his ruling in the afternoon.

Sir Richard had incurred much criticism for the indecisive nature of his Arms-to-Iraq report, but there was nothing indecisive about this summing up; it was, in fact, meticulously argued from start to finish.

He rejected my claim and application for an injunction hands down. He ruled that any General Meeting of members of an association had total executive power to decide the future of the association and of their prospective candidate as they might wish. He made no order on costs. After brief consultation with my legal team I emerged to face the TV cameras and the press. I told them:

> A number of serious constitutional issues were at stake here. The proce- dures used to oust me as prospective candidate for Reigate could equal- ly be used to obliterate Conservative backbenchers with independent minds in many other constituencies across the land. I therefore thought it right to test the matter before the Courts, and though the case has gone against me today, I have no regrets over doing so. It is not my intention to appeal.
>
> But the question remains: should a local Tory faction who can muster 272 votes be allowed to deny to 64,800 electors the freedom to choose whether to return a Member of Parliament who has served them well and who has no smell of scandal attached to him?
>
> I will certainly think hard on this, and will make a further statement when I have come to a conclusion. So just watch this space.

I was deliberately keeping them guessing over what my next moves would be.

I, my family and a few friends returned to my Westminster office. Sarah, who had been totally supportive throughout, was very low; I tried to humour her ('Some you win, some you lose'), but it made lit- tle difference. My family decided to remain with me for the rest of the evening, so we went for dinner at Grumbles in Pimlico, where we dis- cussed my next steps.

Alexander was the political realist; I had come to the end of the road, and might as well accept it. 'Look what's always happened to former MPs who stand as Independents,' he argued. I replied I was certainly not thinking of standing as an Independent, but possibly as a straight Conservative, as opposed to 'The Conservative Party Candidate'; there was no copyright on the word 'Conservative'. Sebastian saw no point in that; at best I would split the Tory vote and let in either the Labour or Lib-Dem candidate. Sophie-Maria knew the principle for which I had fought to the bitter end, and said I should do whatever left me hap- pier. 'But how could you finance a campaign?' she asked, to which I replied: 'Well, how about standing as Conservative and Referendum?' Schooled no doubt by *Private Eye*, none of them had a high opinion of Sir James Goldsmith.

Finally, I put my argument in these terms: 'Look, you know I've been a fighter ever since I entered politics. I've fought from the back benches for everything in which I've believed. Surely it would be better now at least to go down fighting, rather than slink away like a wounded dog?' With this point my daughter agreed; Sebastian thought I might be right, while Alexander reserved judgement.

With this we returned to our separate homes. Before deciding finally, I knew I had to wait till the following week to see whom the Reigate Tories picked as their new prospective candidate; if he or she were an old chum of mine who shared my position on Europe, then there was no way I would stand. But if not ... Perhaps I would then approach my old friend Jimmy Goldsmith after all.

CHAPTER ELEVEN

Going Down Fighting

'This above all – to thine own self be true
And it must follow, as the night the day,
Thou canst not then be false to any man.'
William Shakespeare, *Hamlet*, I.iii

'My support for Sir James [Goldsmith's] initiative is natural, for I
am in harmony with the sturdy defence of Parliament advanced by
my predecessors in the Speaker's Chair. For me to remain silent now
would be an act of treason, for such cowardice would betray the noble
heritage handed on to me by former Speakers of the House of
Commons. God bless you in your efforts as you battle for Britain.'
Lord Tonypandy, Referendum Party campaign video (1997)

FEBRUARY 28, 1997. I am sitting in a London taxi, on the way
to meet Sir James Goldsmith at the house he has hired in Wilton
Place, Knightsbridge. As frequently happens, the interrogation begins
as soon as the journey commenced. 'You're an MP, aren't ya?' 'Yes,' I
reply, 'for Reigate.' 'Tory then, right?' 'Correct.' I do not ask my cabbie
where he stands; I know from experience that is the next thing he will
tell me. 'I was Tory meself, but not this time. 'Ad enough. D'ya know
who'll I vote for, if they put a candidate up where I live? This
Referendum lot.' Well, I think, that sounds like a good start to my day,
but I had better not tell him whom I am on my way to see. Where does
he live, I ask? 'Westminster.' 'Oh, well,' I say, 'they've got a good candidate there: Alan Walters. Used to be economic adviser to Margaret
Thatcher.' 'Ah,' he replies, 'she *was* a leader, wasn't she?' I agree. We get
to Wilton Place, and I pay him. He's earned his tip, I think. I am admitted to the house by a butler.

I had known Jimmy Goldsmith for some time, and at his request once arranged a meeting for him with Tory MPs in the Grand Committee Room off Westminster Hall, which I chaired; as an MEP he had formed strong views on the future direction Europe should be taking, and wanted to put them to Tory backbenchers. I invited a cross section of Euro-enthusiasts as well as Euro-sceptics, and a stimulating discussion ensued. Though I agreed with much of what Goldsmith said, his idea that Europe and the West should not be encouraging open trade with what were then called the 'tiger economies' of the Pacific Rim ran counter to all my own free-trade prejudices.

Then, early in 1996, when the Referendum Party was up and running, I received the same letter that he sent to all MPs, telling of his party's intention to field candidates in the coming election, but not in seats where sitting MPs had committed themselves publicly to supporting a national referendum on whether Britain should remain an independent nation state. What, he asked, was my position on this? I replied, pointing to my record of rebelling in the hope of securing a referendum before the Maastricht Treaty was ratified, and endorsing his call for a proper referendum on this fundamental question. However, I added that my views might not be relevant, since I was facing a deselection challenge in Reigate, which if I lost would result in my resignation; in these circumstances I would be unlikely to be a candidate in the next election. He clearly found my letter interesting, and invited me to lunch in a private room at Mark's Club in Charles Street on 16 April. It was a most agreeable lunch, the only other person present being Patrick Robertson, his publicity adviser. Goldsmith began by suggesting I joined his new party, but I guessed he was not being serious, and we soon got down to discussing the practicalities of my Reigate situation. He assured me there would never be any question of a Referendum Party candidate standing against me.

By 28 February the Reigate association had selected their candidate from a short list of three. The first was Tony Favell, who lost his seat at Stockport in 1992 and was PPS to Major as Chancellor until he resigned because he no longer agreed with his master's European policy; the second was Chris Butler, former MP for Warrington. Both were good friends of mine, had been members of the 92, and shared my views on Europe; there was no way I would have stood against them. But instead, the association chose Crispin Blunt, a former army officer whom I had met very briefly when he was special adviser to Foreign Secretary Rifkind, who had the advantage that for a short time his parents had lived in Chipstead. I also discovered that Blunt enthusiastically supported Major's 'wait-and-see' policy; the way was thus clear for me to stand.

My meeting with Goldsmith was at my instigation, not his, though of course it was obvious why I was coming to see him. The house in Wilton Place was certainly opulent, with marble pillars and busts in recesses, very much Second Empire, and a comfortable library. Goldsmith welcomed me to the drawing room and sat me in a deep easy chair. Again, the only other person present was Robertson. I told him the story of my taxi ride, which clearly amused him, then we got down to negotiations.

I told him of my decision to contest the election, perhaps as a 'Conservative and Pro-British Candidate', though preferably, with his agreement, as 'Conservative and Referendum Candidate', I thought this would appeal to many Conservative voters who knew my record as their MP, while at the same time attracting others who were strongly opposed to the UK being sucked into a federal Europe. But Goldsmith argued against this; he would welcome me as a straight Referendum Party candidate. He thought the inclusion of the word 'Conservative' would narrow my appeal too much; the Referendum Party's appeal was pitched across the entire political spectrum, targeting former support-ers of all parties and supporters of none. Though it later became obvi-ous that most of the RP's activists were natural Conservatives, Goldsmith did not want his party to be tainted by any apparent con-nection with Major's Government. Indeed, Referendum candidates were expressly forbidden to campaign on any other issue; securing a national referendum on our future position in Europe was our sole objective, and if that could be achieved the party would disband.

I pointed out that such a requirement was somewhat unrealistic in my case; after all, I already had a track record promoting other causes over twenty-three years, and could hardly express a neutral view on matters such as lower taxes, preserving the green belt and cracking down on criminals. Goldsmith saw my point and conceded that on this I could enjoy a 'special dispensation' – but I had to campaign solely under the RP's banner or invent another of my own. I agreed to this – and the deal was done. I would resign the Conservative whip when we were ready to make the announcement, sit for the remainder of the Parliament as a Referendum MP, fight the election under the RP's ban-ner and have access to its considerable campaign resources; an experi-enced agent would be assigned to me in Reigate.

That conversation pointed up what I later came to believe was a Referendum Party weakness; many of its candidates would have been more successful had they pressed not only the basic message, but also other issues of importance to their local communities. After all, if they were elected MPs, they would remain so until a national referendum could be achieved, but in the interval would be expected to vote on a wide variety of other matters. It would have helped electors to know their local Referendum candidate's views on many of these issues. The ban also inhibited the party's leaders from getting quotes into the press or on TV on other issues as they came up during the campaign; quotes on farming, pensions, VAT and the rest could so often have been angled to take in the European dimension.

But this criticism is delivered with the wisdom of hindsight. Before I left Wilton Place Goldsmith and I toasted our deal with, as I recall, some decidedly good claret.

———————··◦∞◦··———————

Goldsmith founded his new party in November 1995, with the avowed aim of securing a national referendum to decide whether Britain should remain an independent nation state with close trade ties with the rest of Europe, or be sucked into a European superstate. His first task was to recruit and train around a thousand potential candidates in order to actually field some 600, but until this was achieved the RP kept a low public profile. First, though, he had to explore whether he could achieve his objective through other means, perhaps by persuading Major and other senior ministers that the promise of a full referendum should be part of the next Tory manifesto. Remember that, in earlier times, Goldsmith had donated considerable funds to Central Office, and was well known to many of these people. In subsequent conversations with him I learned much about the secret meetings he had held with senior ministers and with other Euro-sceptic Tory MPs.

For example, in June 1994 while the European Parliament Elections were in progress, Peter Lilley and his wife Gail were flown by helicopter from their home in Normandy to the Goldsmith retreat of Chateau de Montjeu in Burgundy. There they had no formal negotiations, simply conversations covering the entire European scene, which Goldsmith found rewarding, confirming his respect for Lilley, and before boarding the helicopter to return home Lilley agreed to keep in touch. Whether Major knew of this holiday interlude I do not know, but I would not be surprised if he did.

There was also an invitation to Portillo to join in a discussion over lunch at Wiltons on Jermyn Street, which Portillo accepted; Goldsmith wanted to give him encouragement to stay true to his Euro-sceptic credentials in Cabinet, but he also dropped the hint that if a full-blown national referendum were to become official Tory policy, he would per-sonally clear Central Office's £17–18 million overdraft. This was not the best channel through which to convey such an offer, for until April 1996 Portillo was opposed to a referendum commitment even on a sin-gle currency, let alone one of the kind that Goldsmith was proposing. These two Euro-sceptics just did not hit it off together; according to Goldsmith his guest remained 'buttoned-up.' This goes far to explain why in 1997 Portillo faced Referendum Party competition in Enfield Southgate, while Lilley was not opposed in Hitchin.

It was the week after the Tory conference in 1995 that Major invited Goldsmith to a highly secret meeting at 10 Downing Street. It was here, according to Goldsmith, that he was assured by the Prime Minister that he too wanted a full referendum, but had difficult col-leagues whom he needed time to persuade. When Goldsmith left the meeting he was in no doubt that Major's intention was to get a com-mitment to a full-blown referendum included in his next election man-ifesto. Major asked Goldsmith to hold his horses so that he could achieve this without appearing to be bowing to pressure; this was the kind of politics at which Major was so adept, saying what he knew his listener wanted to hear while concealing his true purpose – if he had one. But one has to allow for the fact that perhaps Major's under-standing of the deal was different; indeed that, at that stage, he did not even grasp the difference between a referendum of the kind Goldsmith was proposing and a much more restrictive one on the sole issue of a single currency. However Goldsmith, being the kind of man he was, took Major at his word, and so proceeded only slowly in building up the Referendum Party.

Enter here an intermediary, who arranged that over Christmas Goldsmith would receive a phone call from Downing Street to his home in Cuixmala in Mexico; in this call Major told him he had 'noth-ing to fear from us' – whatever that meant. Major pleaded for Goldsmith's continued co-operation in holding back the full launch of the RP to give the PM time. Goldsmith agreed, and waited for signs that Major would fulfil his undertaking; he waited ... and waited ...

According to Alistair McAlpine, in a postscript to his memoirs, *Once a Jolly Bagman*, included in the paperback edition:

> This intermediary subsequently overreached himself, probably without any official endorsement, when he offered Goldsmith a peerage if he withdrew his party from the field. Goldsmith, of course, thought this was one of the funniest things that had ever happened to him, since to him a peerage meant nothing.

Who was this intermediary? I can reveal it was none other than our old friend, Alan Clark.

Finally, in early March, inside information told Goldsmith that Major *was* planning to promise a referendum, but only on the much narrower question of whether to join a single currency – what Goldsmith called a mere 'technical aspect' of the Maastricht Treaty. Only then did Goldsmith conclude he had been taken for a ride; his mistake had been to take Major at his word. On 14 April Major finally persuaded his Cabinet, despite Clarke's protestations, to agree to hold this much narrower referendum in certain circumstances; it seems he thought this would stitch up Goldsmith, who had been led to expect something much more. On 11 March Goldsmith took full-page adverts in every national newspaper, announcing that the RP would field some 600 candidates, backed by a campaign chest of £20 million – which turned out to be a considerable underestimate.

An equally unproductive discussion took place that month with John Redwood, then of course a backbencher, in Goldsmith's temporary suite at the Dorchester Hotel. Hywel Williams, then Redwood's chief-of-staff, admits in his book *Guilty Men* that he leaked news of the meeting in advance, and the suggestion was made that Redwood was acting as intermediary for those Tories who might lose their seats through Referendum Party intervention. There were thus batteries of cameras lined up outside the Dorchester, and Williams gives an amusing account of how Redwood and he 'spent a quarter of an hour driving aimlessly up and down Park Lane and around Marble Arch and Hyde Park Corner because we realised we would be too early. It would not do to appear too eager.' A discussion duly took place but yielded nothing of substance; according to the Goldsmith camp, they saw it purely as a Redwood publicity stunt.

Relations with another of the 'bastards', Norman Lamont, were far more amicable. They had several meetings, at one of which Lamont came up with the helpful idea that a Referendum rally might be organised in Hyde Park. There was also a suggestion that Lamont, if he failed to secure selection at the last minute as prospective candidate for Harrogate, would stand somewhere else for the RP. There was another Tory backbencher who applied to stand under the Referendum banner, but Goldsmith considered the MP too much of a loose cannon and turned the proposal down.

But there were clandestine approaches from government ministers too. Some time after he became a Minister of State at the Foreign Office in 1995, Nick Bonsor visited Goldsmith in his Wilton Place home at his own request, 'just to discuss objectives'. His Secretary of

State, Malcolm Rifkind, must have known of this exercise, and in all probability Major did too. The discussion was cordial, but nothing came of it.

The conclusion from all this is that relations between senior Tories, some of them ministers, and Goldsmith were far closer than many have since dared to admit. Some sympathised with Goldsmith's objectives, others thought they could cut a deal, while the Prime Minister thought he could keep Goldsmith waiting at the door of the church while a different marriage ceremony was being conducted at a chapel down the road.

As the election approached, Goldsmith decided he would stand at Putney, where Tory David Mellor had a majority of 7,526. A London constituency was obviously convenient, but apart from that Mellor was a strong Europhile and his sleazy affair with an out-of-work actress had made him deeply unpopular with his constituents. With the wisdom of hindsight, Goldsmith would probably have done better elsewhere, for at Putney the wise money was already on Labour to win.

My own deal with Goldsmith was sealed on 28 February, 1997, but it was not announced to the world till the afternoon of 8 March; all those party to the agreement were amazed that for a full week no suggestion of it leaked, despite persistent inquiries by journalists. The reason was that the deal was known only to about a dozen people: my immediate family and the very highest echelon of the RP. Those working at the Referendum HQ could not understand why their senior executives were periodically closeted in private conclave; something big had to be brewing, but what? As for me, I did not even tell my loyal secretary, Sarah Farquharson, which went against the grain with me, but I reasoned that if she knew the secret it would put her under impossible strain; she was engaged to be married to Mark Allatt, another close friend and prospective candidate, so if she kept my confidence it would only strain other loyalties.

We agreed that I should offer an exclusive article to one of the quality Sundays, and we chose the *Sunday Times*. I drew their political editor Andrew Grice aside in the Commons committee corridor and made my offer; he checked with his editor, and a deal was agreed: the paper would get an exclusive article, and the RP would not issue a press release to the media in general till late Saturday afternoon. The news editor was not happy with this timing, so as compensation we threw in an exclusive picture too. The *Sunday Times* sent their star photographer to Wilton Place on Saturday evening, where Goldsmith, Lord McAlpine and I posed for photographs in the elegant library; I recognised the photographer, who a few weeks back had snapped me sitting precariously on the windowsill of my second-floor office, determined not to jump. Goldsmith and I were in sober suits, Alastair looked as if he had just come from a race meeting, which perhaps he had.

Goldsmith wanted to release the news at the climax of a Referendum rally in Glasgow, which he did. The press release was issued under embargo a bit earlier, quoting Goldsmith:

> Sir George's decision demonstrates that, in this last-chance election, country must come before party. After we have secured a referendum on Britain's whole future in Europe we will then return, like Sir George, to our traditional political allegiances.

I added:

> Whether Britain can regain her sovereignty is the supreme issue in the coming election. I am sick to death of equivocation over Europe and the single currency. Protecting our country and the freedom of its people are what I have always been in politics for.
>
> I have done all I can to make the Prime Minister understand that scrapping the pound is rejected in principle by most of his party and most of the country too. He will not listen. Instead we have constant fence-sitting, attempts to be all things to all men ...
>
> The Conservative Party is national or it is nothing. A truly *Conservative* Prime Minister would long ago have proclaimed his abhorrence of a single currency – 1999, 2001 or whenever. Instead we have witnessed an abdication of national leadership without parallel in the history of Britain over a hundred years ...
>
> The millions who value our national freedom above all else must rise above party to win back our national sovereignty ... Let us seize this chance to put country before party, and pull our nation off this escalator to a European Super-State.

The day before, on the Friday, I told four of my most loyal supporters in the Salfords and Sidlow Branch, Douglas and Tarzi Simpson, and Bill and Ena Westnedge, of my intention; the latter couple had already resigned from the association in protest over my deselection, and the Simpsons were to follow suit soon after. Both pledged me their support as Referendum candidate. On the Saturday morning, after I had sent a letter to Alastair Goodlad resigning the Tory whip, I went to tell Joan Spiers, who agreed my decision was the only honourable thing to do. Then, as I was driving to tell another loyal supporter, Danny Kee, I answered a call on my mobile, and pulled into a lay-by to complete the conversation. It was Simon Walters, political editor of the *Sunday Express*; he had the press release, but needed to 'check a few further details'. I did what I could to help him, but was amazed the next morning to find he had cobbled all the material together into a leader-page article with the headline 'Why I am quitting the party I love', and *under my by-line*. It was a very smart piece of journalism, though whether it was strictly ethical was open to question; I doubt whether the editor of the *Sunday Times* was amused. However, the *Sunday Express* did subsequently make generous payment, as though I had been the author of the article.

However, I really did have fun in my exclusive article for the *Sunday Times*. Under the headline 'Why I must bow out of this daft pantomime on Europe', I wrote:

> I have been an instinctive Conservative since the days when, as a young lad, I helped my mother deliver Tory leaflets near our home. I have campaigned in every election I can remember. Tory values are in my blood. So why have I resigned the Tory whip and joined the Referendum Party?
>
> I am a conviction politician, [but] I cannot stand any longer the equivocation that characterises the Government's approach to European issues and especially the single currency. Through this Parliament I have done as much as I could to impress on the Prime Minister that scrapping the pound, joining a European Super-State, is anathema to most of his party workers and his countrymen ...Yet John Major just will not listen. Instead the cheeks of his bottom hold the top of the fence tightly in their grip.
>
> Last week we descended to pure pantomime – Widow Twanky Clarke shouting 'Oh yes we will!', Aladdin Stephen Dorrell shouting 'Oh no we won't.' [Wet minister Dorrell had actually presented himself as a Eurosceptic!] This is no way to lead a party, let alone a proud country ...
>
> Do we want the UK in a Federal Europe? Or do we want the UK to return to an association of sovereign nations in a common trading market? It is downright theft for politicians to barter away the freedom and birthright of our people. The *people* must decide ...
>
> What is the point of sending one set of politicians or another to Westminster to fulfil their promises when they lack the sovereign power to do so and have to obey whatever orders come from European Union institutions? ... I look forward to voting Tory again, once I know that the party's promises can be enacted free from Brussels diktats or European Court decrees.
>
> I also hope that when I return to voting Tory it has become again a tolerant party. In recent years a nasty Stalinist streak has crept in. All you have to do is to question the current orthodoxy and you are deemed to be a bastard, even a traitor.
>
> It was not always so ... Under Margaret Thatcher I defied three-line whips. Margaret understood this and it never affected our friendship. I hope she understands now why I am joining the Referendum Party. I think she will. All we can do is be true to what we believe.

I did call on Margaret Thatcher in her office some three weeks later

– and of course she understood. She had in her hand an advance copy of the Conservative manifesto, published that day; in the margin of the section on Europe, where it was trying to face both ways on Britain's future as an independent nation state, she had scribbled highly caustic comments. Denis came in and poured us a drink; as I left both wished me luck, Denis commenting that luck was something of which I appeared to be badly in need.

On Sunday 9 March when I was interviewed by John Humphrys on BBC TV's *On the Record*, I was perfectly honest:

> It's hard to find a Conservative MP who actually thinks [the party is] going to win the next election. John Major might, but he's about the only one. Tory seats are going to go down the pan with an almighty flush. The writing was on the wall at the Wirral [by-election], and Tory back-benchers are by no means illiterate.

My resignation meant the Government was in a minority of three, but I made it clear I had no intention of joining with Labour to defeat it. Indeed, I was determined the following week to join my old colleagues in the division lobby on a three-line whip. I went into the lobby in the company of old friends Bendall and Carlisle, expecting some unpleasantness – but not a bit. Several Tories wished me well, saying that if they had been forced into in my position they would have done exactly the same. Two or three had already expressed their sympathy to the press.

On the Thursday I decided to try to get called upon in Prime Minister's Questions, and sat in my usual position on the Tory benches. Then a very odd thing happened; just as Major was about to rise I was passed a 'green card' from a badged messenger stating that Goldsmith was waiting to see me in the Central Lobby. I had made no arrangement to meet him, so stayed in my seat. As I kept standing up to catch Madam Speaker's eye the Labour benches became eager with anticipation; 'Call George' Dennis Skinner kept shouting to her. In the end she did; as a hush settled everywhere I asked a by no means barbed but serious question about the European Movement using taxpayers' money (provided by the Commission) to propagandise those same taxpayers into opting to join a single currency. Major sidestepped it quite neatly. Afterwards I went to the Central Lobby to follow up my green card – but no Goldsmith in sight. It was a hoax, doubtless perpetrated by a Tory whip to lure me out of the Chamber at a crucial moment. Dirty tricks like that, I thought, were the sort of things I would miss.

My next task was to attend to my local press. In the previous chapter I explained how Steve Taylor, political correspondent for the *Surrey*

Mirror in Reigate, was an irritating thorn in my side. He believed it was the duty of a journalist to make trouble, just as I did when I was a provincial journalist. But now that I was no longer the established Tory MP, my interest lay in making trouble too. I therefore arranged to take Taylor to a Reigate restaurant for lunch; I hoped we would smoke a pipe of peace, and that is exactly what we did. The truth was that in this situation we needed one another, and so we reached a tacit understanding to do what we could to throw Crispin Blunt and his Tory machine on to the defensive.

Someone else I took into my confidence the day before I declared my hand publicly was Diane Pike, the secretary who ran the Reigate association office, and who had been trained to be my election agent. She had helped me over constituency research work, and I had always got on well with her; I knew, too, how she felt that she had been taken for granted for years by the likes of the Major-General and several others who should have known better; when she was in hospital for quite a serious operation she was never sent a bunch of flowers or even a get well card by the executive council that relied upon her so heavily. On Fridays she worked only in the morning, so I took her for a lunch at a pub well away from the constituency and told her what I proposed to do. She listened intently, then said: 'Well, I must say I've often been tempted to turn my back on the lot of them myself.' That was when I leaned forward and said: 'Diane, I'm going to make you an offer you can't refuse. Come and work in my campaign team. I've Goldsmith's guarantee that you'll be paid your current salary for the rest of the campaign, after which he'll guarantee you employment on at least the same terms within easy reach of your home.' Diane lived with her husband in Orpington, which meant quite a long journey to Reigate and back each day.

She replied: 'I have to say I'm *very* tempted.' I suggested she talked it over with her husband, and the following week I got Goldsmith's offer confirmed in writing. She then gave a dumbfounded Major-General a month's notice, telling him why. It was obviously impossible for the association to ask her to work her notice out, and the following week she was with me. For me this was a major coup; though obviously she did not bring any files or materials with her, she knew the association's organisation backwards, better than anyone else; she was also the only person who knew how to operate the state-of-the-art computer I had persuaded a wealthy businessman to donate to the association. For a couple of weeks she had regular phone calls from the Major-General asking where he could find things.

For the election I was allocated Paul Denyer-Hampton as my agent, in addition to his duties as southern regional agent for the RP. Denyer-Hampton had been Tory agent to Chris Chope at Southampton Itchen in 1992; he lived on a short fuse, but had tremendous vitality. In no time at all he was scouring Reigate for empty shop premises, of which there was quite a choice. He lighted on a shop in the main street, a stone's throw from the Old Town Hall, a lease contract was signed, and within days Referendum HQ sent in shopfitters to make it totally presentable. There was a front showroom where visitors and inquirers could be received, and a large office behind equipped with computer, printer, phones and – quite importantly – a shredder. Denyer-Hampton, Diane Pike and I moved in on 20 March.

I always held three surgeries in different parts of the constituency each month; on the third Saturday it was always in the association office, on the first floor above Redhill Constitutional Club. But what should I do on Saturday 15 March? After all, Parliament was still sitting, I was still Reigate's MP, with a duty to my constituents. I made discreet inquiries, and not surprisingly was told in no uncertain terms that I was not welcome to hold my surgery in its normal place. We therefore hired a combi, plastered it with posters announcing 'George Gardiner's Surgery', and set up business on the curb outside the Constitutional Club. I advised several cases, and was visited by people I had never seen before offering me help in the election. My usual surgery was taken by Councillor Phil Hitchins, who had previously been so staunch in my support, and who normally helped me at Redhill surgeries anyway. He had no callers, and on his way home he stopped for a chat. I then watched him drive away, whereupon I went into the Constitutional Club, of which I was of course a member, with Denyer-Hampton as my guest. We endured a degree of ribbing from the regulars at the bar, but it was all good humoured; I think they were tickled by our audacity.

As a Referendum MP I made only one speech in another constituency, and that was at Cheltenham, supporting Alison Powell, a very competent candidate.

Goldsmith always thought big; this was not *because* he was a billionaire, rather it explains *why* he was a billionaire – he had always thought that way. He was a gambler, but his gambles were very carefully calculated, which is how he built up such a fortune. In planning his campaign he thought big as few political leaders had ever done before. He knew he had to get his case across to the public quickly; he lacked the press empire that enabled the likes of Lords Beaverbrook and Northcliffe to achieve this in days gone by, but like them he relied first upon the printed word. He ordered 25 million copies of a special full-

colour newspaper, to be sent to every household in Britain, explaining
the danger posed by ever closer integration in the European Union, and
what his party was doing about it. Millions of these must have gone
straight into wastepaper bins, but equally, millions were read. He was
on his way.

But even more audacious was his Referendum Party video. Never
before had a political party in Britain attempted the mass circulation of
a twelve-minute video in the run-up to a general election campaign.
Goldsmith sent six million tapes to households via the post office over
a two-week period in those constituencies where the RP had prospective candidates. In seats where realistic calculations pointed to the candidate having only a slim chance, the videos were delivered to one in
four households, evenly spread over areas; where the chances were better, the ratio was one in three; in high-profile seats, like Reigate, the
ratio was one in two. The cost of producing six million videos at short
notice ruled out production in the UK; instead, he commissioned a
special assembly line in the US, and transported the videos to England
in three jumbo jets. They were attractively packaged, bearing the slogan: 'The most important video you'll ever watch.' The video itself was
billed: 'The story the politicians don't want you to hear', and on the
side: 'If you care about Britain, please pass this video on.' It was grip-
ping material, and many who received the tape shared it with neighbours who had not. Few could have been unmoved by Lord
Tonypandy's emotional plea, delivered in his clear Welsh lilt, which I
quote at the head of this chapter. The video became a talking point as
no party political broadcast has ever been. The total cost of each video,
including production, packaging, transport and posting was around £1
– so this was £6 million out of Goldsmith's war chest straight away.
Central Office spent some £20 million on their election advertising –
much of it counter-productive.

Goldsmith also brought big thinking to Reigate, deciding to hold a
mass rally to promote the Referendum Party on 27 March, the
Thursday before Easter. His staff booked a large secondary school's
assembly hall in the southern part of the town, and took half-page
advertisements in local newspapers over a wide area. Douglas Simpson
delivered leaflets to all homes within easy walking distance. On the days
contractors installed strong lighting and colourful backdrops on the
stage, microphones and stereo equipment, and a huge video screen
projecting pictures of the speakers into a large lobby outside. A further
public-address system projected the proceedings to the car park.

The meeting was to be chaired by Bill Westnedge, a ruddy dairy
farmer from Sidlow. He was a well-known and respected figure locally,

a magistrate until reaching retirement age, and chairman of the local branch of the National Farmers' Union; years ago he had bought a Tudor barn and had it reassembled at his farm, with rolling lawns and a pond outside, and frequently lent it out as a venue for fund-raising events for good causes and for the Conservative Party. Bill was straight as a die, and was totally sickened by the devious way in which I was deselected. Goldsmith was to be flown in by helicopter, landing in a field on Westnedge's farm; Bill, his wife Ena, who looked exactly as you might expect a farmer's wife to look, and I were there ready to greet him. They both warmed instantly to Goldsmith, as he did to them; one of Goldsmith's endearing qualities was that he had the same interest and regard for individuals from every walk of life, however grand or humble they might be. I have seen him display the same interest and affection with children, captivating them instantly. After taking tea and munching Ena's cakes we were driven to the rally.

We arrived to find the school packed. More than a thousand people, seated and standing, filled every inch of the main hall, the large doors had been thrown open into the lobby, where more were packed tightly, while at least 200 stood in the car park picking up proceedings from the loudspeakers. Many had come from neighbouring constituencies, but my guess was that well over half came from my own. I spotted many old Tory friends in the audience. The first speaker was Peter Atkinson, RP prospective candidate for Sutton and Cheam; I was to follow him, building up to the finale from Goldsmith. But first a dramatic thirty-minute video (from which the twelve-minute version mentioned above was taken) was shown on the dangers of further European integration and the deception of past leaders like Heath. Introduced by and concluding with loud and stirring music, it raised the audience's enthusiasm for what was to follow. After the video the chairman and speakers took our places at a table on the platform. An egg was thrown, but the aim was wild. More serious was quite a sizeable stone, hurled with such intensity that it made a severe dent in the panelling behind; thank goodness that did not make human contact either. The thrower then struggled to get out, shouting colourful anarchist slogans. When I came to speak, the adrenalin was running high. I began by referring to my local situation:

> I was deselected as Conservative candidate by 272 votes to 213. It was not as if I had ever been lazy in responding to my constituents. It was not as if I had ever been picked up drunk from the gutter [Nick Scott had just been deselected in these circumstance in Kensington and Chelsea]. It was not as if I had even seduced the chairman's wife ... [a pause, then almost under my breath] *Heaven forbid*!

From this point on, the audience was on my side. I explained how I had always supported a proper national referendum on our future relations with Europe, then continued:

> But voting Referendum does not mean being disloyal to your traditional party. It's a bit like having dual citizenship – you can belong to the Conservative Party, or the Labour Party, *and* be a member of the Referendum Party too. I would expect Referendum MPs in the Commons to form a broad alliance with those in other parties who believe in the same end, regardless of the diktat of their leaders.

I then dealt with the charge that the RP was a single-issue party:

> Of course whether Britain is drawn further down the escalator into a United States of Europe or remains a proud nation state is the *fundamental* issue, but a whole range of other issues are absorbed in that. Our freedom to manage our own currency, to decide interest rates appropriate to our own economy, to set our own taxes, to refuse to be to taxed to pay for unfunded pensions across Europe, to sell our beef to countries across the world who wish to buy it, to avoid heaping all kinds of social costs on our employers large and small ... all these are part of what we're arguing about. So a single-issue party? No – rather a party concerned with *all* the issues that shape our national life.

Then Goldsmith, on top form, explained meticulously and rationally the need for some Referendum MPs in the next House of Commons. He never minced his words:

> Voting Conservative will be voting for a corpse. It is too divided even to be effective in Opposition. John Major has been a totally feckless Prime Minister. As for the Labour Party, it will surrender the last vestiges of national independence. The choice here is simply between a party that has betrayed the nation or a party that will complete the task.

We then answered questions, and everyone went home agreeing they had not seen such a lively political meeting for years. I was congratulated afterwards by several old Tory friends, and my spirits were high. Yet Parliament was still not dissolved, and the election campaign proper had not yet even begun.

When Parliament did dissolve on 8 April, few outside the senior staff at Referendum HQ and Goldsmith's close friends and family knew the true state of his health. The cancer of the pancreas from which he had suffered in earlier years had returned; as the election campaign began his doctors gave him no more than four months to live. Only those close to him knew that every weekend he flew in his private jet to Paris for chemotherapy treatment, which left him by Monday totally nauseous, doing his best to sleep on the return journey. Come Tuesday he was back campaigning with vigour, addressing meetings with Cornish fishermen or wherever he was required across the country. No-one could ever doubt Goldsmith's selfless dedication – or his courage.

The tone of my campaign was set over lunch in the White Hart with Denyer-Hampton and Diane on 20 March. Above all, I wanted it to be *fun*. I would work in the mornings in our new office, drafting our own leaflets and welcoming volunteers who called in to the front shop. It was obviously impossible for my Commons secretary to help, so I released her on holiday before terminating her contract. Nick Morritt had succeeded Chris King as my research assistant, and would be on hand to help.

Many in the constituency had signed up as RP members long before me; some of them had retired early or were housewives, and they formed a daily core of voluntary workers. As well as the Simpsons and the Westnedges, quite a number of Tory activists already well known to me volunteered to help too. We hired a people carrier, equipped it with a powerful public-address system, and used it to ferry small canvassing teams to different parts of the constituency; I usually joined them in the afternoons, but deliberately spent more time than I ever had in elections before out on the pavements of shopping centres, especially on Fridays and Saturdays. Towards the end of the campaign we had the help of more canvassers from Referendum HQ, since there was little left for them to do there; four of five of them stayed in a local boarding house. Several elections ago I had mastered the technique of recording a brief message interspersed with passages from opera on a continuous tape, which would play on the loudspeaker while I was on the street. For this election I relied heavily on the exultant 'Carmina Burana' chorus known as 'O Fickle Fortune' – appropriate in my circumstances, I felt.

Convention requires an adoption meeting to drop 'prospective' from a candidate's title, at which point his campaign is deemed to have started and its costs must be kept within the legal limits. This presented certain difficulties for an RP candidate, since the party had no formal membership as such, only records of all those who had volunteered to help. I decided that my adoption should be divided between two meetings, one on the steps of Reigate's Old Town Hall, the other outside the entrance to Banstead's Council Office. As I told the press: 'It's an old tradition for candidates to be adopted on the steps or balconies of town halls, and I'm happy to revive it.' My supporters from the two ends of the constituency gathered on 9 April, when Westnedge proposed my adoption, and I made a brief speech against the passing traffic:

> I am honoured to carry the hopes of so many citizens of Reigate. They are the true patriots, who above all else want Britain to regain her full sovereignty as an independent nation state. They are putting country before party. I will not let them down.

The RP produced some arresting posters, and after a week I had full-colour ones of my own, many mounted on boards; one showed me with Helen, the other me hugging a bulldog; I also used the bulldog on my calling card, licking me across the face. I counted a number of farmers, all friends of Westnedge, among my supporters, so my posters were displayed from trees and hedgerows throughout the constituency. One prime site was on fields either side of Junction 8 on the M25 at the top of Reigate Hill, where one board with a slogan several yards long could not be missed. For what it was worth, there is no doubt we won the poster war, with Labour coming second.

Apart from Blunt and myself, the other candidates were Andrew Howard, a young and bright Labour councillor, and Peter Samuel, a slightly older Lib-Dem; also an Independent and a man from the United Kingdom Independence Party, both of whom barely surfaced in the campaign; UKIP took only 290 votes, which would otherwise have come to me.

In the mornings our shop near the Old Town Hall was a hive of activity; many of my old friends in the Tory Party who had swallowed hard before working for Blunt, including a couple of borough councillors, would drop in for coffee; all of course knew Diane, and there were times when it seemed like a Tory committee room in days gone by. My competitors Howard and Samuel – the Lib-Dems had a shop further down the street – looked in occasionally too, just to check how things were going and pass on gossip. But the joy of my situation was that many of my former loyal supporters who were still working in Blunt's machine kept in regular touch by phone, telling me exactly what was happening; I thus had a fifth column working within his ranks. In one area I even had someone who, while delivering his leaflets, was also delivering mine.

My newly created alliance with Taylor on the *Surrey Mirror* was proving fruitful. The campaign saw marvellous headlines and stories: of my surgery on 15 March, 'Dumped MP holds a roadside meeting' (with a good picture); 'More Tories turn away from party' (with a picture of Blunt with Redwood on a flying visit to buck up morale – but why choose an old picture of Winston Churchill as background, when I know the association office had one of Major?); 'Sir George has got Tories worried ... 'People love an underdog' admits top Conservative'; of a Tory cash appeal to members of the Constitutional Club, some alas deceased, 'Tories ask the dead for cash'; of an appeal by Blunt to party members to turn out in force to support him at two joint meetings of candidates, 'Outrage over Tory bid to rig meetings'; 'Stinging attack on Europe yes man'; of the behaviour of the Tory hard brigade at a joint meeting organised by the National Union of Teachers – 'Tory activists howled down their former MP Sir George Gardiner when he tried to address a meeting in his new role as Referendum Party candidate. They defied pleas from other members of the audience to let Sir George speak'; then finally, 'Tories plan purge of their unfaithful'. I sometimes wished I was still a journalist myself!

When Crispin Blunt was interviewed by the Tories' executive council prior to his adoption, he was asked a standard question put to all applicants: 'If you're selected you'll have very little time to make yourself known before the election. How will you set about the task?' His reply was classic: 'Well, you could put up a donkey as the Conservative for Reigate, and it would win!' Accordingly, at the final selection meeting one of my old supporters rose to put his question: 'Mr Blunt, what precisely did you *mean* when you told the executive that even a donkey would win in Reigate?' He replied that he regretted his words, and assured his audience they did not indicate complacency. But the damage was done; more than 200 people were now party to his unwise remark. Inevitably this was leaked, and it was the Reigate freesheet, the *Independent*, who ran the front-page exclusive headline: 'Tories' new man sparks "donkey" controversy'. This, I decided, was too good to miss.

When I had my campaign-planning lunch with Denyer-Hampton and Diane on 20 March, they could barely believe their ears when I said I wanted a donkey for my campaign. My idea was to buy one, graze it on Westnedge's farm, then bring it up to the shopping centres before selling it at the end of the campaign. However, buying a donkey at short notice is not easy, so we hired a splendid beast for three days, together with its handler. It was called, somewhat unoriginally, Neddy, but we gave it a new name – Crispin. Across its back we hung a plastic sheet I had ordered specially, printed on both sides: 'Meet Crispin – who thinks he can be an MP'. We paraded it on two Fridays and one Saturday in the shopping centres of Reigate, Redhill and Banstead, while helpers handed out leaflets explaining Blunt's remark – 'the official Conservative candidate's assessment of Reigate voters'. Volunteers manning the Lib-Dem shop came out on to the pavement to admire it, and when he heard about it their candidate raced up the street to see for himself. Children loved the donkey, though no rides were permitted, Reigate Safeway got stuffy and asked us to leave their car park, and it brought me into conversation with many who otherwise might have scuttled past. Press coverage was blanket. This was what I meant by good razzmatazz campaigning.

We reached the point in the campaign where all the candidates publish their own personal election addresses. The wording of these had assumed new importance, thanks to the Tory whips pinning MPs to the wall during the Maastricht Bill with the argument that they had never committed themselves against the treaty in their election addresses of 1992. The national press were quick to pick up that around half of Tory candidates were committing themselves to oppose joining a single currency, in defiance of Major's 'wait-and-see' line; this was exactly as I and John Townend had predicted the previous summer, though our warnings to Major had gone unheeded. Paul Sykes, a Yorkshire millionaire, contributed to the election costs of every Tory candidate who did so. Indeed, even ministers and officers at Central Office were breaking ranks; Angela Browning, a Treasury minister, was the first to declare against a single currency, followed by Angela Rumbold, a vice-chairman of the party, who declaimed in her address 'No more power to Brussels. No to a single currency', junior health minister John Horam and James Paice from Education and Employment. As far back as June 1995 I had warned Major that the 'wait-and-see' line could never hold through a general election; now the party line was crumbling completely.

I was pleased with my own election address. It was like those designed by Central Office, though with a different message and featuring the Referendum maroon colour. In it I declared:

> I believe in Conservative values, as I always have. But I appeal to the voters of Reigate, of all parties and of none, this time to put COUNTRY before PARTY – and vote for a say on where we go in Europe.

I imagine mine was the only election address in the country to include a picture of the candidate with the stunning Joan Collins, whom I had earlier brought to show round the Children's Trust hospital and school at Tadworth Court; she has a daughter who suffered brain injury as a child.

The national press had always taken an interest in the RP since it burst into the open in 1995, but once the election was upon us that interest appeared to dry up. They saw us a one-issue party and, as I explained above, never sought quotes from us on other issues that related to the European question; besides this, with Goldsmith receiving chemotherapy and recovering from it over three days each weekend, he was not then on hand to perform this task.

However, the real scandal in election coverage lay with the BBC, ITV and the television companies; here there seemed to be a conspiracy of silence that barely recognised even the existence of Goldsmith or his party. The BBC authorities hated him, especially after he once wiped the floor with a belligerent David Dimbleby on one of its interview programmes; Goldsmith's sharp intellect could dance rings around any interviewer. In my experience the only presenter who thought fast enough to generate a good interview with Goldsmith was John Humphrys. Even when a programme specifically covered the European issue, only spokesmen of parties who were either integrationist or sat on the fence were featured; Euro-sceptics were frozen out. The most disgraceful example was LWT's *Jonathan Dimbleby Programme* that was specifically devoted to Europe; on the panel were Rifkind and his shadow Robin Cook, and spokesmen for the Lib-Dems and even the SNP – but where was the one man who had brought Europe to the fore as an election issue? It was as if he just did not exist. Goldsmith was never an Establishment man, and here we saw the Establishment ganging up to ensure his exclusion from the nation's TV screens. The RP, despite having some 600 candidates and around 230,000 registered supporters, was allowed only one party political broadcast lasting just five minutes.

The high point of the RP's campaign was a vast rally on Sunday 13 April at London's Alexandra Palace. More than 10,000 supporters converged by coach and train from every corner of the kingdom on a nice spring day. The mood was not exuberant, but even so there was almost a carnival atmosphere; the nearest I have seen to it since has been at the Countryside Rally and March in London. Co-chairmen were Alistair McAlpine, the RP's treasurer, and farmer and journalist Robin Page, himself no mean orator. The BBC's cameraman had to be placated after Page, to roars of approval, referred to the 'Brussels Broadcasting Corporation' – a description which at the time of writing this book is equally valid. I spoke, recycling my arguments from the earlier rally in Reigate, and there were interesting speeches from zookeeper and gambler John Aspinall, environmentalist David Bellamy, historian Andrew Roberts and actor Edward Fox. When Goldsmith spoke he was in pain, though he managed to conceal it despite occasional sharp intakes of breath as a spasm hit him. He asked me to leave beside him, and was mobbed by excited supporters, taking half an hour to get to the door.

Everyone went away in high spirits, but how much time did that evening's TV news bulletin devote to the biggest political rally held in the UK since the days of Winston Churchill? Just eight seconds.

An enduring feature of every election campaign are boasts by the candidates, or by their agents, of how encouraging their canvass returns are; not only are their traditional supporters standing firm, but thousands more are swinging their way, that kind of thing. It is all part of the PR battle – but the truth is that no-one ever really knows. It is not just because many say 'Yes, we'll be there to support you' either deliberately to deceive the canvasser, or simply to get rid of him; the fact is that only rarely does the most efficient canvassing machine ever make contact with more than half the households in their constituency during the period of the election campaign, and usually the proportion is far less. I have watched what happens as Conservative candidate in a safe seat like Reigate; of course you mount the most effective canvass you can, generally between 6 p.m. and 9 p.m., but in computing your figures you include all those who were canvassed by keen candidates in local government elections up to three years back, and often they were very optimistic canvasses too. Only experienced canvassers can detect reluctance in a known supporter, or even whether they are simply being fobbed off. A wise candidate, though he may boast to the press of strong canvassing figures, does not necessarily believe them himself.

This said, our canvassing returns in the first two weeks of the campaign were encouraging; in our case it was particularly useful to ask how the man or woman on the doorstep had voted before, and the disillusion among many former Tory voters was only too obvious. Many said they would 'give this Referendum Party a go', and were probably helped towards this in the knowledge that this particular RP candidate had served them well in the past. But we did not just canvass usual Tory areas, and made the intriguing discovery that we had a degree of support on the council estates, often from men who had served in the war or their widows. Perhaps Goldsmith was right to expect cross-party support after all. I spent more time on the streets than in any previous election, and if all those who came up of their own volition to tell me how they admired the principled stand I was taking would actually vote for me, then I was in with a chance. Yet I never forgot the fact that, even in the course of three weeks, opinions can and do change.

It was not till the final week that I detected a shift in mood. Despite all their declared reservations, people were going back to their traditional allegiances, often for purely negative reasons: they were afraid of splitting the vote and letting the old enemy in. Certainly I knew a number of Tory association friends who began by promising me their vote, but towards the end told me quite honestly they just could not split the Tory vote and see either a Labour or Lib-Dem MP for Reigate. In any election there are a surprising number who use their vote *against* someone, rather than in any enthusiastic support. Yet a further factor this time was that, though some traditional Tories started by seeing a strong Referendum Party almost as a means of reforming the Tories and getting rid of Major, once it became clear that Labour was going win by a landslide that motive disappeared; these were by and large the Tories who decided in the end simply to stay at home.

When I went to the count I knew what to expect. The Conservative vote compared with 1992 dropped by 11,097, while Labour's rose by 4,232, almost entirely at the expense of the Lib-Dems. I ended up with 7 per cent of the vote. It thus fell to Blunt to make the first speech, thanking the returning officer, polling clerks, the police and the rest, but in his understandable elation forgot to commiserate with the losing candidates. Howard too drew inspiration from the Labour landslide engulfing us as Tory seat after Tory seat fell to his party. So it fell to Samuel, the perfect gentleman, to thank me for all the work I had done as MP on Reigate's behalf, and for bringing some novelty to the campaign. I think that from the corner of my eye I saw the Black Witch clapping – but I am not sure.

When Blunt came to make his maiden speech in the Commons he went beyond conventional requirements in praising my dedication to Reigate, singling out especially my work for the Children's Trust at Tadworth Court. I wrote to thank him, and told him I had no intention of 'getting in his hair'; I know how many of my colleagues were cursed by having a predecessor airing his views in public to their embarrassment. When Hague was elected leader I rejoined the Tory Party (did I ever leave it?), and established reasonable relations with my successor. I know my donkey stunt was cruel – but then that's politics, isn't it?

On 19 July 1997 Goldsmith died – as McAlpine puts it, 'in the same bed in which he was born'. On 13 November a celebration of his life was held in St John's Church, Smith Square. St John's is now used more often as a concert hall than as a church, and was the perfect setting for a celebration in which sadness and joy went hand in hand. Margaret Thatcher, Henry Kissinger, John Aspinall, David Frost and Goldsmith's brother and daughter gave moving addresses, and at the end Chief Mangosuthu Buthelezi, another old friend, came to the rostrum and led a chant of hope by a small Zulu choir. There were other choirs too; the celebration sprang to life when a Mexican maraca band seated on the platform suddenly produced sombreros from behind their backs, while their lead singer brandished his pistol in the air as they sang 'El Rey' (The King). Later they rendered 'El Nino Perdido' (The Lost Child), in which a lone trumpeter advanced from the back of the church while the muted trumpets, guitars and voices responded to his call from the platform. No-one could hear this without feeling a tight ball in the throat. Goldsmith's tastes were cosmopolitan; he had little understanding of religion, but the flame of democracy lit his path through life. The occasion was a fitting memory for a gentle giant of a man.

The Referendum Party was his child. It cost him £35 million, and secured 811,827 votes – which worked out at £43 each. In the end, 547 RP candidates stood but not one was elected, and 505 lost their deposits. Was the entire exercise therefore a dismal failure, as Goldsmith's critics claim? I think not. So what *did* the RP achieve?

First, it brought the issue of Britain's future relations with the European Union to the forefront of the election campaign. Of course there were other issues – the NHS, education, sleaze, 'time for a change' – but Europe was undoubtedly there. That would not have been the case without Goldsmith; given half a chance the other party leaders would have swept the issue under the carpet, just as they did in 1992.

Goldsmith's critics point out that the RP secured only 2.6 per cent of the total national vote, but this is a misleading statistic. Remember that candidates were fielded only in seats where the retiring MP had not proclaimed himself in favour of a full referendum, so electors in seats previously represented by a Euro-sceptic, whether Labour or Tory, had no chance to vote Referendum at all. As it was, the average vote secured by RP candidates overall was 3.1 per cent, and in the south of England more than 4 per cent. My own share was 7 per cent. The RP never took off in Scotland or Wales, where the SNP and Plaid Cymru scooped up nationalist feeling, leaving the RP as effectively an English nationalist party. Nevertheless, the RP netted a total of 811,827 votes – no mean feat in an almost total media blackout. The UKIP, less well organised and under-funded, netted 106,028; putting these two together, the *openly* Euro-sceptic vote was not far short of a million.

But Goldsmith's biggest achievement of all was to secure for the British people the promise of a national referendum before their political leaders could surrender our currency and what remains of our independence to a future United States of Europe. Of course this is far short of the full referendum he wanted, but the British people would not have been given even this chance but for the threat he posed. Had Major not felt the political need to try to outflank Goldsmith, there would have been no Tory pledge of a referendum on a single currency; and without that pledge Blair would never have made the same commitment so as not to be outflanked himself. If Labour wins the next election the propaganda pressure to join the euro will certainly be intense – yet our people have the guaranteed chance to escape and preserve their democratic freedom if they so wish. This is the historic legacy of James Goldsmith.

CONCLUSION

Slow Death of Democracy?

'Smile on us, pay us; but do not quite forget.
For we are the people of England, that have never spoken yet.'
G. K. Chesterton, 'The Secret People' (1915)

'National loyalties cannot be eradicated; in the end the grass grows
through the concrete.'
William Rees-Mogg, article in *The Times* (1999)

SO THERE ENDS the tale of my political life. The title of bastard was conferred on me only in late middle age, by no less than the Prime Minister of the day. I do not complain; far from it – since it became the name for all those Tory MPs who were totally opposed to Britain's further subservience to European Union institutions, I take pride in it. Indeed, looking back over my career in journalism and politics, and taking the word in its colloquial rather than its literal sense, it could be argued that I have been something of a bastard all along. My life has had other dramas too, like my adventure from teenage agnosticism through the Anglo-Catholic church to Rome, but these are not for the pages of this book.

It gives me some satisfaction that the principle for which I was burned at the stake by a Conservative faction in Reigate has since, under William Hague, become official party policy, endorsed – as we always knew it would be – by an overwhelming majority of grassroots members. The Tory Party is back where it should always have been, putting Britain's interests and position as an independent nation state above all else. The tide of public opinion might ebb and flow over the years, but this is the rock from which the Tory beacon will shine; if the party were to desert it there would be no point in it continuing to exist.

Hague has come in for some criticism for not making this commitment total, talking about 'the foreseeable future' rather than 'never'. Of course no leader can bind his successors in circumstances that none can foresee, but I can see no reason why Hague should flinch from using the N-word. It is already implicit in the argument of the Euro-enthusiasts, since once a country has signed up to full economic and monetary union the act is irreversible, meaning that country can never regain the independence it has traded away.

It still comes as a surprise to many in the Tory Party, and indeed to many in the press, that two years into the 1997 Parliament, Blair and his Government still ride high in the opinion polls, despite all the evident cronyism and scandal. As I write, this comes as no surprise to me at all. I believe the Tory Party is caught in a trap largely of its own making. After the shattering 1997 defeat there was an inclination in the party – and certainly among its leaders – to argue that 'our policies were right but they were badly presented', that 'Major was too decent a chap to survive the dishonesty of Blair', that the defeat was 'all because of disunity in the party'. Such arguments might be consoling, yet they are totally wrong, and if the party's leaders and thinkers still believe them the Tories are likely to be in opposition for a long time. For the reason why the voting public still support New Labour is that they see the last Tory Government as so atrocious, so incompetent and so lacking in any sense of direction from the top, that almost *anything* seems better.

Yet the opportunities for the Tory Party are there; despite devolution to Scotland and Wales, the Labour Government is the most centralising, control-obsessed, meddling, nannying regime since World War II, and a point will come where the public's irritation will outweigh its memory of those disastrous Major years. As for Blair, the higher the pedestal on which he is placed, the more shattering will be the eventual fall. Meanwhile there is time and scope for the Tories to rethink their policies from the bottom up, devolving right down to local communities, below county and even district council levels, the power to make the decisions that affect people's daily lives; the closer to the individual family the better.

But for how much longer will the outcome of general elections really count? I remarked in my Foreword how often the Blair Government sidesteps Parliament, almost as though it did not exist. The Prime Minister is rarely seen in its voting lobbies, policy statements are revealed more often to press conferences than at the despatch box, working hours are shortened while Government backbenchers are encouraged to absent themselves for a week or more at a time. The Commons often appears to be a cosy club rather than a watchdog over the country's administration.

This is made all the worse by the constant deluge of European Commission directives which Parliament has no power to amend or reverse, while the Government has to bow to rulings from the European Court which may run totally counter to its own election promises. During the BSE scare it came as a shock to many politicians to realise that the European Commission could actually forbid us, not only to export certain goods to Europe, but to any country across the world. British democracy, as we knew it only ten years ago, has already been severely eroded. Indeed, the 'democratic deficit' is there throughout the European Union; the European Parliament is a pygmy institution, a gravy train that almost encourages corruption, and is no brake on the rampant designs of the Commission. What we are witnessing can only be called European government by bureaucracy. If we go on this way we might as well make the House of Commons a museum, its benches enlivened by waxworks of former politicians; I hope that Heath is there in the front row, his grin frozen on his face.

However, sooner or later, British voters will have the chance to jump off this escalator to a bureaucratic European superstate, since all parties are committed to a national referendum before the pound is scrapped and we join the European single currency. The people of England, or rather Britain, will get their chance to speak. Until then, the Blair Government is committed to a massive propaganda offensive – using, of course, taxpayers' money – to get a Yes verdict. The old brainwashing technique of telling people that joining the euro is inevitable, whatever their own views might be, will be exploited shamelessly, as if they had no choice in the matter at all. As the referendum draws near, the public will need to be very vigilant to ensure that media coverage is evenly balanced – not between political parties, which would grossly distort the picture, but between the Vote Yes and Vote No campaigns, which will draw their members from all parties and from none. It cannot be left to the Tory Party alone to fight this battle for Britain; there are many in the Labour Party, and believe it or not in the Lib-Dems too, who want to retain a democratic nation state, and they need to be assured they are not fighting for a purely Tory cause. Lord Owen's New Europe Group and Paul Sykes's Democratic Movement are key elements here, but there are other equally worthy bodies that must come together in a co-ordinated campaign.

If the national verdict in that fateful vote is No, then it is hard to see how its consequences will stop simply at saving the pound. Before long it will be necessary to renegotiate Britain's relationship with the developing European Union, so that we may both benefit from mutual free trade and co-operation on common environmental issues and crime problems like drug trafficking, but the British Government and Parliament may be freed from the rulings and diktats of the European Court and Commission.

If the verdict should be Yes, then, in Hugh Gaitskell's memorable words, that will be 'the end of a thousand years of history'. But even if such a tragedy were to befall us I doubt whether such a bureaucratic structure could avoid decay any more than could the old Ottoman Empire. I am the eternal optimist; I agree with William Rees-Mogg, quoted at the head of this passage, that national loyalties will never be eradicated, that 'in the end the grass grows through the concrete'. My concern at seeing the power of democratic decision snuffed out in France, or Spain, or ultimately in the Czech Republic, is almost as great, as seeing it snuffed out in my own country. However much concrete might spew across the face of Europe from Brussels, in the end – perhaps through civil disobedience or civil war – the sweet-smelling grass of traditional national loyalties and pride will break it up from beneath. But by then, this particular bastard will be long gone.

PUBLISHED SOURCES

In writing this book I have drawn on the following works:

Baker, Kenneth, *The Turbulent Years*, Faber & Faber, 1993.
Clark, Alan, *Diaries*, Weidenfeld & Nicolson, 1993.
Gorman, Teresa, *The Bastards*, Pan, 1993.
Gove, Michael, *Michael Portillo*, Fourth Estate, 1995.
Howe, Geoffrey, *Conflict of Loyalty*, Macmillan, 1994.
Junor, Penny, *The Major Enigma*, Michael Joseph, 1993.
Knight, Jill, *About the House*, Churchill Press, 1995.
Lawson, Nigel, *The View from No 11*, Bantam Press, 1992.
McAlpine, Alistair, *Once a Jolly Bagman*, Phoenix, (revised edition)
    1998.
Neil, Andrew, *Full Disclosure*, Macmillan, 1996.
Prior, Jim, *A Balance of Power*, Hamish Hamilton, 1986.
Ridley, Nicholas, *'My Style of Government': The Thatcher Years*,
    Hutchinson, 1991.
Seldon, Anthony, *Major: A Political Life*, Weidenfeld & Nicolson, 1997.
Thatcher, Margaret, *The Downing Street Years*, HarperCollins, 1993.
Tebbit, Norman, *Upwardly Mobile*, Weidenfeld & Nicolson, 1988.
Watkins, Alan, *A Conservative Coup*, Duckworth, (second edition)
    1992.

INDEX

Individuals are referred to without titles, since many changed during the period covered in this book. Peers who were known by their title throughout are referred to as such.